Moral Revolution
and Economic Science

Recent Titles in
Contributions in Economics and Economic History
Series Editor: *Robert Sobel*

ELLEN FRANKEL PAUL

Moral Revolution and Economic Science

THE DEMISE OF LAISSEZ-FAIRE IN NINETEENTH-CENTURY BRITISH POLITICAL ECONOMY

Contributions in Economics and Economic History, Number 23

GREENWOOD PRESS
Westport, Connecticut • London, England

HB103
A2
P38

Library of Congress Cataloging in Publication Data
Paul, Ellen Frankel.
  Moral revolution and economic science.

  (Contributions in economics and economic history;
no. 23 ISSN 0084-9235)
  Bibliography: p.
  Includes index.
    1. Economics—Great Britain—History. 2. Laissez-
faire—History. I. Title.
HB103.A2P38   330.15'3   78-73797
ISBN 0-313-21055-1

Library of Congress Catalog Card Number: 78-73797
ISBN: 0-313-21055-1
ISSN: 0084-9235

First published in 1979

Greenwood Press, Inc.
51 Riverside Avenue, Westport, Connecticut 06880

Printed in the United States of America

10 9 8 7 6 5 4 3 2 1

This book is dedicated to
Jeffrey Elliott Paul
and
Raymond Brett

Contents

Acknowledgments

I wish to express my appreciation to a number of individuals and institutions for their advice and support throughout the writing of this book. Judith Shklar of the Harvard University Government Department deserves my particular gratitude for her patience and critical advice during the writing of this work, and a special word of thanks goes also to William Schneider who provided much encouragement to me during the publication process. Kenneth Templeton, director of the Institute for Humane Studies deserves a special note of thanks for the fellowship which provided support while I revised this manuscript as a visiting fellow at Harvard. Gerald O'Driscoll of New York University, Murray Rothbard of New York Polytechnic Institute, and Abraham Hirsch of Brooklyn College all provided valuable critical comments on portions of this work. Dotti Pierson, secretary of the Miami University Political Science Department, was extremely diligent and unfailingly cooperative during the typing of the manuscript. Cuffy Paul deserves my particular gratitude, for without his tolerance, understanding, and forbearance, this manuscript might never have been completed.

Ellen Frankel Paul

Moral Revolution
and Economic Science

Introduction

The question of the proper scope and limitations on governmental intervention in the economy has been one of the fundamental problems for
political theory for at least the last two centuries. Perhaps the most fertile
field for the study of this question can be found in the economic, moral,
and political writings of late eighteenth- and nineteenth-century British
theorists. Modern economics was born in Britain. But its birth did not
occur in isolation, for the men who devoted their scholarly endeavors to
the newly emerging science of political economy were the very same men
who wrote and often taught moral theory and political theory. In that
period, unlike our own, economic issues were not discussed in purely
pragmatic terms or in splendid disregard for questions of moral ends and
human nature. For these men—Smith, Bentham, Ricardo, Mill, Jevons,
Marshall, and their lesser followers—a concern for the question of the
proper limits of state action in the economic sphere was uppermost in
their minds, and they were aware of the complexity of the question as
having both a moral-political aspect and a purely economic aspect.

British political and economic theory of this period poses an additional fascination, for in that brief span of time one seemingly invincible
doctrine raised itself to dizzying heights, dominating the intellectual
scene, and then succumbed to the onslaughts of its putatively disproved
and vanquished enemy. Why did the dominant intellectual *zeitgeist*
change from one of relative laissez-faire in the early part of the century
to one of growing acceptance of expanded governmental intervention in
the economy by the end of the century? Can the cause of this intellectual
revolution be attributed to alterations in "pure" economic theory—the

basic laws and conceptions of the science of political economy—or rather to a fundamental change in moral perspective?

Thus, our principal question is precisely this—the extent to which this radical change in outlook was caused by alterations in pure economic theory or rather by changes in moral theory. Related to this question is a subordinate one, which concerns the ongoing debate on the scope and method of political economy, that is, to what extent can the science of economics *qua* science give prescriptions for practical application by legislators? Is it, as in Adam Smith, thought of as an appendage to the art of politics and hence useful for the guidance of political leaders? On such a view, political economy would have a direct, didactic relationship to both political theory and practical politics. Or is it, following the Mill-Senior-Sidgwick approach, conceived of as a pure science, providing laws and an abstract conceptual framework but offering little guidance for practical problems and even less certainty for settling policy disputes or making predictions?

As our analysis unfolds, the centrality of Utilitarianism to the downfall of laissez-faire in political economy and the emergence of its statist adversary will become apparent. Utilitarianism served as the catalyst which, particularly under the direction of John Stuart Mill, precipitated the disrepute of laissez-faire among the intellectuals of the time. Just as Utilitarianism as an ethical theory became successively less rigid and formalistic and more subjective and idealistic, as Mill took the mantle from Bentham and later as Sidgwick followed Mill, so these men as economists became more tolerant of governmental intervention in the economy. Thus, by the end of the century, governmental intrusion became a positive phenomenon to be encouraged and expanded (Wicksteed and Marshall), rather than a Mercantilist holdover to be suspected and minutely scrutinized (Smith and Bentham).

Thus, the movement was from suspicion and curtailment of governmental action in the early part of the century, followed by a more tolerant attitude toward such intrusion, although within carefully defined areas, in the middle of the century, and, finally, succeeded by a positive approval of state involvement by the end of the century.

A rather striking historical trend will emerge from this study. While both the natural rights tradition and the Utilitarian School advanced two theoretically divergent foundations for essentially the same system of economic freedom (laissez-faire), as time went on they came to hold ever more disparate conceptions of the proper role and functions of the state. The natural rights position, being the more absolutist of the two on metaphysical grounds, remained essentially intact in its opposition to an economic role for the state. Through Adam Smith and such French economists as the Physiocrats Mercier de la Riviere and Frederic Bastiat to the Englishman Herbert Spencer, the suspicion and condemnation of state economic action remained unchanged. Meanwhile, the Utilitarian attitude towards state intervention became much more permissive until the desirability and efficacy of the economic system of laissez-faire itself was brought into question.

The explanation for this alteration in Utilitarianism while the natural rights position retained its purity can be found in the difference in the grounds upon which the two theories initially opposed state economic intrusion. The Utilitarians' opposition to state intervention in the marketplace was founded primarily upon the conviction that such actions would be counterproductive, that is, they would produce precisely the opposite of the desired effect in most cases. Rather than increasing wealth by redirecting human effort into more productive channels, governmental action would serve only to dislocate the natural allocation mechanisms of the marketplace and, in addition, stifle private initiative. The natural rights advocates' primary argument against such intervention rested on their contention that such activities by governments constituted a direct violation of the individual's rights to liberty and property. Although it is quite true that the Utilitarians also opposed governmental intervention on a "violation-of-freedom" argument and that the natural rights theorists opposed intervention on a "non-feasibility" argument, such considerations were of only secondary importance to both groups.

This work does not purport to be a strict intellectual history of the period. Rather, it focuses upon the seminal figures of each phase of the nineteenth century, the purpose being to discover how these dominant influences altered economic and moral theory in such a way as to expand the role of government and adulterate the largely laissez-faire economics of Adam Smith. Our efforts, consequently, will center upon the following theorists: (1) Adam Smith—as the great founder of political economy who set the stage upon which future economists would perform. It was Smith in England who originated the modern science of economics by distinguishing it from other disciplines (ethics, jurisprudence, and politics) and defining its essential concepts (value, price, cost, exchange, etc.).

And it was Smith who gave the paradigmatic case for economic nonintervention. All nineteenth-century English economists took Smith as the
founder of their science, and they felt impelled to justify their departures
from his system. (2) Bentham—who vehemently denounced the natural
rights foundation for the defense of limited government and replaced it
with a utility underpinning; Malthus—who introduced the problem of
population to economic theory and dissented from Say's Law; and
Ricardo—whose theory of rent served to accentuate the class-analysis
aspect of political economy. (3) Senior, Mill, and Sidgwick—who separated
economics into two aspects, an art and a science, and moved political
economy as a discipline towards a more tolerant and permissive attitude
concerning an expanded role for government in the management of the
economy and in the distribution of its product. (4) Jevons, Wicksteed,
and Marshall—who instigated and developed the Marginalist revolution
in value theory and examined its effect upon the question of the economic
role of government.

Throughout our treatment of these political economists, we will be
focusing upon several major additions to pure economic theory and we
will attempt to determine what role they played in undermining the
hegemony of the laissez-faire principle. Of particular interest are the following developments:

(1) Malthus' population theory which was tremendously influential
    in its time. It also brought out the depressing, pessimistic side
    of a free-market economy, with the contention that if affairs
    were left to run their own course, the result would be dismal
    indeed.

(2) Ricardo's doctrine of rent which emphasized the inherent antag-
    onism of interests between classes as an inextricable part of the
    economic system and one to be exacerbated rather than relieved
    by progress.

(3) Mill's separation of distribution and production, in which he
    viewed the latter as subject to natural laws and the former as
    mutable, to be altered at the discretion of men and govern-
    ments. Implicit in this entire approach was a disapproval of
    the way in which a free economy distributes its participants'
    products.

(4) Jevons' replacement of a labor theory of value with a marginal utility theory of value. This finally shattered the dominance of Classical economics with its generally negative attitude toward governmental economic action.

Why did orthodox political economists in late nineteenth-century Britain evolve so far from the limited government stance of Adam Smith? Was this great transformation in policy prescriptions caused primarily by changes in pure economic theory or rather by a revolution in moral principles? It is this complex question, one which holds great interest for its bearing on contemporary debates over the extent of governmental incursions into the marketplace, that this work will examine.

Chapter 1

Adam Smith:
The Great Founder

It is both necessary and fitting that we begin our investigation with Adam Smith, the founder of modern political economy and Classical economics in England, for despite the claims of Quesnay and the Physiocrats to the title of originator, it was Smith's *An Inquiry into the Nature and Causes of the Wealth of Nations* that captured the spirit of the new industrial and commercial system and presented its theoretical defense in a form which dominated the thought of the most influential writers of economics for the greater part of the next century. No examination of the thought of nineteenth-century political economists concerning the question of the relationship between economic theory and the state's role in the economy could be complete without first examining the framework from which their conceptions developed and the source of the theoretical positions which they espoused.

This framework is found in the *Wealth of Nations* as are the theories and principles which shaped political economy right up until the Marginalist revolution of the 1870s. To name but a few of the theoretical positions of Smith's which retained their hold over later economists of the Classical School and even became linked in the history of economic thought with the names of these followers as their own unique contributions, we have the following: (1) the labor theory of value which held sway among orthodox economists through John Stuart Mill and Henry Sidgwick, and with its reformulation by Ricardo, influenced socialist writers such as William Thompson and Karl Marx; (2) the theoretical correlation of population trends, agricultural output, and wage rates, with the conclusion that wages tend toward a subsistence minimum; later, this was to become

Malthus' and Ricardo's theory through whom it influenced Mill; (3) the beginning of the wages-fund doctrine which did not finally subside until J. S. Mill acknowledged its critical defeat in 1870; (4) the forecast of the tendency of profits to a minimum as a society improves (this prediction was later expanded by Ricardo into the view that a stationary state would be the eventual result of progress, a prediction with which J. S. Mill concurred); and (5) a class analysis of the shares of the nation's annual production in which the three classes of wage earners, profit takers, and rent collectors were distinguished and their various interests isolated and evaluated in relation to the interest of society as a whole in the maximization of wealth.

THE MORAL UNIVERSE OF SMITH'S ECONOMIC MAN

Before embarking upon our investigation of Adam Smith as political economist, it will prove salutary to pause for a moment and examine both the moral system and teleological position which Smith brought to the study of economics, for in these areas he differed markedly from the Utilitarian moral code in which Bentham was soon to entwine British thought on politics and economics. Despite numerous scholarly interpretations of Smith which categorize him as a utilitarian in morals, it will be argued that he falls more consistently into the natural rights camp.

The Smith of *The Theory of Moral Sentiments* has often been perceived by critics as a different species of moralist from the Smith who penned the *Wealth of Nations.* The one promulgated a system based upon moral sentiments and the sympathetic feelings among men, and the other advocated an extreme individualism in which men are motivated solely by self-interest. Upon a close examination of these two works, it will become apparent that there is but one Smith and that the *Wealth of Nations* fits rather nicely into the moral framework of the *Theory of Moral Sentiments.*[1] The former demonstrated that by merely employing one aspect of man's nature, and that the most selfish and antisocial, men can function quite adequately and indeed socially in both the economic sphere and the political sphere. But men are more than their self-regarding sentiments; they are desirous of pleasing others, of gaining the approval of others, of both being and seeming to be honorable and virtuous. And so there is more to life than economics and politics. There is the life afforded in a society based upon friendship and mutual observance of the higher virtues. However, such considerations fall outside the domain of political economy which is concerned strictly with the maximization of wealth. It is the singular beauty of the economic realm, Smith believed, that it permits men to function on the lowest level of virtue, that of self-interest, which is still a virtue in its proper place, and yet secure the greatest benefit for the whole society. There are no passages extolling self-love or the selfish pursuit of men's own interests to the detriment of others in the *Wealth of Nations*,[2] but there is an examination of this part of man's nature as it performs its proper function.

If men are to a certain degree self-regarding, they are so constituted for a definite purpose. In Smith we are far, indeed, from a Benthamite world view. Nature, for Smith, is harmonious and economical,[3] and thus, men's selfish desires are implanted in their breasts for a positive and useful purpose. Smith accepts the natural law conception of nature and of man, and whether he is dealing with the subject of morality, justice, government, or economics, he is constantly striving to determine the natural principles which govern men's conduct in such pursuits.

> In every part of the universe we observe means adjusted with the nicest artifice to the ends which they are intended to produce; and in the mechanism of a plant or animal body, admire how everything is contrived for advancing the two great purposes of nature; the support of the individual and the propagation of the species.[4]

In addition to these selfish instincts, nature has provided man with "principles of his nature" which interest him in the welfare of others and make their happiness necessary to him. Through imagination only can we identify with the feelings of others and share a fellow feeling with them. Thus, man can through sympathy, pity, and compassion enlarge his feelings beyond himself to engage those of his family, neighbors, countrymen, and even all mankind, though in diminishing degrees as the connection to himself becomes more and more attenuated.[5] In addition to this capacity for empathy with the feelings, motives, and sentiments of others, nature endowed man with other attributes which make him fit for society; that is, a natural desire to be the proper object of love and concomitant dread of being the deserved object of hatred, an original desire to please and an aversion to offending his fellows, and a desire actually to be virtuous and not simply to be thought of as virtuous.[6]

The mechanism by which men emerge from the isolation of their own sentiments and judgments is a combination of this capacity for sympathy with others' feelings through the use of our imagination and the natural need to love and be loved, to garner the praise of our neighbors. But the socialization process, Smith hints, is never complete and must be constantly regenerated and the instinct for raw self-advancement neutralized by a realization that such avarice will endanger our need for approval and the empathetic understanding of others.

The socialization process, then, is an ongoing one, but the self-regarding sentiments of men are implanted within them by nature for a definite and socially necessary purpose. Every man, Smith the individualist maintains, is by nature principally recommended to his own care. He is fitter to take care of himself than is any other person.[7] "Every man, therefore, is much more deeply interested in whatever immediately concerns himself than in what concerns any other man."[8] This natural propensity of mankind for self-preference would induce him to prefer a large hurt to someone else to a small injury to himself. Fortunately, the social attributes of men intervene at this point to warn them that they cannot pursue their own interests by injuring others or they will forfeit the good opinion and praise of others. But it is not simply from an enlightened self-interest that men avoid injuring others (as it would be, for example, on a Benthamite calculus), for Smithian man naturally desires the sympathy of others. "We must here, as in all other cases, view ourselves not so much according to that light in which we may naturally appear to ourselves, as according to that in which we appear to others."[9] Thus, the individual must "humble the arrogance of his self-love," for it seems absurd to the multitude because to them he is but one, and bring it down to the level at which other men can go along with it. Reason, conscience, and principle intervene to prevent us from pursuing an insignificant advantage to ourselves at the cost of the greater interest of mankind. Reason tells us that we will be the fitting object of ridicule if we so act. It is not love for our neighbor which prevents us from injuring him for our own benefit, Smith argues, but a stronger love, the love of what is honorable and noble, of the grandeur, dignity, and superiority of our own character. Thus, a higher selfishness comes to replace a lower, as we come naturally to prefer an image of ourselves as being just and virtuous to one of being a crass and mendacious self-seeker. Smith goes even further when he claims that we have a natural aversion to inflicting injury upon others unless they have committed a prior injustice.

Justice, according to Smith, is the necessary ingredient of society without which it could not survive, and thus, the observance of its dictates can be extorted by force. Unlike beneficence, which is always free and cannot be properly commanded, justice is necessary to the existence of society, and its observance requires no reward while its breach incurs punishment.[10] "Mere justice is, upon most occasions, but a negative virtue and only hinders us from hurting our neighbors."[11] From the nature of man, his self-regarding motivation and his need to live in society in order to survive and function as a man (Aristotle's social animal), the "most sacred laws of justice" emerge. They are, in order of priority: (1) those laws which guard the life and person of our neighbors, (2) those which guard his property and possessions, and lastly, (3) those which protect his personal (i.e., contractual) rights.[12] Without justice the "immense fabric" of human society would crumble into "atoms,"[13] so to enforce the observation of justice, nature, according to Smith, has not relied on men's reason[14] but has implanted in each human breast a consciousness of ill desert and a terror of merited punishment as the twin safeguards of human association. Thus, while men are naturally sympathetic to a certain degree, the feeling is greatly attenuated when the personal connection is not great, and consequently this principle of justice is necessary to curb our own interest when it would injure others. The principles of justice are implanted in the human heart to conserve society and curb harmful selfishness, and reason intervenes to make us choose the greater interest of mankind to our own trifling interest.

But how do men first come to recognize the requirements of justice and, indeed, to make all different kinds of moral distinctions, to approve and disapprove of their own actions and those of others? It is not by reason, which cannot make the original perception of what is right and wrong. Nor is it by a "moral sense" in the way in which such was conceived by Hume and Hutcheson, Smith's mentors. Rather, it is by an original experience which each individual has of how the actions of others and of his own feelings and actions affect him directly, that is, whether they please or displease him directly. From these primary experiences and the reactions of other men to his actions, the individual forms general rules of conduct.[15] The mechanism is, then, one of induction from experience.

> They [the general rules] are ultimately founded upon experience of what, in particular instances, our moral faculties, our natural sense of merit and propriety, approve or disapprove of.[16]

These general rules serve as a corrective for the partiality which men have in their own cases. Smith suggests, as a further corrective, the hypostatization of an "impartial spectator" to whom we can appeal in our minds to judge whether we are about to act in a way which will garner the sympathy of other men.

This impartial spectator is not the standard of what is moral as it may appear to be on a cursory reading, but rather a mental construct by which the individual can be guided in his moral judgments when his own interest is so intimately involved in the case that his objectivity might be severely undermined. The impartial spectator prevents Smithian man from being prejudiced in his own case, while Smith's ethics as a whole are prevented from being solipsistic or different for each man by the assumption that all men have the same natural sentiments implanted in them by nature or God, which dictate the same moral judgments to all men once partiality is excluded. While these sentiments can be perverted in some men, they can not be wholly expunged. Hence, Smith claims, the general rules, while drawn from experience and induction by each individual, are Laws of the Deity,[17] although impressed by nature.

The most virtuous man, for Smith, is not the man of a merely commercial spirit, the man he describes in his *Lectures of Justice, Police, Revenue and Arms,*[18] but is more an Aristotelian man. He governs himself by self-command, thus reining in his selfish or unruly impulses and regulating his conduct by the strict demands of the three primary virtues of prudence—to regulate his own happiness properly; justice—to exhibit the minimum of concern for others' happiness; and beneficence—to act positively for the happiness of others.[19] He joins the most perfect command of his own original and selfish feelings to a most "exquisite susceptibility" to both the original and sympathetic feelings of others; he possesses both the gentle virtues and the great, awful, and respectable virtues.[20]

And hence it is that to feel much for others and little for ourselves, that to restrain our selfish and to indulge our benevolent
affections, constitutes the perfection of human nature, and can
alone produce among mankind that harmony of sentiment and
passion in which consists their whole grace and propriety.[21]

Smith even goes so far as to say that it is a precept of nature that we
must love ourselves only as we love our neighbor.[22] But this is an ideal
standard, and a more suitable one to judge our actions by, he suggests,
might be the approximation to this standard which is commonly attained
in the world.[23] Perhaps Smith set the ideal so high because he realized
that it went so strongly against the grain of man's original, selfish sentiments. If men were so strongly pulled in one direction, it could only help
reinforce the weaker, sympathetic feelings to state the case so emphatically
for acting virtuously toward our fellows; few men would go overboard in
trying to exceed the limits of beneficence. But Smith, always the realist,
finally drew back from the excesses of his own rhetoric by cautioning
that while the virtuous man, like the good soldier, must be willing to
sacrifice his own interest to society and his society's interest to the
greater interest of the state or sovereignty and that in turn to the interest
of mankind, such self-sacrifice is usually unnecessary, because the Divine
Being conducts the universe to produce the greatest possible quantity
of happiness, and hence, the job of caring for all of mankind is best left
to Him. Men perform their proper functions when they attend to their
own happiness and that of their families, friends, and country; such mun-
dane duties, he admonishes, must not be neglected for the contemplation
of the sublime.[24]

In summation, then, we can say of Smithian man that he is (1) a being
who inhabits his proper place in a natural order which is efficient and
harmonious, (2) a moral being who can attain his true nature and potentialities only in society, (3) a social creature who acquires a moral code
by experience and induction, although it is founded upon and judged by
his innate moral sentiments which are given to him by nature, (4) a composite of original, selfish sentiments which are, in their way, necessary
to his survival and that of society but also endowed with sympathetic
feelings for other men, and finally, (5) a being who requires for his happiness the praise and approval of his compatriots in addition to his own
estimation of himself as a virtuous man worthy of such accolades. It is

interesting to reflect, in passing, that Smithian man desires wealth not for the ease and comfort which it will afford him but for the approval it will garner for his actions in the estimation of other men, for it is a universal peculiarity of men, Smith observes, that renders them more sympathetic to the actions of the rich man than the poor.[25] "Upon this disposition of mankind to go along with all the passions of the rich and powerful is founded the distinction of rank and the order of society."[26] This disposition to admire and accept the actions of the rich and despise those of the poor is also the "most universal cause of the corruption of our moral sentiments."[27]

The commercial man of the *Wealth of Nations* is not essentially different from this moral man; he inhabits the same natural universe of laws, efficiency, and harmony. But the commercial man is the virtuous man in only one of his aspects. He does not go beyond the private virtue of prudence or the limited social virtue of justice (i.e., refraining from injuring others) into the positive virtue of beneficence. But he need not, for such is not the proper concern of men in their strictly economic function which is to secure the well-being of themselves and their dependents. Beneficence cannot be compelled or purchased; it must be a free gift. So while commercial man may be beneficent in his private capacity, such considerations are not properly entertained in a discussion of economics. Smith, in his lecture *Of Police*,[28] speaks of the introduction of commerce into a country as serving to foster probity and punctuality, such being attributable to self-interest and the realization that one has more to lose in a reputation for cheating than he has to gain by a particular fraud. But the commercial spirit is also confining, because the necessary division of labor in industrialized society limits men's perspectives. In this respect, Smith yearns for the virtues of the past—honor, glory, and the martial spirit—which have passed on with the arrival of commercial man. And so the tone of the *Theory of Moral Sentiments,* which first came to print in 1759, and the *Lectures,* of 1763, is less accepting of this new man than is the *Wealth of Nations* of 1776. The commercial man is a part of the virtuous man—he is not complete—but it is the genius of nature that he need not be the wholly virtuous man for society to function or for the economic system to operate for the maximization of wealth. For simply by pursuing his own private interests, the original and selfish sentiments of the *Theory of Moral Sentiments,* he will in the economic realm choose those endeavors which will best serve society.

Herein lies the connection between the two great works which make them the work of a single and largely consistent theorist. With this key Smith's political economy fits rather neatly into his moral system and his conception of the universe.

THE FOUNDATION OF CLASSICAL ECONOMICS

During the course of the *Theory of Moral Sentiments,* Smith projects the need for a comprehensive study of the general principles which ought to be the foundation for the laws of all nations. *An Inquiry into the Nature and Causes of the Wealth of Nations* is Smith's attempt to discover and formulate these general principles of legislation in the economic realm. Political economy as a discipline had, for Smith, the specific purpose of discovering the nature of wealth and the means by which wealth can be maximized for a nation. As a science, then, it is valued for its practical instructions concerning how an economic system ought to be operated and not simply for its theoretical analysis of abstract laws or its observations concerning existent systems. As a branch of the science of a statesman or legislator, political economy has a heuristic and meliorative function, that is, it must instruct the statesman on how best to secure its two great objectives: (1) to supply a plentiful revenue or subsistence for the people, or more fittingly, once one grasps the true system of political economy, to enable the people to provide such an abundance for themselves, and (2) to provide the state with a revenue sufficient to perform its proper public services.[29] Thus, the study of the science of political economy should provide concrete principles by which the legislator can establish a system whereby both the people and the sovereign shall be enriched.

Smith did not draw the distinction between "positive" and "normative" economics which was later made by Senior and Mill for the purpose of restricting economics as a discipline to the sole practical function of predicting the outcome of various policies (the "positive" aspect) and leaving all questions of competing value systems or objectives to be adjudicated by citizens or their representatives (the "normative" aspect).[30] In fact, the rationale behind such a circumscription of the science would have been very nearly incomprehensible to him, since he thought the objectives were implicit in the way the discipline was defined, that is, as an instrument for maximizing the wealth of the nation and that the means for attaining this end would be discovered in the study and should be applied in the real world by the political powers.[31] The kind of normative questions that so troubled later economists—for example, should wealth be distributed equally to all?—were not problems for him because of the moral framework of natural law and a quasi-natural-rights position which he brought to economics. Smithian economics would instruct the sovereign on the laws that should be enacted and those that should be repealed in order to maximize national wealth within a moral framework of individualism and self-reliance; it would provide the best system for the production of wealth, which is assumed to be the sole normative purpose to be pursued by the sovereign. Hence, disputes about values and collective objectives do not arise in a political economy so conceived.

The men who inhabit the world of the *Wealth of Nations* are Greek men in the same sense that they were so in the *Theory of Moral Sentiments*, if we mean by "Greek" that they are, in Aristotle's term, "social animals." Just as the man of the *Moral Sentiments* was dependent for the formulation of a moral code upon others to mirror his acts by proffering their approbation or disapprobation, so the man of the *Inquiry* is dependent upon a great multitude of other men for his material survival as a result of the advancement of the principle of the division of labor.[32] It is remarkable, Smith writes, how the support of the most humble workman in his customary life-style involves the assistance and cooperation of thousands of workmen. Thanks to this system of cooperation brought about by the division of labor,

> it may be true, perhaps, that the accommodations of a European Prince does not always so much exceed that of an industrious and frugal peasant, as the accommodations of the latter exceeds that of many an African King, the absolute master of the lives and liberties of ten thousand naked savages.[33]

The division of labor, which accounts for the great improvement in the productive powers of labor, was originally brought about not by any conscious, reasoned, or willed act of men, but rather, resulted from the realization of the advantages which arise from the specialization of trades. In the early stage of civilization it was soon apparent that all men could be better off if each pursued a trade in which he had a natural propensity and subsequently engaged in exchange with others of his surplus in order to acquire the balance of his needs. The system of exchange and eventually the replacement of barter by a monetary system were natural developments from the division of labor, which itself was a natural outgrowth not of human wisdom and design but of a human propensity.

> It is the necessary, though very slow and gradual consequence of a certain propensity in human nature which has in view no such extensive utility; the propensity to truck, barter, and exchange one thing for another.[34]

This propensity may be an original principle of human nature; however, Smith thinks it more likely that it was a necessary consequence of the faculties of reason and speech. This attribute is common to all men and only to men. We owe to this drive the specialization which greatly multiplies the productivity of man's labor and diffuses through all society a "universal opulence" which extends even to the lowest ranks of people.[35]

Men in society, then, require the continual assistance of other men, few of whom they actually know, and fewer still whom they could call upon as friends. It is vain, warns Smith, to expect help from others by appealing to their vanity. "It is not from the benevolence of the butcher, the brewer, or the baker that we expect our dinner, but from their regard for their own interests."[36] One gains another's willing assistance by appealing to his "self-love," by showing him that it is actually to his own advantage to do what one wishes of him. And so, a bargain is struck. "We address ourselves, not to their humanity, but to their self-love; and never talk to them of our own necessities, but of their advantage."[37] In the *Moral Sentiments* we were told that men have but little regard for people who have no immediate connection with them, and here we are instructed in the natural way in which such indifference and self-preference is overcome in the economic realm where men are dependent for their survival and comfort upon the willing cooperation of other men. The mechanism of exchange accomplishes this without coercion[38] by making each man serve his own self-interest and his own needs by producing goods for the immediate satisfaction of others. The disposition to exchange enables us to get from people who are totally indifferent to our welfare the means for our happiness, "by treaty, by barter, by purchase."[39]

Smith accepts the Lockian-Liberal notion of men as naturally equal, attributing the difference apparent in men more to the specializations which they pursued in life than to any great natural disparities in ability. These differences are more the effect than the cause of the division of labor. "The difference between the most dissimilar characters," Smith remarks in a light vein, "between a philosopher and a common street porter, for example, seems to arise not so much from nature as from habit, custom, and education."[40]

Smithian man, then, is roughly equal by natural abilities and equipped with a propensity to exchange; he is also motivated principally by self-interest in his economic dealings, and he is provided by nature, slowly and spontaneously, with a system which perfectly suits him and one which naturally makes his inherent self-seeking fit him for society. And from this desire of every man to seek his own advantage and to improve his condition arises all public and private wealth. In fact, the drive is so strong that it is often able to overcome the extravagances of bad governments and the imposition of improper laws of political economy.[41]

The extent to which Smith remained in the natural law-natural rights tradition has been hotly disputed,[42] with some interpreters such as Lord Robbins[43] viewing him as being much closer to a pragmatic utilitarianism, and with others, for example T. W. Hutchison,[44] maintaining that he was still fairly well infused with a natural law perspective. On balance, the latter view of Smith appears to be the more credible when one considers the consistency in outlook evidenced in the *Moral Sentiments,* the *Lectures,* and the *Wealth of Nations.* In the two former works he continually speaks of the need to discover the natural rules of justice which underlie the positive laws of different states,[45] while in the latter, it will be argued, the same philosophical position is maintained.

In his *Lecture on Justice,* Smith argues for natural rights but in a way that differed from Locke in that he drew a distinction between the rights to life and liberty, declaring them to be natural rights, and the right to property, which he considered an acquired right dependent upon the sufferance of society. "The rights which a man has to the preservation of his body and reputation from injury are called natural. . . ."[46] This distinction between the natural rights of life and liberty (*iura hominum naturalis*) and the acquired property rights (*iura adventitia*) was a critical alteration of the Lockian formulation in which he portrayed all these rights as having force before the creation of civil government. Smith's distinction between natural rights and property rights is articulated in the following passage:

The origin of natural rights is quite evident, that a person has
a right to have his body free from injury and his liberty free
from infringement unless there be a proper cause, nobody
doubts. But acquired rights such as property require more explanation. Property and civil government very much depend on
one another. The preservation of property and the inequality of
possession first formed it, and the state of property must always
vary with the form of government.[47]

In the *Wealth of Nations* the same philosophical assumptions are made
concerning the existence of natural rights and natural laws of justice, although, not being a disquisition on justice, the distinction between civil
and property rights is not discussed. If anything, the impression one draws
from this work is even more Lockian than that which emerges from the
Lecture on Justice. Here, in fact, Smith unambiguously declares that the
property which every man has in his own labor is the foundation of all
property and is sacred and inviolable.[48] Consequently, Smith condemns
all legislation which interferes with the free bargaining between workmen and employers. To hinder a man from employing his labor in whatever manner he wishes without injuring his neighbor is a violation of this
"most sacred property"; it is a violation of the just liberty of both the
workmen and their potential employers. In a similar vein, Smith condemns
legislation on apprenticeships as a violation of property in one's own
person. This is most definitely Locke and not Hume or Bentham.

In addition, then, to the pragmatic, utilitarian arguments for a free
economy which are displayed throughout the *Inquiry*—arguments to the
effect that the maximization of national wealth can best be achieved by
leaving men free in their economic choices and that all other systems
which aim at this end by other means are self-defeating—there is running
through the volume a natural rights defense of economic freedom which
cannot be ignored. The law should let people judge of their own interests,
Smith repeatedly intones; laws which are violations of natural liberty
are unjust.[49] In discussing the prohibition by governments on the exportation of corn, for example, he speaks of such acts as tantamount to
sacrificing the "ordinary laws of justice to an idea of public utility, to a
social reason of state; an art of legislation which ought to be excused
only, which can be *pardoned* only, in cases of the most urgent necessity."[50]

Free trade is pragmatically desirable, Smithian economics contends,
and therefore, it should be practiced by every enlightened state, but it

also argues that any violation of the maxims of free trade is a violation of natural liberty and justice and should be condemned for that reason alone. Furthermore, Smith employs the same natural rights argument when he condemns all acts which prohibit people from trading freely as "a violation of the most sacred rights of mankind."[51] The evidence shows clearly, then, that a natural rights defense of the free market was an integral part of Smith's orchestration.

How was Smith able to consummate this marriage of natural rights with a utility defense of economic freedom? It was accomplished through the economic argument that self-interest will prompt men to enter those trades in which the profit will be greatest and that these trades are the most profitable precisely because they fill the most urgently felt needs of society. The argument proceeds as follows: (1) every individual continually exerts himself to find the most advantageous use for his capital—this is a deduction from the principle of self-interest, and consequently, (2) that in looking out only for his own interest, he is naturally and necessarily led to prefer that employment which is most advantageous for society as a whole. The individual, then, is the best judge of the most efficacious investment for his industry, much more so than the statesman or the lawgiver, because his interest is more immediate than theirs; it is he who stands to gain or lose by the transaction, not the legislator.[52] Without the intervention of any laws, private interest disposes men to distribute their stock among employments in the proportion most agreeable to the welfare of society.[53]

Therefore, all regulatory systems, such as the mercantile system, derange this natural mechanism and thus can only be injurious to society. Profit serves as a natural criterion by which to judge the efficacy of one's investments; if too much capital is drawn into one employment, then profit goes down and funds are withdrawn to other lines of endeavor. The system is self-correcting. By artificial, legislative regulations one only succeeds in diverting capital to less profitable productions (that is, those less desired by the ultimate consumers), thus curtailing consumer satisfaction. A natural rights argument would lead to a system of economic freedom by the following steps: (1) all men have the natural rights of life, liberty, and property, and therefore, (2) they must be free to transfer, exchange, sell, or will their property as they wish. The argument from self-interest to division of labor and a system of exchange simply illustrates how what is naturally right and just leads of necessity to what would be considered most beneficial on a purely pragmatic, utilitarian calculation. For this is the same Smith of the *Moral Sentiments,* who maintained that nature was both harmonious and economical. What is just and right, consequently, *must* be what leads to the happiness and material welfare of mankind, for man is a natural part of a natural *telos,* and he is fitted with those attributes, namely self-interest for the economic realm, which will enable him to play his part successfully. And so, Smith can write that the establishment of perfect justice, liberty, and equality will secure the greatest prosperity to all classes,[54] that is, there is a natural harmony of interest between the different classes of society. Men have a natural right to do precisely those things which upon examination will prove to be most beneficial for themselves and for their fellows—a harmonious and efficient nature insures this outcome. It could not be otherwise. The extent to which Smith was a consistent advocate of this, his dominant view, will be discussed subsequently.

Now, as we come to examine Adam Smith's contributions to what would later be considered pure economics, the following tenets will be considered both because of their central role in Smith's own system and because of the influence which they were to have upon the future course of economic theory: his theory of value and price; his analysis of the origins and nature of profit, wages, and rent; his treatment of the way in which classes were delineated and their interests distinguished; and his projections as to the effects of improvement in the economic sphere.

The labor theory of value which Smith propounded remained *the* theory of value until the development of the marginal utility theory in the 1870s, and as such it influenced the economic and social thinking of such diverse theoreticians as Karl Marx and Jeremy Bentham. To elicit a clear view of this theory, however, is not a simple task, as Smith's formulation contains elements of at least two types of labor theories which he muddled together and which were only later distinguished by Ricardo.[55] Smith combines both (1) a "labor-cost" theory of value, that is, that a commodity's value is what it has cost the laborer in time to produce the object, and (2) a "labor-purchase" (or "labor-command") theory of value, that the value of an item produced by labor is determined by what it will exchange for or how much of the products of other men's labor it will purchase. What Smith seems to be saying, although it is never quite in focus, is that labor-cost is the real, original, and underlying cause of value and that labor-purchase is the rough equivalent employed once civilization advances and appropriation has made some men capitalists and others their employees. Thus, it will be argued, for Smith labor is both the cause of value and the measure of value.[56]

To backtrack for a moment, let us examine certain other features of Smith's value theory which are explicitly stated and of equal importance. Smith, in attempting to define value, draws the distinction between (1) value is use, that is, the utility of a certain object in satisfying human wants, and (2) value is exchange, the power of purchasing other goods which the possession of that object conveys.[57] What the economist is concerned with, Smith contends, is exchange value, and thus, he rejects utility as the standard of value. He made such a move largely because his conception of utility was of "total" utility and not of the later notion of "marginal" utility. He was driven to this conclusion by the consideration of such examples as the diamond-water paradox, a paradox, one might add, only on (1) an objective theory of value, one which does not consider the subjective evaluations of individual consumers, or (2) a theory which neglects to consider the role played by scarcity in the formulation of value. In this paradox water, a good of inestimable value in use, is worth little or nothing in exchange, while diamonds, a commodity of scarcely any value in use, are worth a great deal in exchange value. From this objective definition of value—value in exchange being defined as the power of purchasing other goods—Smith moves on to the "cost" theory of value, of which we spoke previously. "The real price of everything, what everything really costs to the man who wants to acquire it, is the toil and trouble of acquiring it."[58] (Here, Smith treats the "real price" and "exchangeable value" as equivalent terms.) "What everything is really worth to the man who has acquired it; and who wants to dispose of it or exchange it for something else is the toil and trouble which it can save himself. . .,"[59] the implication being that, once a good is destined for sale, the regnant principle of exchange value is the labor-purchase theory of value, that is, the value of a good destined for exchange is equal to the quantity of labor which it will purchase. Labor—whether it be the original labor that went into the production of a commodity or the labor which that good when exchanged will enable the producer to command, is not clear—is the real measure of the exchangeable value of all commodities. All the wealth of the world was originally purchased by labor. Labor, then, is both the cause and measure of value.

Labor is, however, not the medium in which value is commonly estimated because it is difficult to equate the hardship entailed in different occupations or the varying amounts of ingenuity they require. Consequently, the equation is never precise, and the adjustment is left to "the higgling and the bargaining of the market."[60] Furthermore, goods are most frequently exchanged for each other and with the advancement of society, for money, and these commodities or money come to be regarded as the measure of value. But Smith's contention is that while these commodities and money (gold and silver) vary in value through time, labor (in the sense of sacrifice of ease on the part of the laborer) never varies in value, although it may purchase larger or smaller quantities of goods—it is the real price of all goods. While labor may appear to the employer to cost more at some times than at others, it is actually the goods which he uses to purchase labor that are cheaper or dearer. Labor is the unchanging real price of all commodities; money is the nominal price because it fluctuates in value.

When it came to the actual exchange of goods in the marketplace, Smith drew a distinction, one which was later adopted by both Ricardo and J. S. Mill, between natural price and market price, the former being the long-range price around which the market or actual price would tend to gravitate. Natural price, as determined by labor cost, rent, and profits (or what it really cost the manufacturer to bring it to market), would not be affected by factors of supply and demand, while the variation in the market price from this natural price would be solely attributable to that source. There are problems with this two-tier price system, as Malthus for one realized, the principal one being that it artificially excluded all questions of consumer preference from the establishment of the long-range or natural price. The natural-price notion seems to be a holdover from the Medieval notion of a "just price."

In moving from labor-cost to labor-purchase, Smith offers an inadequate explanation of profit which was to haunt the Classical economists and provide ammunition for socialists such as Marx to undermine the capitalist system as it was defended by this kind of an argument. Profit, on the account proffered by Smith, seems as though it were somehow mysteriously slapped on by the capitalist as men emerged from the labor-cost-governed, primitive society. It was all too easy for Marx to come along and denounce this as an act of expropriation by the capitalist and demand the full product for laborers.

What Smith did was to draw a false distinction between (1) an early trade state of society which precedes the appropriation of land and the accumulation of stock, in which the proportion between the quantities of labor necessary for acquiring different objects appears to afford the only rule for determining their exchange value, and (2) an advanced stage of society in which men have accumulated stock and in which they employ laborers. In the latter stage only does profit arise as the worker produces his salary plus a part for the profit of the employer as payment for hazarding his stock in the venture. (Note the typical classical confusion between profit and interest.) These profits are—and here Smith gets into even deeper trouble—regulated by the value of the stock employed and are not the wages of the labor of inspection and direction.[61] Thus, whenever Smith speaks of profit, it is as if the capitalist were entitled to his 5 percent or 10 percent or whatever the customary, "natural" rate of profit might be, and his share would be governed solely by the quantity of stock which he originally invested. From the commodities which a capitalist's laborers produced, he would receive X percent on his capital, and hence, the laborers would not be entitled to the whole product of their labor.[62] The problem with this theory is that it makes profit appear to be arbitrarily determined, as though each venturer of stock would automatically receive profit on his investment regardless of whether the business was managed efficiently or whether there was any demand for the good.

Similar problems are to be found with Smith's account of the determinants of price, in which he isolated labor, rent, and profit as discrete components of price. Though all were ultimately measured by labor, each was considered as a separable entity with both profit and rent tacked on with the advent of an advanced society based on accumulation of stock and land appropriation. From the produce of labor, chunks were to be deducted for both profit and rent. Smith himself was not unaware of the apparent arbitrariness of this arrangement, as he disparages landlords as those who desire to reap where they have not sowed,[63] and he describes rent on land as naturally a monopoly price.[64] In fact, as Paul Douglas observed,[65] Smith offers four different accounts of how the landlord is able to collect rent: (1) because he demands it, (2) because he holds a monopoly, (3) because he has a differential advantage, and (4) because nature is bountiful. His account of profit was similarly confused. Smith's account hardly provides an adequate description of, let alone a justification for, profit or rent.

By isolating wages, profit, and rent as separate components of price, Smith was led to the separation of men into discrete and even hostile

classes of rent collectors, wage earners, and profit seekers, thus undermining the very notion of the harmony of interests which was the dominant thrust of his political economy. His approach was adopted by his
followers, and much of their effort was wasted down a blind alley as they
attempted to discover the proper distribution between these three factors
of production. This class analysis, when driven to its limit, led to a
Marxian, class-antagonism paradigm of the workings of the capitalist
economic system.

Let us ponder this question of class a bit further and examine what
has happened to the harmony-of-interests claim previously discussed. For,
it will be recalled, Smith's conception of nature led him to conceive of
the economic order as essentially harmonious. However, in the course of
the *Inquiry,* certain discordant notes are struck. While the landlord's
interest is inseparably connected with the general interest of society, as
is that of the wage earners, the interest of the merchant or manufacturer
is not so intimately connected. This state of affairs is the result of the
fact that the rate of profit does not, like rent or wages, rise with the
prosperity and fall with the declension of society; rather, it is naturally
low in wealthy countries, high in poor ones and highest in countries going
fastest to ruin.[66] A political problem emanates from this economic source
in that those classes, the landlords and laborers, which are most in harmony
with the interest of the whole society are precisely those least equipped
to project their interest into political action, while the class which is least
intrinsically interested in the general good, the merchants and manufacturers, is best equipped to influence legislation. The proprietors of
land can never mislead their fellows in deliberations concerning commerce
or police, if only they know their own true interest, but they are, thanks
to their occupation, indolent and unfit for public office. Likewise, the
wage earners are incapable of comprehending their own interests and
their relationship to the remainder of society. The profit seekers, on the
contrary, have a much better understanding of their own interest, which
is to widen the market and narrow the competition. Consequently, those
best situated by inclination, experience, and position to influence legislation are precisely those whose interest does not coincide most nearly
with the public interest and who may even have an interest in oppressing
society.[67]

Smith does not abandon the harmony-of-interests generalization entirely in the case of merchants and manufacturers as evidenced by his
discussion of the role of the inland corn dealers; at this point he notes

that by pursuing their own interests in times of shortage—that is, by holding out part of the supply until the price rises—the corn trader actually serves the society's interest by acting as an automatic, self-governing allocation system, thus stretching the insufficient supply over a longer period of time.[68] Government interference, Smith cautions, would only turn a dearth into a famine.[69]

A partial reconciliation may be effected between Smith's harmony-of-interest position and his contention that class interests may diverge and even run counter to the general interest. It can, perhaps, be argued that Smith can be made more consistent by interpreting his cautions against conflicting class interests and conflicting class and general interests as warnings against exacerbating existing differences by permitting classes to influence legislation. While Smith does decry class-inspired legislation, he seems to do so more on a natural rights or violation-of-justice basis than on an empirical argument based on class interests, for example, his contentions that to hurt one class of citizens in order to help another is contrary to the justice and equality of treatment which the sovereign owes to all different orders of his subjects,[70] and that laws should let people judge their own interests because to do otherwise would be a violation of natural liberty and, as such, unjust.[71] What we can say, then, is that Smith had three separate arguments for limiting the use of state power by classes for their own interests: (1) the harmony-of-interest contention, in which the interests of all classes are seen as compatible; hence, state intervention could serve only to unbalance the natural mechanism; (2) the disharmony-of-interest argument, wherein the class of manufacturers and merchants is seen as having interests which can in some cases run counter to the interest of society, thus leading us to conclude that the state should be limited in its economic intervention so as to avoid making matters worse by fostering class legislation by the profit seekers, the most politically active and economically aware class; and, finally, (3) the natural rights and violation-of-justice position which would dictate a limitation of legislation in the economic sphere because such laws would necessarily violate certain people's rights or nullify their claims to equal justice under the law.

Arguments (1) and (2) are obviously inconsistent in their basic assumptions, although all three arguments, as employed by Smith, lead to the same conclusion. It is only possible to reconcile (1) and (2) if we take the harmony of interests among classes to mean that they all enjoy greater prosperity and thus have an interest in the establishment of perfect justice, liberty, and equality. While Smith says this,[72] it is a minimal claim, and he seems to be maintaining much more when he repeatedly claims that by pursuing one's own interest, one benefits society. All we can conclude, then, is that Smith interweaves several incompatible foundations as justification for minimal state intervention in the economy, and that he was apparently unaware or untroubled by these inconsistencies because they all led to the same conclusion—that of limited government.

Smith's arguments for general laissez-faire are further buttressed by the orientation of his economics. It is consumer-oriented. Consumption is, according to Smith's conception, the sole end and purpose of all production. Consequently, the interest of the producers ought to be attended to only insofar as it may be necessary for promoting that of the consumer.[73] Smith considers that a self-evident maxim. On these grounds he condemns the Mercantilist system which sacrificed consumers to producers by legislating bounties and restraints on importation.

As we turn now to Smith's theory of government, the importance of his harmony-of-interest analysis will become apparent. It led him to promulgate a "minimal-state" theory of government which, while not the much maligned "night-watchman state," argued for the circumscription of state interference in the economy. In the *Lectures*, Smith follows Hume in denying the validity of a Lockian type of contractual basis both for the foundation of government and for the source of our obligation to obey its dictates.[74] Rather, he maintains, there are only two principles which can induce men to enter into civil society: (1) authority, or (2) utility. The former is constituted primarily by superior wealth, but encompasses also all other facets in which some men may excel their fellows, for example, superior ability, age, strength, mental capacity, long possession of power, ancient family, and so on, while the latter principle dictates that men ought to submit to governmental decisions for the good of the whole, for public more than private utility, and in order to prevent the greater evil of anarchy. Government came about only with the appropriation of herds and flocks which introduced inequality of fortunes. "Till there be property there can be no government, the very end of which is to secure wealth and to defend the rich from the poor."[75] The genesis of government, then, is through a natural process as men emerge from their primitive state into a herding phase, eventually culminating in a commercial society. This development occurs without the intervention of human planning in a Lockian or Hobbesian sense, and this is certainly not surprising considering Smith's general conception of nature and man's place in it. Just as individual economic relationships proceed in a manner most amenable to progress without such effects being consciously intended by the actors, government develops spontaneously to insure an orderly and nonviolent nexus in which men can pursue their objectives.

If the operations of the market combined with the natural propensity of men to truck and barter in the pursuit of their own self-interest and advancement will insure the maximum output of wealth for the nation as a whole, and no other systems, such as a Mercantilist system of intervention in favor of the producers, or an agricultural system which views manufacturers as unproductive, will do anything but thwart this system of natural liberty, as Smithian economics contends, then government must not interfere with this natural mechanism so as to cause its derangement. What role remains, then, for government to play? Clearly it has no need to propound positive policy objectives such as furthering full employment, maximizing output, encouraging a high rate of growth, or stimulating an advantageous balance of trade, because such ends are best secured by the free play of the marketplace.[76] Positive intervention by government on behalf of any of these goals would only serve to divert investment from its naturally most profitable course, profitable precisely because it served the most urgent wants of the people. But the "simple system of natural liberty" does require for its efficient operation the restriction of force, because only then can men pursue their interests with the assurance that they can retain the fruits of their labor. Freedom and security, Smith constantly reiterates, are the two requisites for the maximization of national wealth.[77]

Dugald Stuart, in his introduction to the *Wealth of Nations,* quotes from a manuscript of Smith's from the year 1755 (over twenty years before the publication of Smith's political economy, interestingly enough) in which Smith succinctly summarized his leading principles on government in the process of enumerating what he considered to be his original contribution to the subject. It will be helpful to cite this passage here, for it captures the essence of Smith's conception of both the natural workings of the economic system and of the state, which is itself a natural outgrowth.

Man is generally considered by statesman and projectors as the material of a sort of political mechanics. Projectors dis-

turb nature in the course of her operations in human affairs;
and it requires no more than to let her alone, and give her
fair play in the pursuit of her ends, that she may establish
her own designs. . . . Little else is requisite to carry a state to
the highest degree of opulence from the lowest barbarism, but
peace, easy taxes, and a tolerable administration of justice;
all the rest being brought about by the natural course of
things. All governments which thwart this natural course, which
force things into another channel, or which endeavor to arrest
the progress of society at a particular point, are unnatural, and
to support themselves are obliged to be oppressive and tyrannical.[78]

Both Mercantilism and the agricultural system of favoritism fail because they subvert the very purpose they were meant to promote, that is,
they hinder the progress of society by restricting the production of wealth.
Therefore, argues Smith, the system of "natural liberty is proved," since
all systems based on principles of state intervention in the economy would
be susceptible to the same criticism of being self-defeating. Neither by encouragements for capital to seek investments which it would not naturally
pursue nor by restraints against certain categories of investment can the
government accelerate the progress of society towards greater wealth and
greatness.[79] "All systems of preference or of restraint, being thus completely taken away, the obvious and simple system of natural liberty
establishes itself of its own accord."[80] Every man must be left free to
pursue his own interests and to compete with all other men, so long as
he does not violate the laws of justice. Consequently, the sovereign is re-
leased from the intolerable burden, which he cannot perform advantageous-
ly or even adequately in any case, of intervening in the economic order
where no human wisdom or knowledge can ever be efficacious. He no
longer is responsible for superintending the industry of private individuals
or directing their efforts to the interest of society, because this is already
accomplished without his intervention.

Thus, the sovereign, according to this system of natural liberty, has only
three duties: (1) the duty of protecting the society from the violence and
invasion of other independent societies, (2) the duty of protecting as far
as possible every member of society from the injustice and oppression of
every other member, that is, the duty of establishing an exact administration of justice, and (3) the duty of erecting and maintaining certain necessary public works and certain public institutions which it can never be in

the interest of any small number of individuals to maintain because the profit would not repay the expense.[81] Naturally, to support these projects, the government requires revenue to be raised by taxation. Smith offers as an illustration of how government can correctly perform its functions the following case—of a landlord and farmer for whom the government can provide assistance (*a*) negatively—by allowing both to pursue their own interests in their own way, (*b*) positively—by providing to them the most perfect security to ensure that they shall enjoy the full recompense of their own enterprise, and (*c*) positively—by procuring to them the most extensive market possible for their products through the establishment of easy and safe communications by land and water within the country, as well as the most unrestricted freedom of exportation to foreign countries.[82]

There is, quite obviously, a problem with Smith's analysis of the duties of government, and the problem lies precisely in his third injunction (3) to the effect that the government has a duty to engage in public works and institutions when private incentive is insufficient to secure the desired good. Why does the mechanism of natural liberty break down in these cases—or does it?[83] What Smith does here is to smuggle in a utilitarian standard to cover these cases in which the market purportedly will not provide adequate services; examples of which are the construction of streets, canals, harbors, embassies, and fortifications for the encouragement of trade and commerce; the education of youth and the general population; and the maintenance of the church. He had been arguing all along that the system of natural liberty will accomplish all the utilitarian kinds of objectives (the principal one being the maximization of the wealth of society as a whole) and that these goods can be achieved, and can only be achieved effectively, by adhering to this system of individual freedom and nonviolation of the claims of others to justice, that is, their equal claim to enjoy the fruits of their own industry without threat or violence. If the free play of the market, which Smith wholeheartedly endorses, fails to provide roads or schools (which is extremely doubtful as evidenced historically by the existence of private railroads and private schools), by what justification can the government step in to build the roads and schools? By Smith's own logic, such intervention can not help but commit both the economic sin of diverting capital from its most profitable avenue of employment (that which satisfies the most pressing wants) and the political and moral sin of coercing men through taxation to pursue ends other than their own. It is only because Smith is confused about his ultimate principles that he can advance such an argument. That he combines and obfuscates the distinction between a natural rights defense of the system of natural liberty and a utilitarian defense is apparent. This confusion led Smith to make what is in effect a despotic claim, that when the market fails to provide the canals, roads, and schools which he, Smith, deems desirable, then he is justified in using the coercive force of the state to compel all individuals to contribute to these projects.

In a consistent rendition of the natural-liberty system, one would argue that the fact that these projects were not undertaken would be sufficient evidence to prove that they were not desired enough by the consumers to make their production possible on a profitable basis. Consequently, no case could be made for the government engaging in such enterprises. To argue, as Smith does, that these socially advantageous projects (socially advantageous by what standard and in whose judgment is never specified) should be undertaken when the market fails to provide them is to undermine the whole edifice, based on private interests leading naturally to social advantage, which he attempted to construct. If it is once conceded that some higher force, the government, may legitimately intervene when some putative social good is not being produced by the marketplace, then it is but a logical step to say that the market is not producing some other desired effect, say the equal distribution of incomes, or full employment, or whatever, which someone might consider socially desirable, and therefore, the government must intervene to accomplish this goal.

This is precisely the kind of reasoning that Smith considered totally illegitimate. And it is ironic that he himself sewed the seeds for just such claims by future proponents of a utilitarian-based defense of the free market. On a theoretical level, Smith understood perfectly well that you can not have it both ways, that you must, in order to secure men's purposes, either defer to the market and the infinite array of individual choices which it encompasses or establish some other ultimate authority, the government, to make men's choices for them. Clearly, he intended to opt for the former solution because it cohered with the "natural" workings of the world, thus providing the only security for individual well-being and social wealth. But when it came to describing the role of the government in safeguarding this system, Smith fell into contradiction by proposing a positive role for government which went beyond upholding justice, and thus he succeeded only in undermining his defense of the "natural" system. While governmental duties 1 and 2 are defensible on natural-justice grounds principally and only incidentally on grounds of utility, duty (3) can only be justified, and not even correctly so, on utilitarian grounds.

From this third duty of government—which we have criticized as being (1) inconsistent with Smith's system of natural liberty and justice for all, and (2) indefensible on even utilitarian grounds because Smithian economics teaches that the happiness of the whole can best be achieved through the interplay of individual, free choice—Smith drew the justification for certain instances of governmental interference which he deemed acceptable in certain clearly delineated cases. Hence, he allows for several circumstances in which it may be advantageous to restrict foreign in favor of domestic industry, for example: (1) when a certain industry is necessary for the defense of the nation (e.g., the Navigation Acts are permissible), (2) when a tax is imposed on a domestic industry it should also be levied on foreign industry, and (3) when a foreign country imposes taxes on your exports, you may do likewise but only in hopes of getting the imposition removed.[84] Similarly, there were other exceptional cases in which the government may properly intervene: monopolies may be legitimately granted to joint-stock companies in unexplored areas on a temporary basis; in the case of banking where the liberty of a few endangers the liberty of the whole society, the few ought to be restrained by law; the rate of interest should be determined by the state (a position which he later recanted under Bentham's prodding); and education should be provided for those who can't afford it. It should be noted, once again, that all these governmental incursions are justified by Smith on the grounds either that they are desirable and necessary or that the market will fail to provide these services. Both claims are subject to serious dispute, even on utilitarian grounds.

Smith's discussion of taxation suffers from similar difficulties. Taxation is necessary not for the maintenance of justice, which Smith says can be sufficiently supplied by court fees levied on the users, but for the defense of the society and the dignity of the sovereign and for public institutions and public works; activities, we have argued, of questionable legitimacy on Smith's own terms. Nevertheless, Smith argues that those institutions or public works which are beneficial to the whole society may without injustice be defrayed by the general contributions of the whole society.[85] He cites the expense of maintaining roads and communication, educating children, and instructing in religion. The preferred method of payment would be by those who directly receive the benefit or by voluntary contributions, but the national treasury can be utilized if these sources fail to provide all the requisite funds. It is a peculiarity of early liberal theory that taxation for social projects was not considered to be a violation of anyone's claim to equal justice or a transgression of the right to one's own property. Smith thought that the citizen was bound to contribute taxes to the sovereign,[86] and, in fact, he goes much further when he remarks that every tax is a badge of liberty, not of slavery, because it shows that the taxpayer has no master,[87] a view of taxation subsequently rejected, and with good reason, by Jeremy Bentham.

Smith offers the following guidelines for the least oppressive manner in which taxes can be imposed: (1) subjects should contribute taxes in proportion to their respective abilities, that is, in proportion to the revenue which they enjoy under the protection of the state; (2) a tax should be certain and not arbitrary; (3) a tax should be levied at a convenient time for the contributor to pay it; and (4) a tax should not take from people much more than it gives into the public treasury, that is, the expense of collection should be kept down.[88] These strictures appear reasonable enough—and, indeed, they were influential, appearing intact in the works of Smith's followers Ricardo and Mill—once one grants the justice of taxation itself and the justifiability of the public works for which the taxes were raised, both dubious claims. But Smith strays even further from a night-watchman conception of the state when he suggests that a tax on homes and luxuries could be justified in order to discourage opulence and induce people to invest their money in other, more productive avenues.[89] This is most definitely a utility-based approach, which attempts to direct men's efforts into channels approved by some higher authority who knows better than the natural workings of the market what will benefit society. Smith's contention that rent provides the best base for taxation, because taxes on profits or wages would be ultimately borne by the consumer anyway and would be difficult to assess or collect, is open to the objection that such governmental interference is discriminatory and even redistributive in effect. It should be noted, in passing, that Smith objected to inheritance taxes, not as violations of property rights but as taxes difficult to assess or collect. A flawed theory of property rights is the fundamental source of all these idiosyncrasies.

Smith's discussion of legitimate governmental practices was most consistent with his pure economic theory when he came to discuss the ques-

tions of freedom of trade and colonial policies.[90] Here his "let alone"
philosophy achieves full play. To prohibit people from trading freely is
a "violation of the most sacred rights of mankind,"[91] and it is also an
utterly feckless policy because no conceivable regulations can increase
the quantity of industry in any country beyond what its capital will
maintain; rather it can only be redirected without any guarantee of
producing a more advantageous result.[92] Wealth, Smith lectures the
Mercantilists, does not consist in gold and silver but in the commodities
which they purchase.[93] Freedom of trade without governmental intervention will supply us with all the requisites of existence, as well as gold and
silver, these latter being regulated by the effective demand for them in
each country. Gold and silver are the most effortlessly self-regulating
commodities. "Upon every account, therefore, the attention of government never was so unnecessarily employed, as when directed to watch
over the preservation or increase of the quantity of money in any country."[94]
Foreign trade, free from governmental interference, is to be heartily approved for its beneficial effects, including (1) the exchange of superfluities
for things in demand which are not produced in one's own country, (2)
the incentive it offers to improvements in productive powers, and (3)
the stimulus it provides to progress in the division of labor.[95]

In regard to the colonial question, Smith considered the policies of
his day to be injurious both to the colonies themselves and to the mother
countries, and he remarks that Britain's colonies fared somewhat better
than Spain's only because of the greater security and freedom permitted
in the former, but that nevertheless, Britain's trading policies were largely
monopolistic in intent. This viewpoint carried through the entire Classical School; imperialism was anathema to all of them. It is, then, in his discussions of free trade and errors in the Mercantilist system and colonial
policies that Smith remains most consistent with both his philosophical
formulations and his pure economic principles.

CONCLUSION

In the preceding discussion of Smith's economic, moral, and political
works, we have seen that he can hardly be accused of erring on the side
of consistency, although a general compatibility was perceived between
his world view as propounded in the *Theory of Moral Sentiments* and
in the *Wealth of Nations.* In the latter work Smith's ambivalence regarding

ultimate principles is most apparent, appealing at times to a natural rights-natural law foundation and at other occasions to a utility standard. There is, then, a marked disjunction between his philosophical premises (i.e., individualism and the natural harmony of interests between non-rights-violating men) and his discussion of governmental activities, in which he becomes much more of a commonsense, pragmatic utilitarian (e.g., his assertion that the government has as one of its legitimate functions the undertaking of public works and institutions).

Another disjunction exists between Smith's moral Aristotelianism and his decidedly un-Aristotelian attitude toward politics. Where Aristotle stressed man's nature as being principally political, the result of his status in a particular society and the moral view implanted in him by that society, Smith emphasized man's individuality and his natural independence from government as a rights-bearing entity even before government was instituted. Smith, then, was an heir of Locke in politics and Aristotle in morals. Aristotle's man was not truly human unless he was a member of a *polis,* while Smith's man of the political economy was bound to his fellows as a result of the division of labor and his own realization that consequently self-interest necessitated such an association. Aristotle's political society embraced a teleological purpose and Smith's did not. Thus, Aristotle's view of politics was far more interventionist because his men had to be molded into a society in order to achieve their communal moral end. Smith's man could be left much more liberty by government because his moral ends were private only. Politics was a positive good for Aristotle, whereas for Smith it was merely a necessary construct without which there could be no guarantee that the play of individual interests would be restricted to peaceful means. Aristotelian man could not be truly man without the state. Smith's man could be properly such with or without government.

Smith's conception of the purpose of political economy as being the instruction of legislators in the best means of maximizing national wealth held the seeds of future problems. While in Smith's own economics the conclusion was that the politician desirous of achieving this maximization of wealth should leave the economic sphere alone in most instances, he did, however, acknowledge cases in which private interest would not accomplish desirable social goods and where government action would be acceptable. But when future economists came to question the efficacy of private initiatives in achieving social goals over much wider areas than Smith acknowledged as deficient and furthermore questioned the sanctity of wealth maximization as the sole national objective (considering other factors, such as the distribution of wealth, as equally worthy national goals), then Smith's conception of political economy as the handmaiden of the legislator was to have far different effects than Smith intended.

The confusion engendered by Smith's labor theory of value and his mistaken notions about the origin of profits caused a great deal of trouble for Classical economists and in addition provided ammunition for future socialist writers in their attempts to discredit the free-market economy. One can find little to disagree with Paul Douglas' assertion (except to deny the "inevitability") that Smith's formulation of the national product among the factors of production "was such as almost inevitably gave rise to the doctrines of the post-Ricardian socialists and to the labor theory of value and the exploitation theory of Karl Marx."[96] Smith's claim that in the early stages of society the laborer would receive the whole of his product led quite naturally to the socialists' clamor that the laborer in an industrialized society should once again receive all that he produces.

We can conclude this investigation into the origins of Classical economics by reiterating two crucial points. First, Smith failed to provide a theory of legitimate governmental intervention in the economic realm consistent with his economic principles of individual self-interest leading to the harmony of interests when men were left free to pursue their own ends. Second, his conception of political economy was far more intimately connected with a natural law—harmony of nature ontology than would be the works of his followers, although he was not a consistent exponent of such a view.

NOTES

1. For other recent arguments which maintain a similar position see: R. H. Coase, "Adam Smith's Views of Man," *Journal of Law and Economics,* October 1976, 19 (3), pp. 529-46; T. D. Campbell, *Adam Smith's Science of Morals* (London: George Allen and Unwin, 1971); R. Anspach, "The Implications of *The Theory of Moral Sentiments* for Adam Smith's Economic Thought," *History of Political Economy,* Spring 1972, 4 (1), pp. 176-206; A. L. Macfie, *The Individual in Society: Papers on Adam Smith* (London: George Allen and Unwin, 1967); H. C. Rechtenwald, *Adam Smith: Sein Leben und Sein Werk* (Munich: Beck Verlag, 1976).

2. Differing viewpoints on the role of self-interest in the works of Smith are presented by: A. W. Coats, "Adam Smith's Conception of Self-Interest in Economic and Political Affairs," *History of Political Economy,* Spring 1975, 7 (1), p. 132-6; G. Stigler, "Smith's Travels on the Ship of State," in Skinner and Wilson, eds., *Essays on Adam Smith* (Oxford: Clarendon Press, 1975), pp. 235-46; R. H. Coase, "Adam Smith's Views of Man," *Journal of Law and Economics,* October 1976, 19 (3), pp. 529-46; Thomas Wilson, "Sympathy and Self-Interest," in T. Wilson and A. Skinner, *The Market and the State: Essays in Honour of Adam Smith* (Oxford: Clarendon Press, 1976); pp. 73-99.

3. Adam Smith, *The Theory of Moral Sentiments.* The Glasgow Edition of the Works and Correspondence of Adam Smith. Vol. 1, ed. D. D. Raphael and A. L. Macfie (Oxford: Clarendon Press, 1976), (II.i.5.9), p. 77.

4. Ibid. (II, ii.3.5), p. 87.

5. Ibid. (I.i.1.2), p. 9.

6. Ibid. (III.2.7), p. 117.

7. Ibid. (II.ii.2.1), pp. 82-83.

8. Ibid.

9. Ibid., p. 83.

10. Ibid. (II.ii.1), pp. 78-82.

11. Ibid. (II.ii.1.9), p. 82.

12. Ibid. (II.ii.2.2), pp. 82-83.

13. Ibid. (II.ii.3.4), p. 86.

14. Interesting discussions of the role of reason in Smith's conception of man appear in: Coase's "Adam Smith's Views of Man," in which it is argued that Smith has a low estimate of the position of reason as compared to instincts in man (a position in accord with that of Jacob Viner), e.g., "Adam Smith would not have thought it sensible to treat man as a rational utility-maximizer. He thinks of man as he actually is—dominated, it is true, by self-love but not without some concern for others, able to reason but not necessarily in such a way as to reach the right conclusion, seeing the outcomes of his actions but through a veil of self-delusion" (pp. 545-6). See also: H. Spiegel, "Adam Smith's Heavenly City," *History of Political Economy,* Winter 1976, 8 (4), pp. 478-93, in which Smith is portrayed as a spiritualist, having elements predating Enlightenment reason.

15. Smith, *Moral Sentiments* (III.4.7-8), pp. 159-60.

16. Ibid. (III.4.8), p. 159.

17. Ibid. (III.5.3), p. 163.

18. For a recent reappraisal and analysis of newly discovered lecture

notes on the Glasgow Lectures see: Ronald Meek, "New Light on Adam Smith's Glasgow Lectures on Jurisprudence," *History of Political Economy,* Winter 1976, 8 (4), pp. 439-77.

19. Smith, *Moral Sentiments* (VI.iii.1), p. 237; and (VI. concl. 1), p. 262.

20. Ibid. (III.3.34), p. 152.

21. Ibid. (I.i.5.5), p. 25.

22. Ibid.

23. Ibid. (VI.iii.23), p. 247.

24. Ibid. (VI.ii.4-6), pp. 236-7.

25. Ibid. (I.iii.), pp. 43-50.

26. Ibid. (I.iii.2.3), p. 52.

27. Ibid. (I.iii.3.1), p. 61.

28. Adam Smith, *Lectures in Justice, Police, Revenue and Arms* (from a student's notes of the year 1763, first published by Edwin Cannan, Oxford, 1896), in Herbert W. Schneider, *Adam Smith's Moral and Political Philosophy* (New York: Harper Torchbooks, 1948), p. 317.

29. Adam Smith, *An Inquiry into the Nature and Causes of the Wealth of Nations,* ed. R. H. Campbell and A. S. Skinner, The Glasgow Edition of the Works and Correspondence of Adam Smith, 2 vols. (Oxford: Clarendon Press, 1976), Bk. 4, Introduction, p. 428.

30. T. W. Hutchison, *'Positive' Economics and Policy Objectives* (Cambridge, Mass.: Harvard University Press, 1964), Ch. 1, p. 16; see also J. S. Mill, "On the Definition of Political Economy; and on the Method of Investigation Proper to it," in *Essays on Some Unsettled Questions of Political Economy,* 2nd ed. (1st ed. 1836; rpt. London: Longman, Green, Reader, and Dyer, 1874), and N. Senior, *An Outline of the Science of Political Economy,* 6th ed. (1st ed. 1836; rpt. New York: Farrar and Rinehart, 1939).

31. For an interesting discussion of Smith's scope and method see: T. Hutchison, "Adam Smith and the Wealth of Nations," *Journal of Law and Economics,* October 1976, 19 (3), pp. 507-28. Hutchison contends that Smith, in contrast to James Mill and Ricardo, kept a tight rein on abstract reasoning, preferring what is described as a descriptive and historical approach. The whole is held together by a dynamic model, "the simple system of natural liberty."

32. The following works present detailed evaluations of the role that division of labor plays in Smith's political economy: V. Foley, "Smith and the Greeks: A Reply to Professor McNulty's Comments," *History of Political Economy,* Fall 1975, 7 (3), pp. 379-89; R. Hamoway, "Adam Smith, Adam Ferguson, and the Division of Labour," *Economica,* August 1968, N.S., 35 (139), pp. 249-59; R. Lamb, "Adam Smith's Concept of

Alienation," *Oxford Economic Papers,* July 1973, 25 (2), pp. 275-85;
R. Meek and A. Skinner, "The Development of Adam Smith's Ideas on
the Division of Labour," *Economic Journal,* December 1973, 83 (322),
pp. 1094-1116; R. Meek, "Smith, Turgot, and the 'Four Stages Theory,' "
History of Political Economy, Spring 1971, 3 (1), pp. 9-27; N. Rosenberg,
"Another Advantage of the Division of Labor," *Journal of Political
Economy,* August 1976, 84 (4), pp. 861-68; E. G. West, "Adam Smith
and Alienation: A Rejoinder," *Oxford Economic Papers,* July 1975, 27
(2), pp. 295-301; West, "Adam Smith and Rousseau's Discourse on In-
equality: Inspiration or Provocation," *Journal of Economic Issues,*
June 1971, 5 (2), pp. 56-70; West, "The Political Economy of Alienation:
Karl Marx and Adam Smith," *Oxford Economic Papers,* March 1969,
N.S., 21 (1), pp. 1-23; P. McNulty, "A Note on the Division of Labor in
Plato and Smith," *History of Political Economy,* Fall 1975, 7 (3), pp.
372-8.

33. Smith, *Wealth of Nations,* (I.i.11), p. 24.

34. Ibid., (I.ii.1), p. 25.

35. Ibid. (I.i.10), p. 22.

36. Ibid. (I.ii.2), pp. 26-7.

37. Ibid.

38. Thus, I dissent from Samuels' interpretation (see: W. J. Samuels,
"Adam Smith and the Economy as a System of Power," *Review of Social
Economy,* October 1973, 31 (2), p. 125), when he states, "Smith understood the economy as a system of mutual coercion. . . ." Rather, I think
all that he describes as coercion in Smith is to be interpreted as simply
a bargaining process.

39. Smith, *Wealth of Nations* (I.ii.3), p. 27.

40. Ibid. (4), pp. 28-9.

41. Ibid. (II.iii.31), pp. 342-3.

42. For a variety of interpretations of natural rights in Smith see: T.
Lewis, "Adam Smith: The Labor Market as the Basis of Natural Rights,"
Journal of Economic Issues, March 1977, 11 (1), pp. 21-50 (in which it
is argued that Smith felt that the market was the crucial instrument by
which men come to recognize natural rights); W. Gampp, *Economic
Liberalism,* vol. 2 (New York: Random House, 1965); J. Cropsey, "Adam
Smith," in *History of Political Philosophy,* ed. Strauss and Cropsey
(Chicago: University of Chicago Press, 1963); Cropsey, *Polity and Economy*
(The Hague: Martinus Nijhoff, 1957); R. Lindgren, *The Social Philosophy
of Adam Smith* (The Hague: Martinus Nijhoff, 1973), pp. 61-63 (in which
a natural-rights interpretation of Smith is rejected).

43. Lionel Robbins, *The Theory of Economic Policy in English Classical
Political Economy* (London: Macmillan and Co., 1952).

44. T. W. Hutchison, *'Positive' Economics and Policy Objectives.*
45. Smith, *The Theory of Moral Sentiments* (VII.iv.36-37), pp. 340-2.
46. Smith, *Lectures on Justice, Police, Revenue and Arms,* p. 285.
47. Ibid., p. 286.
48. Smith, *The Wealth of Nations* (I.x.c.12), p. 138.
49. Ibid. (IV.v.b.16), p. 530.
50. Ibid. (IV.v.b.39), p. 539.
51. Ibid. (IV.vii.b.44), p. 582.
52. Ibid. (IV.ii.4-10), pp. 454-6.
53. Ibid. (IV.vii.c.87-97), pp. 629-33.
54. Ibid. (IV.ix.17), p. 669.
55. Paul H. Douglas, "Smith's Theory of Value and Distribution," *Adam Smith, 1776-1926* (Chicago: University of Chicago Press, 1928), rpt. in *The Development of Economic Thought,* ed. H. W. Spiegel (New York: John Wiley and Sons, 1964), "Douglas on Smith," pp. 71-102. On the other hand, Kauhshill ("The Case of Adam Smith's Value Analysis," *Oxford Economic Papers,* March 1973, 25 (1), pp. 60-71) views Smith as presenting a consistent theory.
56. "Labour is the real measure of the exchangeable value of all commodities. . . . Labour was the first price, the original purchase money that was paid for all things." Smith, *Wealth of Nations* (I.v. 1 and 2), p. 47. Hence, Smith did not make the modern distinction between a measure of value and a theory of value (i.e., cause of value). Labor performed both functions.
57. Smith, *The Wealth of Nations* (I.iv.13), pp. 44-5.
58. Ibid. (I.v.2), p. 47.
59. Ibid.
60. Ibid. (4), p. 49.
61. Ibid. (I.vi.6), p. 66.
62. Ibid. (7), p. 67.
63. Ibid.
64. Ibid. (I.xi.a.5), p. 161.
65. Douglas, "Smith's Theory of Value and Distribution."
66. For a discussion of profits in Smith which analyzes his aversion to high profits (because they are a deterrent to efficient capitalist performance and the result of noxious combinations or government-granted monopolies), see: N. Rosenberg, "Adam Smith on Profits—Paradox Lost and Regained," *Journal of Political Economy,* Nov./Dec. 1974, 82 (6), pp. 1177-90.
67. Smith, *The Wealth of Nations* (I.xi.p. 1-10), pp. 264-7.
68. Ibid. (IV.v.a-b.3), pp. 524-5.
69. Ibid. (IV.v.b.7), p. 527.
70. Ibid. (IV.viii.30), p. 654.

71. Ibid. (IV.v.b.16), pp. 530-1.

72. Ibid. (IV.ix.16-17), pp. 669-70.

73. Ibid. (IV.viii.49), p. 660.

74. Smith, *Lectures on Justice, Police, Revenue and Arms,* Division 1, "Of Public Jurisprudence."

75. Ibid., p. 291; see also Smith, *Wealth of Nations* (V.i.b.12), p. 715.

76. Cairncross presents an interesting analysis of some modern objectives of economic policy that the market does not fulfill and speculates how Smith might respond to them. See: A. Cairncross, "The Market and the State," in T. Wilson and A. Skinner, *The Market and The State.*

77. Smith, *The Wealth of Nations* (IV.v.b.43), p. 540.

78. Dugald Stuart, "Dugald Stuart on Smith's *Wealth of Nations,*" in Adam Smith, *An Inquiry Into the Nature and Causes of the Wealth of Nations* (London: George Routledge and Sons, 1908), pp. xi-xii.

79. Smith, *The Wealth of Nations* (Clarendon), (IV.ix.50-1), p. 687.

80. Ibid. (51).

81. Ibid.

82. Ibid. (V.ii.c.18), p. 833.

83. E. G. West ("Adam Smith's Public Economics: A Re-Evaluation," *Canadian Journal of Economics,* February 1977, 1011, pp. 1-18) disputes what he takes to be the two conventional explanations of Smith's justification for intervention: (1) the pragmatic interpretation which views these as exceptional cases of government superiority, and (2) the theoretical view which links him to modern public goods analysis. He argues instead that "Smith's prescription for public works was usually the extension of *private* provision through public *companies enjoying new privileges* of joint stock and limited liability" (p. 1). West's argument is rendered dubious by the fact that the issue of sanctioning limited-liability companies was not really raised until the middle of the following century. On the other hand J. Spengler ("Adam Smith and Society's Decision-Makers," in Skinner and Wilson, *Essays on Adam Smith,* p. 409) interprets Smith in a traditional way which leads to an opposite interpretation from West's. He views Smith as highly critical of joint-stock companies and exclusive companies granted monopolies to govern colonies. Even if West's interpretation were correct, Smith would still be departing from strict noninterventionism by arguing for such companies privileged by law.

84. Smith, *Wealth of Nations* (IV.ii).

85. Ibid. (V.i.h-i.4-6), pp. 815-6.

86. Ibid. (IV.vii.31), p. 654.

87. Ibid. (V.ii.g.11), p. 857.

88. Ibid. (V.ii.b.2-6), pp. 825-827.

89. Ibid. (V.ii.e.7), pp. 842-3.

90. For a detailed discussion of Smith's pure theory of international trade, his absolute-advantage approach, see: H. Myint, "Adam Smith's Theory of International Trade in the Perspective of Economic Development," *Economica*, August 1977, 44 (175), pp. 231-48; also, A. Bloomfield, "Adam Smith and the Theory of International Trade," in Wilson and Skinner, *Essays on Adam Smith.*

91. Smith, *Wealth of Nations* (IV.vii.b.44), p. 582.

92. Ibid. (IV.ii.3), p. 453.

93. Ibid. (IV.i.17), p. 438.

94. Ibid. (15), p. 437.

95. Ibid. (31), pp. 446-7.

96. Douglas, "Smith's Theory of Value and Distribution," p. 73.

Chapter 2

The Followers of Adam Smith: The Early Period—Bentham, Malthus, and Ricardo

The tension in Smith's attitude toward governmental intervention generated by his predominant strain of natural rights and his subordinate, instrumental utilitarianism was resolved by Bentham, decisively and consistently, in favor of the latter. It was to Bentham's credit that he made the choice. His avowed declaration of allegiance to Smithian political economy, however, was mitigated by this introduction of the "general-happiness" standard as the regnant principle in both the moral and political realms. Although not himself aware of the revolutionary implications of the utility principle for Smithian political economy, Bentham's principle was to have far-reaching effects which came to full fruition only in the work of his philosophical heir John Stuart Mill.

In addition to this change in moral outlook wrought by Bentham, the first quarter of the nineteenth century witnessed several critical developments in pure economic theory which shaped what came to be known as English Classical economics for the remainder of its hegemony. Malthus' population theory—the proposition that population tends, when unchecked, to multiply faster than the food supply—and the consequent subsistence theory of wages advanced by Malthus and Ricardo, impressed upon the free-market system a pessimistic and gloomy cast. Also, the Ricardian theory of rent provided added impetus to the detractors of the competitive system in that it predicted the gradual enrichment of the nonproductive, landowning class at the expense of both the capitalists and the laborers. In the ensuing discussions of Bentham, Malthus, and Ricardo we will evaluate the effects of these and other alterations upon the body of Smithian political economy.

The climate of opinion in which Benthamism was spawned was quite different from what it would become in the middle of the century when liberalism captured the social and political consciousness of the rising middle class. In this period economic theorists were still confronted by an unreconstructed Parliament dominated by Tory landholders elected from rotten boroughs or quite often openly purchasing their seats. The animus of the early Classical economists against government can be accounted for in large measure by the rampant corruption which the English government of the day exhibited and also by the blatant class domination of Parliament by aristocratic-agricultural interests.

Reaction against the upheaval and subsequent terror of the French Revolution still impressed itself upon conservatives and liberals alike. Both the Tories with their Six Acts of 1819, which sought to prohibit potentially seditious meetings, public libels, and the training of people in the use of weapons, and Bentham, who penned one of his most vituperative attacks upon the Declaration of Rights, displayed the prevalent fear of the educated class in England that such a virulent political disease might spread to the English laboring class. In attempting to deflect such a catastrophe, the entrenched Tories responded in typically conservative ways. On the one hand, they preserved a paternalistic, inefficient Poor Law system to aid and also constrain within their parishes the unemployed and in 1802 passed the first Factory Act to regulate the working conditions of apprentices, and on the other, they enacted the Combination Act of 1800 which classified workmen's attempts to form trade unions as criminal conspiracies. Under the provisions of this act any worker who attempted to combine with others to negotiate with his employer or, heaven forbid, engage in a strike would be held criminally culpable. Employers were likewise forbidden to collude in setting wages, a clearcut example of Tory agricultural interests striking at perceived threats to their political positions from both the laboring class and the newly emerging manufacturing interests. Benthamite influence in politics convincingly displayed itself in 1824 with the repeal of the Combination Acts and the decriminalization of combinations of both workers and employers.[1] Such conspicuous champions of Benthamism as Francis Place, Joseph Hume, and John McCulloch were instrumental in fostering this legislative emancipation, and despite the partial repeal of 1825, they were victorious. From that time until the 1870s, Benthamite liberalism would be the regnant social philosophy among politically influential Englishmen.

THE PRINCIPLE OF UTILITY AND ITS EFFECTS UPON POLITICAL ECONOMY—JEREMY BENTHAM

One decisive indication of the hegemony of Smithian economics around the turn of the eighteenth century may be found in the power it held over a personality seemingly addicted to the elixir of social experimentation and rational systemization, that of Jeremy Bentham. Indeed, Bentham was a figure of a type more prevalent in the twentieth century than in his own time. He was a perpetual tinkerer, enthralled by his own innumerable schemes for restructuring society, rationalizing the legal systems of all nations, exorcising all irrationalities of tradition from government, revolutionizing the penal system through an architectural invention (his Panopticon), and engineering countless gadgets for the ease of mankind and his own amusement.

For such a man as this to declare that Adam Smith had settled all theoretical questions in the science of political economy was quite a testimonial especially when one recalls that Smith's system was in the main an endorsement of laissez-faire policies in respect to governmental intervention in the economy. But Bentham's pledge of adherence to Smithian economics and his claim to have merely adapted Smith's scientific theories to practice must be examined rather critically and skeptically. When such an examination has been completed, it will be evident that political economy underwent dramatic theoretical[2] and practical transformations under Bentham's influence and his enthronement of the principle of utility as the regnant principle in the social sciences as well as in moral theory.

THE MORAL SYSTEM OF BENTHAMITE UTILITARIANISM

The principle of utility, being a first principle and the basis of a whole system of reasoning, is not capable of direct proof,[3] Bentham argues. Rather, all that is required for its adoption is that it be clearly explained and that its rivals be discredited. Once this is done, every reasonable man will recognize utility as the true, if unspoken, principle behind his actions. The principle of utility, like the axioms of mathematics, is established once one has shown that it can not be rejected without falling into absurdity. Acquiescence to this principle is secured, in addition, by exposing the contradictory nature of its two adversaries—the principle of sympathy-antipathy and the ascetic principle.

The ascetic principle is based on a horror of pleasure and would found morality on privation and suffering. It acclaims as the highest virtue the utter renouncement of oneself. Such a moral injunction of self-abnegation when employed as a general principle for society would lead to misery and deprivation and, ultimately, national suicide. Consequently, it must be rejected as anathema to the natural instincts of rational men and, what's more, detrimental to the perpetuation of mankind.[4]

The second logically possible alternative to the principle of utility is also found to be defective. This principle of sympathy-antipathy, or the arbitrary principle, is condemned as not truly a principle at all because it attempts to devise a system based upon the whims of individuals. In fact, it is nothing more than "mere caprice." Upon such a foundation no consistent moral conclusions can possibly be drawn. Under such a "principle" actions are approved or condemned by each individual judging only on his own personal sentiments. An action is approved simply because it pleases me, not because it conforms to the interests of those it affects. The result, clearly, would be an "anarchy of ideas" with no common standard or ultimate tribunal.

Thus, Bentham disposes of all moral systems founded upon "conscience" or a "moral sense" as providing no fixed standard for the moralist. In this category he places: (1) all moral systems which take as their foundation a claim to have discovered an eternal and immutable rule of right, (2) all religions which harken back to some ultimate principle supposedly dictated by God, and (3) all ethical systems built upon a formulation of the law of nature or natural rights or natural equity.[5] This principle in all its many variations has exercised the greatest influence upon governments, and consequently, Bentham expends considerable effort on its condemnation.

For our own immediate purposes, it will be useful to delve a bit deeper into Bentham's arguments against the natural-law and natural-rights positions,[6] because, it will be recalled, Smith remained (despite the influence upon him of another opponent of natural rights, David Hume) in large part a firm believer in the harmony-of-nature conception and in the existence of natural laws and natural liberty.

Bentham advanced, in his *Theory of Legislation,* a compelling theoretical attack upon the natural-law tradition and its derivative, the natural rights of man, an attack which he carried to even greater lengths in his acerbic condemnation of the French Declaration of Rights.[7]

Natural law, being the foundation of natural rights, is the initial concept which Bentham subjects to logical evaluation. It is, he claims, a fiction or metaphor, dependent for its superficial appearance of credibility upon a legitimate term—law—which is the will or command of a legislator. But natural law is merely figurative because nature is represented as a being with dispositions called laws attributed to her. The advocates of natural law speak as though there had been a real code of law which antedated government, and they use this supposed law as an instrument to oppose existing legislation.

The following considerations further condemn the components of natural law, according to Bentham: they are merely laws invented by their several proponents; all their advocates dispute about the content of this code; they all affirm natural law without advancing a proof; the systems of natural law are as numerous as their authors; and they always find it possible to dispute anew. Sentiments of pleasure and pain are, indeed, natural to man, Bentham contends, but it is false and dangerous to call these laws. In fact, it is necessary to make laws precisely to restrain these inclinations. If there were a law of nature directing men to seek their common good, as its advocates contend, laws would be superfluous.

A similar argument is offered against natural rights as a metaphorical subversion of the language but one with gravely deleterious consequences for actual governmental practices. The term "natural rights" trades off the legitimate meaning of the term "right," that is, as the creature of real laws. What is natural to man are means or faculties, and it is a travesty of language to call rights natural. Rights are, rather, securities established by governments to insure the exercise of means and faculties. The right is the guarantee, the faculty the thing guaranteed.

The main thrust of Bentham's attack does not rely upon this theoretical, quasi-linguistic argument, but upon the anti-legal use made of natural rights as a device dangerous in the highest degree to all existing governments. What he fears, then, is the anarchic consequences of this theory. Natural rights, he says, are often employed in an anti-legal sense, with such phrases as "law cannot avail against natural rights"; it is employed in a sense above the law which attacks the law and overturns and annuls it. Natural rights are, he declares, the greatest enemy of reason and the greatest destroyer of governments. There is no arguing with fanatics armed with natural rights because each person understands them as he pleases and applies them as he wishes; they are both inflexible and unintelligible; and they are taken as dogmas from which it is a crime to dissent. Rather than considering laws for their effects, they consider them only in relation to these "chimeras of their imagination." Furthermore, these rights are never proved, but merely asserted to be self-evident.

Their concrete effects are catastrophic: they are employed to nullify established laws; they urge citizens to rise up against existing governments in the name of defending their supposed rights. No state can long maintain itself when every citizen takes upon himself the discretion to resist the law simply upon his own personal judgment.

So much for Bentham's general attack upon natural rights. Now, let us examine his arguments against particular rights claimed to be natural. To begin, first, with property, which Bentham takes to be an established expectation for the enjoyment of a thing possessed, it is apparent to him that such a persuasion can only be the work of the law. But what of the expectation of enjoyment anterior to law? Bentham considers such circumstances very limited and precarious. Rather than property being prior to the law, property and law are born together and die together. The claim that property can not be taken away from men by the law is, hence, a glaring confusion. In addition, the right to property would actually mean that no one had a right to anything because a right by its very nature is exclusive. On the practical level, the natural right to property would exclude all taxation or fines without the consent of the subject and would call for resistance to such laws.

Next, the claim of an unbounded right to liberty, incapable of proscription, ignores the fact that all rights are made at the expense of liberty because there can be no rights without corresponding obligations, no liberty given to one that is not taken away from another. Hence, all laws and also all property rights are repugnant to natural rights, since they limit the liberty of some. Bentham rejects, too, the interpretation placed upon liberty by the natural-rights advocate, that is, liberty defined as the freedom to do what is not hurtful to others. He claims that this is a perversion of language, as the doing of mischief is also a part of liberty. Such a restriction would entail not being able to act until all the consequences of an action were known and one could be assured that no one would be injured. This would make punishment, to take only one case, impossible.

As regards the final, purported natural right, Bentham claims that the right to unbounded security in one's own person would lead to voiding all laws which expose any man to any risk, which designate capital or corporal punishment, and which command military service.

In summation, then, Bentham advances the following major claims against natural rights: (1) on the practical level: (a) they are rights asserted against government and, consequently, anarchic, (b) the right they imply to resist oppression leaves to every individual's discretion whether to offer resistance to the government when he supposes his imaginary rights to be transgressed; and (2) on the theoretical level: (a) they are the un-proven, metaphorical imaginings of various thinkers, each of whom inter-prets them in a different way, (b) they are founded upon an equally fallacious theory of natural law, and (c) the unbounded rights which they claim are incomprehensible and mutually inconsistent.

Thus, under Bentham's influence, political economy would come to renounce the metaphysical and moral foundation which shaped its devel-opment throughout the eighteenth century. Bentham's utility principle rejected both the Physiocrats, with their natural law-natural rights under-pinning for political economy, and Adam Smith, with his "moral sense" basis for morality and his natural-law basis for economics. Both schemes were reprehensible to Bentham as subspecies of the principle of sympathy and antipathy.

If Smith can be considered as principally an advocate of the nature philosophy, the natural harmony of the universe, and man's appointed place in it, as I have previously argued, then Bentham's condemnation of such a conception was destined to place British political economy on a different footing entirely. While Smith's departures from laissez-faire in certain of his suggestions for governmental intervention in the economy would place him in the position of being an inconsistent advo-cate of his principles, Bentham's much more extensive governmental intrusions were founded upon a completely different principle—that of utility. Although Smith occasionally justified the interventions of which he approved by pointing to their utility, he did not employ that principle in any systematic way. But more of this later.

Let us return now to the principle of utility, which lacks nothing fur-ther for its enthronement but to be explained and illustrated. Its two rivals have been dispensed, and they are the only logically possible alter-natives to utility. "My notion of man," Bentham writes, "is, that, success-fully or unsuccessfully, he aims at happiness, and so will continue to aim as long as he continues to be a man, in everything he does."[8] In the much quoted opening passage of his *Principles of Morals and Legislation,* Bentham succinctly and brutally states his view of man's nature:

> Nature has placed mankind under the governance of two sovereign masters, pain and pleasure. It is for them alone to point out what we ought to do, as well as to determine what we shall do. On the one hand the standard of right and wrong, on the other the chain of causes and effects are fastened to this throne.[9]

These "masters" govern us in all we think and do, and it is not in our power to "throw off their subjection"; they dictate what we in fact do, but they also provide a standard for what we "ought" to do.

The moral principle which is a direct outgrowth of this view of the nature of man states that men should (and do in actuality) act so as to maximize their pleasure and minimize their pain. By this principle of utility, or greatest-happiness principle, Bentham means "that principle which approves or disapproves of every action whatsoever, according to the tendency which it appears to have to augment or diminish the happiness of the individual whose interest is in question."[10] Every action whatsoever is rightfully subjected to this test, whether it be that of a private individual or a legislative measure of a government. Just as the principle instructs an individual to maximize his happiness, so it dictates to a community that it is the happiness of the whole which is to be sought.

However, this whole is not some metaphysical, Hegelian entity but a compound "body" made up of the individuals who compose it, and it has no "interest" or "good" apart from the interests or goods of the individuals who compose it.

> The community is a fictitious *body,* composed of the individual persons who are considered as constituting as it were its *members.* The interest of the community then is, what?—the sum of the interests of the several members who compose it.[11]

Consequently, when considering what is in the interest of a community, one must never forget that what one really is talking about is the interests of a series of individuals. Now, a particular course of action is in the interest of A when it tends to add to the sum total of his pleasures or to diminish the sum total of his pains. Similarly, an action is in the interest of the community and thus, conforms to the principle of utility when it has a greater tendency to augment the happiness of the community than to diminish that happiness.

What can be said with respect to the logical consistency of Bentham's argument? Upon a superficial examination, the principle of utility seems solid enough; what is declared to be the moral principle with respect to each individual is, then, taken to be the moral principle for a series of individuals. But is the principle really unaltered in the process? Or have its content and its injunctions undergone a subtle transformation? I believe that it has undergone such an alteration, and, what's more, that Bentham was not aware of this most critical logical leap. Let us look more closely at the two formulations.

(1) *The Principle of Utility as it is Stated for the Individual.* It is that principle which approves actions which augment the happiness of the individual whose interest is in question and disapproves of those actions which diminish his happiness.

(2) *The Principle of Utility as it is Stated for the Community.* "That principle which states the greatest happiness of all those whose interest is in question, as being the right and proper, and only right and proper, and universally desirable, end of human action: human action in every situation, and in particular in that of a functionary or set of functionaries exercising the powers of government."[12] In other words, that which is conformable to the interest of the community is what tends to increase the total sum of happiness of the individuals who compose it.

(I might add that Bentham does not present these as two distinct principles but sees the second as either an outgrowth of the first, or an equivalent of the first. Thus, he indiscriminately calls both formulations "the principle of utility.")

The instructions given by these two formulations with respect to whether a particular action should be undertaken may be the same in many, if not in most, instances. However, this is not true in all cases. For example, if Fred can increase his own happiness by refusing to lend money to six of his destitute acquaintances and instead buying himself a second Lincoln Continental, under the principle of utility number 1, he would be perfectly justified in doing exactly that. But does this example really belong under the individual interest test of number 1, for other interests are involved besides Fred's, six others, in fact. Thus, principle of utility number 2 would have to be invoked and Fred's action condemned.

The formulation of the principle of utility which Bentham employs for his legislative endeavors is the second, that is, the greatest happiness for the greatest number. In his argument for the principle of utility, however, he argues that men are under the twin masters of pleasure and pain and that they *do* act and that they *ought* to act so as to increase the former and diminish the latter; and that all men will recognize this principle as the one which actually governs their behavior. Now clearly, it is the individualist formulation of the principle number 1 which would be so recognized and not the second formulation, which would instruct men in some cases to act so as to diminish their own pleasure, thus instructing them to throw off the twin "masters" of pleasure and pain—an impossibility according to Bentham's own emphatic declaration.

If Bentham had argued instead from the collective happiness to the duties of the individual, his formulations would have been consistent. That is, if he had maintained that the legislative or communal principle of utility decrees that those in power must act so as to secure the greatest happiness of the greatest number, and that individuals must then act so as to secure their own personal happiness within the constraints of the legislation established by those in authority, then he would have provided a more consistent and logically unassailable groundwork for his subsequent legislative program.

Bentham did not do this. Rather, on an ontological level, he proceeded from the individual and his nature to a collective moral principle. But on a practical level, when it came to enunciating his civil and penal codes, he acted as though he had done precisely the opposite, that is, that he had proceeded to establish a collective principle first, from which individual moral duties could later be deduced. Perhaps Bentham was still too much of an individualist to want to validate this latter logical progression explicitly. It would have left much greater opportunity for actions which would sacrifice the individual to society or to his fellows, and it would have done so in ways in which Bentham did not personally desire that individuals be sacrificed. Nevertheless, he traded on this latter progression in many of his schemes, for example, his establishment of economic equality as one of the goals of society (although he was never an extremist), his suggestion at the close of the *Principles of Morals and Legislation* that governments might be well advised to make it a punishable offense to refuse to help someone in danger when the pain would be only slight to oneself, and his endorsement of the Poor Laws.

That Bentham personally refrained from more extreme suggestions for sacrificing some individuals for the greater happiness of others can be attributed more to his own individualistic proclivities rather than to the dictates of the principle of utility in the muddled way in which he formulated it.

The way Bentham formulated his principle of utility, from the individual to the collective of individuals, had certain polemical advantages even if, as we have shown, its philosophical soundness was quite dubious. He sacrificed consistency for flexibility. This obfuscation allowed him to harken back to the supremacy of the individual in instances in which he found such a claim to be desirable and to argue for overriding social considerations in other cases. Since he condemned natural rights arguments as based on mere personal whim and caprice, it is ironic, indeed, that the principle of utility as formulated by Bentham has fallen victim to the same kind of charge.

Leaving these reservations aside, let us see how Bentham proposed to make his pleasure-pain calculations, first for individuals and second for society. To a person considered alone, the value of a pleasure or pain will be greater or lesser depending upon the following considerations: (1) its intensity, (2) its direction, (3) its certainty or uncertainty, (4) its propinquity or remoteness, (5) its fecundity, (6) its purity. In addition, a seventh consideration must be entertained when considering more than one person: (7) its extent. Finally, Bentham advances what he considers to be an exact method for ascertaining the desirability of a proposed action which would affect the interests of an entire community:

I. Beginning with each individual take account of:
    (1) The value of each pleasure in the first instance.
    (2) The value of each pain in the first instance.
    (3) The value of each pleasure produced after the first, i.e., its fecundity of the first pleasure and impurity of the first pain.

(4) The value of each pain produced after the first, i.e., the fecundity of the first pain and impurity of the first pleasure.

(5) The sum of the values of the pleasures and pains and get the balance of either one or the other for the individual.

II. The identical process is then repeated for each individual whose interests appear to be affected.

III. Finally, sum up the individual balances and you arrive at either a collective balance on the side of pleasure, and hence you have exhibited the good tendency of the act, or on the side of pain, in which event you have proved the evil tendency of the proposal.[13]

That this "moral arithmetic" would provide an objective standard by which legislative proposals could, at long last, be judged, Bentham was convinced. But critics from his own time through today have pointed to the impossibility of definitively measuring personal pains and pleasures on such a mathematical scale. The problem would be difficult for an individual, let alone for a legislator called upon to ascertain such figures for each person subject to his prescriptions. Indeed, Bentham himself admitted the difficulty when he recognized that each man does not feel sensations in the same degree because such sensitivity depends upon the "bias" in one's sensibilities.[14] It is true that men make judgments about their own pleasures and pains and the ways in which their actions would affect their own happiness, and so do legislators; but the estimations are rough and approximate in both cases, particularly the latter. This whole problem of how we can quantify utility and, further, whether any interpersonal valuations or comparisons of utility can be made, will become very important when we come later to the marginal utility theorists. For now it is sufficient to note that Bentham thought such comparisons were possible and even essential and that he imagined they could be made objectively and numerically.

This account of Bentham's view of man and the moral system most suited to him would not be complete without mentioning certain recurrent themes which shaped his later endeavors into legislation and its subfield, political economy. He continually emphasized that man was above all else a rational agent and that, as a general rule, the individual was the best judge of his own utility,[15] with exceptions made for children and the insane. And he believed that in most individuals, excepting only the rare humanitarian saint, self-regarding interests would predominate. This is not to deny that men act out of social sympathy or beneficence, these both being members of the category of simple pleasures, but they do so through personal interest, that is, in the expectation of receiving some pleasure in return.[16] In Bentham's own graphic description,

> That which in the language of sentimentalism is a sacrifice of private interest to public interest, is but a sacrifice of a self-supposed private interest in one shape to a self-supposed private interest in another shape; for example, as an interest corresponding to the love of power, to an interest corresponding to the love of reputation—of that reputation of which power is the expected fruit.[17]

To depend on any other principle for the foundation of an economic system but the most powerful, constant, dominant, lasting, and general one of personal interest is, Bentham thinks, to build upon quicksand.[18] However, Bentham did, in his earlier days, particularly in the *Principles of Morals and Legislation,* contend that the motives of a goodwill are the surest of coinciding with the principle of utility, the dictates of which coincide with the most extensive and enlightened benevolence.[19] A more typical and consistent viewpoint of his, in contrast, was enunciated in *The Theory of Legislation,* in which virtue is declared to be the sacrifice of a lesser interest to a greater interest, of a momentary to a durable interest.

THE SCOPE, METHOD, AND SCIENCE OF POLITICAL ECONOMY

Political economy is a subfield of the art of legislation, in Bentham's account, and as a branch of the latter it is subject to certain limitations common to all legislation. Politics and morals share a common end—happiness—yet they have a different extent. The one directs the operations of governments while the other instructs individuals. All actions public and private fall under the jurisdiction of morals, while legislation can not be a guide to men in all matters because it can not act except by inflicting punishments (and only rarely through bestowing rewards, and

Bentham doubts that these exceptions are properly thought of as legislative acts). While morality commands individuals to do all acts advantageous to themselves and the community, legislation is much more circumscribed; that is, there are many acts, both injurious and useful, which the government ought not either forbid or command. The reason for this limitation upon legislation is that in many cases the evil of the punishment would far exceed the evil of the offense. Specifically legislation should not intervene when punishment would be groundless, inefficacious, unprofitable, or needless.[20] "There are few cases," Bentham writes, "in which it *would* be expedient to punish a man for hurting himself; but there are few cases, if any, in which it would *not* be expedient to punish a man for injuring his neighbor."[21] This distinction between morals and legislation is particularly significant for political economy, since Bentham proclaims himself to be a disciple of Smithian economics in which legislative intervention was kept to a minimum.

Political economy, for Bentham, was a distinguishable branch of the general science of legislation, but the laws of this branch were not easily separable from the general laws of politics. In other words, he did not think it possible to have a separate code of purely economic laws.[22] In this conception of the categorization of political economy, Bentham remained true to Smith's formulation, in which the purpose of the science was the instruction of legislators in regard to the most efficacious means of effecting the maximization of national wealth.

He did, however, draw a distinction, which was not to be found in Smith, between political economy as an art and as a science. The purpose of the science was to serve as the foundation of the art. Each art, or practical application, would utilize the prescriptions culled from several sciences. Only as a guide to the art is the science useful, Bentham thought. It is interesting to note that it is precisely this viewpoint which will, at a later date, fall into utter disrepute when such theorists as Nassau Senior, to name but a single example, come to question the very possibility of the science of economics *qua* science providing the legislator with definitive injunctions for action. Clearly this was not Bentham's view. Such a sterile science would have been of no interest to a man of his activist proclivities. His treatise had a far more "utilitarian" purpose, to show what ought to be done in the way of political economy by a government and what not.[23] "Political economy, considered as an art exercised by those who have the government of a nation in their hands," he writes, "is the art of directing the national industry to the purposes to which it may be directed with the greatest advantage."[24] In actuality, though, this art-science distinction was not employed in any systematic fashion by Bentham. In fact, he did little more than call attention to its existence, and it remained for later theorists, such as John Stuart Mill and Nassau Senior, to employ the distinction in any meaningful way.

Also, Bentham followed Smith in not making the normative-positive distinction which was so important to subsequent economic theorizing. The reason he did not make such a distinction can be traced to a different source, however. While Smith's natural-law conception merged "what is" with "what ought to be," Bentham's principle of utility subjected all value consideration to arithmetical calculation.[25]

Bentham claimed that on the scientific questions he concurred with the doctrines of Adam Smith[26] but that Smith's object was the development of the science while his was the unfolding of the art. As we have seen in our discussion of Smith, he did not distinguish between political economy as an art and as a science, and furthermore, his ultimate objective for the science would definitely fall under Bentham's description of art, the purpose being to instruct the legislator in the most likely means of maximizing national wealth and public revenue. Bentham's single, self-professed claim to originality on the scientific level—that is, his formulation of the principle that industry is limited by the availability of capital—is to be found in Smith,[27] despite Bentham's denial. His claim to have employed a different method in his treatise than that demonstrated in the *Wealth of Nations* is a much more credible claim. Smith's method of procedure was largely inductive—proceeding from concrete examples and observations of the workings of existent economic measures and procedures to the drawing of general principles, from which subsequent suggestions for action could be made. Bentham, while acknowledging that induction was the suitable method for scientific pursuits, conceived his purpose differently—he was amplifying on the art, having recourse to Smith's already developed science as his foundation—and so he employed a predominantly deductive method, proceeding from definitions, adding insights into the psychology of economic man, and employing the objectives deduced from the principle of utility to arrive at specific conclusions to be utilized by the legislator. Bentham did not engage in any explicit formulation of his methodology.

Bentham departed from the Smithian model in one critical respect.

While Smith designated only a very general objective for political economy, the maximization of national wealth, which was consistent with his definition of the science, Bentham established the equivalent of this objective stated in Utilitarian terms but in addition formulated specific subordinate objectives. The significance of this change is substantial; it permits far more governmental regulation and intervention than did Smith's approach. The manner in which Bentham accomplished this mini-revolution in Smithian economics while avowing his loyalty to it warrants a closer examination.[28]

The end or object of every government ought to be "the maximum of happiness with reference to the several members of the community taken together, and with reference to the whole expanse of time."[29] The general end of political economy is to show the sovereign the most suitable course to follow in pursuit of the greatest happiness of the greatest number—this is the "end paramount." The subordinate ends to be sought are necessary components without which the maximization of happiness cannot be achieved; they are (1) subsistence, (2) security, (3) abundance (consisting of enjoyment and abundance), populousness, and (4) equality. Independent powers are often in conflict about these subordinate objectives, and the legislator must mediate between them in order to insure the realization of the paramount end. It is further alleged that there is a hierarchy among these subordinate ends, with subsistence as the most fundamental, followed by security, abundance, and equality. Bentham at one point seems to limit the principle of utility as it applies specifically to political economy, when he says that it calls for the maximum of happiness insofar as the more general end is promoted by the production of the maximum of the often conflicting demands of wealth and population.[30] But in his discussion of the role of government in the economy, he uses the principle to justify the government's balancing of all four categories of subordinate ends.

Thus, Bentham held a much more specific set of goals to be achieved by government in the economic realm, and he envisioned a much broader field over which government intervention could range. Such was particularly the case with issues generated by the fourth subordinate end, that of equality, which would spawn the whole issue of redistribution of wealth and the maximization of happiness through greater equality in material possessions. These considerations were to have a pronounced influence over the future course of economics even though Bentham kept such schemes to a minimum. Suffice it to say that a government called upon to maximize happiness by adjudicating between competing claims of individuals and groups for increased emphasis upon either sub-sistence, abundance, security, or equality would have a much greater theoretical foundation upon which to base acts of intervention than would a government called upon simply to maximize national wealth, as in the Smithian model.

Perhaps the contrast between Smith's and Bentham's approaches can be stated in even sharper terms by categorizing Bentham's view of govern-ment as teleological, whereas Smith's was not. That is to say, that while Bentham established *objectives* for the government to pursue—with happi-ness as the paramount objective to be secured with the assistance of the four subordinate objectives—Smith merely proposed *functions* for the government to undertake—providing national security, protecting the individual from violence, and operating certain essential public works.

As we turn now to Bentham's brief scientific endeavors in his early economic writings, his description of the nature and causes of wealth, Smith's influence will be greatly in evidence. It is combined with Bentham's own analysis of utility and interest as developed in his writings on morals. The wealth of the community, Bentham begins, is the sum of the portions of wealth belonging to the several individuals of whom the community is composed.[31] Wealth can be increased only by two means: (1) increasing the quantity of capital, or (2) improving the advantageousness of the direction given to it. The latter depends upon the choice of trades in which the capital is employed and the decisions as to the best mode of carrying out each trade. In both cases the chance of the choice being better will be (1) in proportion to the degree of *interest* which the person who makes the choice has in the result, and (2) in proportion to the chance he has of possessing the requisite knowledge and judgment. It is Bentham's contention that (2) depends upon (1). In other words, the greater the interest, the greater will be the acquisition of the necessary knowledge and skills. And whose interest is greater than that of the individual—certainly not the legislator's. "It is not often that one man is a better judge for another, than that other is for himself," Bentham wrote in his famous tract, *In Defence of Usury*, "even in cases where the adviser will take the trouble to make himself master of as many of the materials for judging as are within the reach of the person to be advised. But the legislator is not, can not be, in the possession of any one of these materials—what private can be equal to such public folly."[32]

The individual's interest is greater in his own affairs than would be the sovereign's. Consequently, in respect to natural and acquired faculties and knowledge, the sovereign must be inferior to the individual and inferior beyond all measure. If, perchance, the sovereign did have privileged information about a particular trade, the best thing he could possibly do would be to see to its dissemination. No exercise of power is necessary. When it comes to increasing the quantity of capital, the government can do nothing, for capital can be increased in a particular country only by frugality or importation.

The previous discussion is drawn mainly from the *Manual of Political Economy,* but in a later work, his *Institute of Political Economy,* Bentham advances a more definitive scheme for categorizing and evaluating the government's role in the production of wealth. This scheme fits within the general framework established in the *Manual;* however, its structural implications are far more statist. In the *Institute,* he says that the method of production undertaken by individuals is either (1) spontaneous or what he calls *sponte acta,* (2) promoted by government—*agenda,* or (3) obstructed by government—*non-agenda.*[33] In different countries the proportion of each varies. In the most opulent countries, the list of (1) is the longest and (2) is kept to a minimum.

Now, in cases of *sponte acta,* the end is promoted by individuals acting without interference by government beyond the distribution being maintained and the civil and penal laws being enforced. Bentham concurs with Smith when he states that men constantly desire to increase their wealth and that no force or special inducement is necessary. All they require is to be secure in what they have produced. Natural need will provide the incentive. "What men want from government is not incitement to labor but security against disturbance."[34]

Advocates of the proposition that national wealth can be increased by coercive measures must argue for two propositions: that more wealth will be produced with such measures than without them, and that the increased comfort from this extra wealth is more than equivalent to the vexation suffered under the coercive measures. In the overwhelming majority of cases, such a proof can not be given. This is Bentham's contention.

Now, the questions of *agenda* and *non-agenda* strike at the heart of our discussion of the proper role of government in the economy. Bentham had much of interest to say on this question. However, before we examine Bentham's position on the government's role in the economy, it will be necessary to discuss his general conception of the role and objectives of government and the means at its disposal for effecting these ends.

GOVERNMENT: ITS OBJECTIVES AND THE MODE OF OPERATION PROPER TO IT

The legislator's object, as we have seen, ought to be the public good, and the foundation of his reasoning ought to be general utility,[35] the greatest possible happiness for the community. This is the only right and justifiable end of government,[36] and it effects that end by punishing primarily and only secondarily by rewarding.[37] In this moral arithmetic which the government performs, everyone's happiness has an equal claim to be regarded. This is true even of the transgressor who must be punished, punished not because his own happiness has a lesser claim to consideration, but because it is necessary for the greatest happiness of the greatest number.[38]

Governments can increase happiness primarily by guarding against pains, meanwhile leaving the care of enjoyments almost entirely to the individual. Such a function can only be fulfilled by creating rights and conferring them upon individuals—rights of personal security, of protection for honor, of property, and of receiving aid in case of distress. In the process of generating these rights, corresponding offenses are necessarily created, as are concomitant obligations. Thus, by logical necessity, the citizen can not acquire rights without obligations and consequently without sacrificing a part of his liberty.[39]

Bentham categorically denies on the evidence of history, the nature of man, and the existence of political society that the paramount end of happiness can be achieved by the "uncoerced and unenlightened propensities and power of individuals."[40] The control and guidance of the legislator is a prerequisite for the attainment of the greatest happiness for society. Just as the physician prescribes for the body, so the legislator acts as the physician to that artificial body, the body politic. He makes "moral calculations" as to which course will prove most likely to increase pleasure and prevent pain.

But this element of control must vary in its intensity and extent in respect to each of the four different subordinate ends. Security is the government's primary work. Subsistence, abundance, and equality require its interference to a much lesser degree. In fact, interference for these ends is "comparatively unnecessary." However, without the security provided by government, political society could not exist.

Subsistence is aimed at indirectly by the government, and it is sufficient, in most cases, for its realization that men be protected while they labor and guaranteed the enjoyment of the fruits of their labor, that is, that security is maintained. For abundance, the government need do even less, since natural motives suffice to make men seek enjoyments. Equality, on the other hand, presents a more complex problem for the legislator. It is clear, on Utilitarian principles, that the law, in seeking to maximize happiness for society, must not seek to give more to one individual than to his fellows. But in fact the government can not act except by conferring rights on some and concomitant obligations on others. Thus, equality of rights, as envisioned by natural-rights theorists, is an impossibility, as it would render all legislation invalid. Similarly, the equalization of property and possessions, while a desirable goal according to the utility principle and the principle of diminishing marginal social utility in the distribution of property, can not be aimed at directly. To do so would be to endanger general security. All the government can do is to ensure that it does nothing to make inequality greater. When there is a conflict between security and equality, equality must yield. The mass of property already existing must not be confiscated by the government, for such action would violate justice which is the first duty of government. The government should rely, rather, on the element of time to provide a prosperous country with movement toward greater material equality, for such will be the eventual effect of a system which aims at security. But to aim at equality directly will only result in the abrogation of all security of property, all industry and incentive, all abundance, and would ultimately require the Inquisitor continually to redirect the distribution.[41]

While Bentham gives different accounts of the hierarchy of the subordinate ends (for example in the *Theory of Legislation* security predominates, while in the *Institutes of Political Economy* subsistence heads the list), his general position can be fairly confidently stated: that the legislator's duty is to secure the greatest happiness of the greatest number, and he is to accomplish this by balancing the often competing claims of the subordinate ends. In pursuit of these objectives it is not necessary that all initiatives emanate from the government: "What concerns him is—that the desirable effect should take place: not that it should have his own agency for the cause."[42]

And what is the justification for the sovereign's right to perform such acts of adjudication? It is simply this—the only true political tie—the immense interest which we have in maintaining a government. Without it no security can be attained and none of the other ends realized. It is this overriding utility (or interest) which is the justification for government, and not such spurious foundations as antiquity, the authority of religion, the condemnation of innovation, the fiction of the social contract, imaginary laws, natural rights, or the principle of antipathy-sympathy.[43]

Although men have a natural interest in combining to form a "social body" and in maintaining such a union once it has been formed, something more is required to make possible the realization of the greatest-happiness principle. It is precisely this—the addition by the legislator of an "artificial interest" to the natural one, so that individuals will be made to perceive the connection between their own personal interest and the interest of others.[44]

However, in promulgating such "artificial" measures, the legislator must remain cognizant of three important considerations. (1) Every law is an evil because it is an infraction of liberty.[45] (2) Laws operate through sanctions or the imposition of pleasures and mostly pains, and all punishment is a mischief because it increases pain.[46] (3) The public interest equals the mass of individual interests, so that the increased pains imposed on some individuals by a law must be overbalanced by the increased pleasures resulting to others.[47] Hence, while it is often necessary for a legislator to impose laws, there is always a reason against every law which in the absence of an overriding opposing reason will be sufficient to condemn it—the reason being that it is an attack upon liberty. A precise accounting of costs and benefits must be made before any laws are enacted. Considering all these factors, then, Bentham arrives at the conclusion that as a general rule the greatest possible latitude should be left to individuals in all cases in which they can injure only themselves, for they are the best judges of their own interests. The power of the law need only be invoked to prevent one individual from injuring another.[48]

> To prevent our doing mischief to one another, it is but neces-
> sary to put bridles into all our mouths: it is necessary to the
> tranquility and very being of society: but that the tacking of
> leading-strings upon the hands of grown persons, in order to
> prevent their doing themselves a mischief, is not necessary
> either to the being or tranquility of society, however condu-
> cive to its well-being, I think cannot be disputed. Such paternal,
> or, if you please, maternal care, may be a good work, but it cer-
> tainly is but a work of supererogation.[49]

Herein lies the importance of the distinction between morals and legislation: it is the function of education, or the duty of the old towards the
young, to impose restraints upon the individual for his own welfare and
not the business of the government.

THE GOVERNMENT'S ROLE IN THE ECONOMY: AGENDA
AND NON-AGENDA

Only government can create a possession so fixed and lasting that it
would merit the name of property. Unlike the natural-rights system in
which property is a right antecedent to the creation of government, in
Bentham's treatment the government is ineluctably tied in to all property
relations. Property itself is the creation of government. "Property and
law are born together and die together," Bentham emphatically declared
in the *Theory of Legislation*. But this is not taken as a *carte blanche* to
governments to distribute property as they will or to engage continually
in acts of interference. Such activities would, of course, be a direct threat
to security and its constituent, justice. In addition, the claims of actual
possession should be honored in the absence of any other overriding consideration. The principle of utility, however, provides the general guidelines regarding limitations to be placed upon governmental intervention.
    Bentham's stated purpose in his *Manual of Political Economy* was to
show what ought to be done and not done by government in the economic
realm. His general conclusion is,

> . . . of the much that has been done in this way and with these
> views scarce anything ought to have been done; and that of
> what ought to be done, as matters stand, almost the whole con-

sists in undoing what has been done, and in obviating the inconven-
iences that would result from the carrying on this process of undoing in an abrupt and inconsiderate manner.[50]

Bentham developed his position more fully some ten years later in his
Institute of Political Economy. Here he enunciated the general rule that
"nothing ought to be attempted by government for the purpose of causing
an augmentation to take place in the national means of wealth, with a
view to increase of the means of either subsistence or enjoyment, *without some special reason* [emphasis added] . *Be Quiet* ought on these occasions to be the motto or watch-word of government."[51] The reasons for
this abstention are (1) that acts of intervention are generally *needless*
because the wealth of the community is composed of the wealth of the
individuals who comprise it, and in general the individual is the best judge
of what is in his interest, and finally, he has the greatest motivation to
pursue that interest; and (2) the governmental measures are more likely
to be *pernicious* in that they obstruct the individual from attaining his
and society's ends, and they are pernicious also because they impose
pains on individuals by such restraints, including the greatest pain of all,
taxation.

In a similar vein, to cite a concrete example of Bentham's principle
in operation, his earlier work, *The Defence of Usury*, contains as a general
proposition the assertion that contracts ought to be free and the liberty
of men left unfettered in their economic relationships. The burden of
proof falls upon those who might want to curtail contracts and place
restrictions on the liberty of men. They must defend their exceptions
on the grounds that such actions will result in a greater measure of
happiness.

His method of procedure in *The Defence of Usury* is particularly important to observe, because it is a perfect example of the way in which
Bentham employed the principle of utility to rule upon the advisability
of a particular instance of governmental intrusion. Only five generic reasons can be found, he contends, to justify such governmental restrictions
upon the free trade of money: that such restrictions are advantageous
for (1) the prevention of usury, (2) the prevention of prodigality, (3) the
protection of the indigent against extortion, (4) the repression of the
temerity of projectors, and (5) the protection of simplicity against imposi-

tion. Bentham then proceeds to prove that the imposition by the government of legal limits on the interest rate can not achieve those ends. Such usury laws are either totally inefficacious in that they will not achieve the desired purpose, or totally spurious in that they will achieve the directly opposite result from the one sought. It is not necessary for us to go into the specific details of his argument, but what is significant to us is the method employed to arrive at the general conclusion that the individual is the better judge of the worth of money to him than is the legislator. It is a purely pragmatic calculation that the proposed objectives can not be secured by the proposed means and that, therefore, the individual should be left free to make the bargain for himself. In other words, no exception to the general rule of free contracts and liberty ought to be tolerated in this case, simply because it would not be efficacious.

While this argument against usury might appear irrefutable on utilitarian grounds, it is particularly revealing that a scant fourteen years later Bentham himself would have discovered a justification for overturning his own arguments on this very same ground of utility. When he came to pen his "Defence of a Maximum,"[52] a new consideration for governmental interference to set maximum rates of interest occurred to him which far outweighed all earlier objections. It was that a government which had such powers could borrow money at comparatively advantageous terms. This admission is striking, to say the least, for it portends Bentham's growing statism and also the malleability of the utility principle.

As we saw earlier, Bentham considered every law an evil *qua* law, as a restraint on liberty. In consequence, every law in the economic realm, which is necessarily a claim to restrain individuals for some good, must be justified on the grounds that it will produce some greater good than the evil it must impose. Precisely this same formulation was adopted at a later date by John Stuart Mill and Henry Sidgwick. The *reductio ad absurdum* of this line of argument is, of course, that it is fine to trounce on liberty in all instances in which some putatively convincing argument can be made that a greater good will result from the sacrifice. The inherent vagueness of the principle of utility, combined with the apparently insurmountable problem of arriving at an objective calibration of the happiness of other people, provides the legislator with practically a *carte blanche* for justifying any particular course he personally favors.

This is far, indeed, from the strictly objective standard which Bentham claimed to have provided, and, in historical fact, in the hands of his follow-

ers his formulation did provide for an ever more expansive role for governmental intervention. They did not have to change Bentham's principle in
any essential way. They merely had to draw different conclusions from
their "moral arithmetic."

Let us take an example of the principle of utility in action to see how
contradictory its dictates can be. Does the principle of utility tell the
legislator to prefer a measure which gives twenty "utilities" to each of
five people or one which lets one man free to keep his eighty "utilities"
while the other four only have ten apiece? There is greater happiness
("utilities") in the latter case than in the former—120 versus 100—yet,
a case can be made that there is greater happiness where there is an equal
distribution, because each individual enjoys the twenty "utilities" at the
margin more than the one individual would enjoy his eighty (an argument,
by the way, which Bentham did make). The slipperiness of the principle
of utility is evident from the fact that J. S. Mill favored the twenty-"utilities"-to-five-people kind of division in his socialistic phases and the
eighty-to-one-person and ten-to-four-people free-market arrangement in
his more orthodox periods. And he invoked the same principle in both
cases. Suffice it to say, then, that the principle of utility as a guide to the
legislator in the proper course to be followed in regulating the economy
provided a much more expandable and interpretable standard than did
the more strictly natural-rights approach of Adam Smith.

But let us return to Bentham, who remained in large part immune to
the extremes to which his principle could be pushed. As we saw earlier
in our discussion of Bentham's treatment of wealth and *sponte acta,* he
held to the Smithian view that government intervention was almost totally
inefficacious in achieving the primary objective of an economic system—
maximizing the production of wealth. By pursuing one's own interest in
regard to matters of personal wealth, the general end of greatest happiness would be attained insofar as happiness consists in acquiring wealth,
and in *most* cases. The main task of government in the economic realm,
then, was to preserve security and specifically to prevent the use of force
and fraud by individuals in place of free competition.

A propensity conducive to the requisite ends, general and subordinate, is implanted in every breast he [the legislator] has
to deal with: it is the endeavour, or at least the wish, of each
individual to see those sacred blessings in his own instance at

least, carried to the highest pitch: the course which each individual will take of himself is therefore the course that will be
most conducive to the end in view, in so far as it can be pursued without thwarting other individuals in their course, and
in so far as his own stock of knowledge is adequate to his
guidance, to the reflecting the proper light upon his steps.[53]

As a direct practical consequence of this theoretical position, Bentham
held that the ordinary workings of trade, whether foreign or domestic,
did not have to be encouraged or overseen by any "paternalistic" intervention by government. Such intervention would be inefficacious because, on Bentham's "scientific" principle, trade is limited by the extent
of capital, and the government can not increase capital. It can merely
take some from one branch of trade, where it is more effectively employed or it wouldn't be there in the first place, and give it to another
branch where it will be less productive. Bounties are condemned.[54]
Hence, over a large range of economic activity there is an explicit presumption against interference by government. But there is no natural-
rights kind of claim which would preclude such acts *a priori;* the result
is that as each argument for government intervention is proposed, it must
be analyzed on its merits. It must be subjected to the litmus test of expediency as directed by the principle of utility.

And that is precisely what Bentham did when he came to examine,
and in some cases approve, certain "exceptions" to his general rule of
"be quiet." Before we examine the elements of *agenda* which gained
Bentham's approval, let us see what kinds of measures which were frequently engaged in by governments nevertheless merited Bentham's condemnation. He termed such measures *non-agenda.* Included among these
were the categories of: (1) Direct Encouragements to Industry, for example, (a) loans of capital to business—condemned because they could
operate only by forcibly taking money by taxation from A to give to B,
and A would suffer greater pain from the loss than B would gain in pleasure, and furthermore, the money would be given to a less productive
industry, (b) bounties on exportation—condemned as even a greater mischief; and (2) Indirect Encouragements to Industry, for example, (a)
prohibitions of rival branches of industry, (b) prohibition of rival imports,
(c) taxation of rival branches of home manufacture, tariffs on foreign
imports, nonimportation agreements, or treaties with other nations gain-

ing advantages for particular branches of industry.[55] Condemned also
are measures to force frugality, that is, to increase capital through a
forced accumulation by means of taxation. He thought that sufficient
accumulation would be achieved spontaneously by the voluntary choice
of individuals. Forced frugality, under these circumstances, would constitute the attainment of national opulence at the expense of justice. The
government clearly has the power to do this, but it is unnecessary in
cases where opulence is the objective (defense and subsistence, however,
are treated differently, as we will see). Attempts by the government to
increase the quantity of money under the presumption that by so doing
real wealth will be increased are rejected because they inflict an uncom-
pensated suffering on people of fixed income and they fail of their
purpose.

Usury laws are not proper governmental measures, and neither are
attempts to increase the quantity of land by colonization; the former is
inefficacious and counterproductive, while the latter engenders vast,
needless expenditures by the mother country, increases taxation, and
results in wars. (It is ironic that even this anti-colonialist stand by Bentham
was negated in a later work, the "Defence of a Maximum," in which he,
now concerned about excess population rather than a dearth, argues that
colonization may be a prudent policy to siphon off excess population
and capital—yet another example of the pliancy of the principle of utility.)
Also, governments ought not to aim at the increase of population directly,
although such increases are desirable because they extend the number of
those who can enjoy happiness. Population is limited by the availability
of the means of subsistence, and the most effective means of maximizing
subsistence is for the government to "be quiet" and leave the work to the
spontaneous actions of individuals. The government can promote this
particular objective primarily by ensuring security, although Bentham
does promote some *agenda* in this area, but more of that later.

Being a Utilitarian, Bentham tempered some of his anti-regulationist
zeal with the warning that all excesses of government can not be abrogated
immediately. A certain measure of regard must be had for the effects of
such wholesale repeal on the expectations and livelihood of those people
who would be affected by the change. In addition, the advocate of repeal
must take into account the other subordinate ends which may be met by
the offending practice.

Now, as we come to examine Bentham's list of *agenda* for government, it will be evident that he permitted and approved many more exceptions to the general rule of "be quiet" than did Smith. It is rather ironic that despite his seemingly ironclad denunciations of various governmental interventions as *non-agenda*, at some point or another and for one reason or another, he would come to approve of the selfsame measures.

Wealth will be increased, Bentham argued, if sufficient power, knowledge, intelligence, and inclination are present in individuals, but where any factor is deficient, the government may interpose itself or not depending on the likelihood of the advantages of such an intervention outweighing the disadvantages. Inclination is least likely to be deficient. Power can be supplied by the government when it repeals coercive laws. Knowledge and intelligence can be augmented by government through a judicious encouragement of its production and dissemination.[56] It is permissible, then, for the government to form establishments for the propagation of knowledge; such ventures might include boards of agriculture, veterinary schools, royal institutions, and universities. It is expedient for the government, in addition, to grant patents or exclusive privileges to inventors, for without such security men will not exert themselves to develop new methods and machinery and wealth will suffer. Although patents are the creatures of government just as are monopolies, they have an opposite and beneficial effect.

There are, he concludes, two extensive cases in which it is generally both necessary and expedient to intervene in the individualistically oriented wealth-production nexus, and that is to give to the increase of wealth a direction which would suit it to the purposes of subsistence and defense (or security). Government must guarantee security in respect of subsistence and defense, and in order to accomplish these objectives it is justified in diverting the excess which individuals would spend on their own enjoyment to these purposes. Thus, while Bentham denounced bounties as a general proposition for the encouragement of wealth, he approved them for the purpose of defense, for example, he sanctioned the English Navigation Acts and allowances given to certain fisheries. Bounties may also be justifiably continued for the purpose of relieving the distress of workmen or masters already employed or embarked upon particular trades which formerly received bounties. Once the necessity for such activities has passed, however, so would the rationale for the forced curtailment placed upon national enjoyment. "Take away the

necessity, there remains wealth purchased at the expense of justice: .
enjoyment given to one man, at the expense of enjoyment taken from
another."[57]

There are certain cases in which governmental power is necessary to
secure the objective of subsistence, and in such cases the government has
a right to act, for example, where corporate powers are necessary for the
allocation of a scarce, vital commodity. Bounties on bread corn are justifiable, for instance, when the following conditions are met: (1) if the government's inaction would lead to a quantity of this essential commodity
that would fail to meet the minimum needs of the society in certain years
of dearth; (2) if the bounty would actually secure the desired effect, by in-
suring the production of more corn in years of scarcity than would have been
produced without its agency. That Bentham did not have a great deal of
confidence in these measures is apparent; yet he did sanction such enterprises if he thought they had a prospect of success. Magazining, he thought,
was the only method which could afford absolute security.[58]

It is on this very question of vital subsistence for the people, the issue
of the scarcity of bread corn and its high price which emerged in 1801,
in which Bentham's departure from liberalism appears most flagrant.
Once again, it is the elusive utility principle which serves as the rationaliza-
tion for his desertion of the "be quiet" axiom. In his "Defence of a Maximum" he argues that the state ought to impose a maximum price for corn.
When confronted by the apparent inconsistency of this position with his
contention in "The Defence of Usury" that no such government-imposed
ceiling was prudent, Bentham had this to say:

> I have not, I never had, nor ever shall have, any horror, senti-
> mental or anarchial, of the hand of government. I leave it to
> Adam Smith, and the champions of the rights of man (for con-
> fusion of ideas will jumble together the best subjects and the
> worst citizens upon the same ground) to talk of invasions of
> natural liberty, and to give as a special argument against this or
> that law, an argument the effect of which would be to put a
> negative upon all laws. The interference of government, as often
> as in my humble view of the matter any the smallest balance on
> the side of advantage is the result, is an event I witness with al-
> together as much satisfaction as I should its forbearance and
> with much more than I should its negligence.[59]

In regard to the objective of abundance of population, Bentham thought that little could be done by government of a positive nature but that government could provide hedges against the depletion of the existing population with such measures as hospitals for the poor and the incurably sick, establishments for the temporary maintenance and employment of the ablebodied poor, and establishments for the prevention or mitigation of contagious diseases.[60]

Equality, another one of the objectives of government, can be achieved through laws of succession or escheat, and so Bentham proposed that all estates of those who die without lineal descendants should devolve upon the government. The legislator may also establish a regular contribution for the needs of the indigent through taxation, as the voluntary contributions of the well-off are not dependable or sufficient. Bentham advanced a scheme for Poor Laws based upon his Panopticon model. In fact, Bentham went so far as to state that the title of the indigent to relief is stronger than the title of the proprietor to his superfluities[61] because the pain of death from starvation would be an evil far outweighing the pain of disappointment to the rich if a portion of their luxuries were taken from them. This is a long way, indeed, from Smith.

Proposals for various financial schemes on the part of the government fascinated Bentham, and around the turn of the century, he advanced several pet notions of his own. He justified such ventures by claiming that there were certain lucrative occupations to the exercise of which individuals were not the most competent. In these cases, superiority on the part of government was attributed both to its ability to afford *security* and its superior *longevity*.[62] The practical conclusion was that the government ought to engage in annuity dealings, social insurance, and money management. The government debt could be used as an investment vehicle, and the government could monopolize the issuance of paper currency.[63] (At that time, 1795, such transactions as the issuance of paper currency were the province of independent banks. Bentham found such a state of affairs deplorable, and he expended a considerable amount of effort in dreaming up schemes for curtailing the powers of the banks.[64]) No Utilitarian or legalistic objections could be found by him to exclude the exercise of these powers by government. Private notes should, henceforth, be forbidden. And at one point he even suggested that the government should go into the banking business.

Taxation provided another category of *agenda* for government. Taxes constitute, Bentham wrote, the "sacrifice made of wealth and opulence, at the expense of enjoyment, to security in respect of defence and security in respect of subsistence."[65] The legislator must seek to minimize this diminution of wealth. He must strive to ensure that the diminution is as small as possible and that the vexation and inconvenience are kept to a bare minimum. The principle of equality in taxation ought to be observed, and that principle dictates that where there is an equal ability to pay, there should be an equal burden levied. So if landowners are taxed, manufacturers, traders, and professional men ought to be similarly taxed. In "Tax with Monopoly"[66] Bentham goes so far as to approve the granting of monopolies to compensate the victims of new taxes, as long as such monopolies would not raise prices. Here he was thinking, once again, of regulating banking and stockbroking.

The legislator must estimate the good to be achieved by the expenditure of money raised by taxation against the mischief produced by the extraction of an equal sum by the most burdensome species of tax employed. Of course, this is not to say that taxes are to be prohibited; rather it is merely meant to caution the legislator that each act of governmental encouragement provided to one individual or industry can come from no other source but the wealth of other individuals or businesses. What he does condemn, however, is the forced extraction of the wealth of individuals for the purpose of increasing the quantity of national capital; while it is demonstrably within the power of government to coerce such "savings," it can only be accomplished by traducing the end of civil society—happiness—and this would constitute an act of oppression.[67]

There is in Bentham's economic writings, which spanned roughly an eighteen-year period from 1786 through 1804, a progression from wholehearted acceptance of fundamental Smithian doctrine to skepticism about certain of its aspects. A conspicuous example of this phenomenon would be Bentham's rejection of the Smith-Turgot savings and investment analysis in which it was argued that interest rates would automatically serve to regulate the two processes, a pure economic principle which he had earlier embraced. Thus, in "The Manual," an early work, the principle leads directly to laissez-faire conclusions, that is, that government can do nothing but harm in intervening in the market to adjust interest rates or promote investments. But when, in later years, Bentham came to renounce the

Smith-Turgot position in "The True Alarm,"[68] this change in pure theory would sanction a movement away from laissez-faire.[69] Now Bentham argued that the government can act beneficially by expanding the money supply without individual savings if unemployed resources exist with the result that the level of economic activity will be augmented. However, the vast majority of *agenda* proposed by Bentham were recommended under the umbrella of the utility principle and not as direct deductions from any alterations that he might have made on Smithian pure economic principles.

In summation, then, Bentham found reasons to justify governmental intervention in certain instances for the following purposes: to establish Poor Laws, hospitals for the indigent, workhouses for the unemployed; to levy estate taxes for redistributive purposes and to decrease the need for direct taxes; to recompense victims of crime when the perpetrator is indigent; to safeguard national security and establish courts and internal police; to disseminate useful information to industry; to label poisonous substances; to guarantee marks for quality and quantity on goods; to set a maximum price for corn; to provide security of subsistence by stockpiling grain or granting bounties to producers; to encourage investment in times of unemployment; to grant patents to investors; to regulate banks and stockbrokers; to promote government annuities and a voluntary government insurance plan; to establish government banks; to establish and enforce a government monopoly on the issuance of paper currency; to engage in public works to put the unemployed to work; and, finally, to establish institutes, boards, and universities. Bentham's "shopping list" of permissible governmental incursions into the economic realm is prodigious, indeed, and far lengthier and more intrusive than was Adam Smith's. This is simply further evidence, if any more was needed, of the expansivity and interpretability of the principle of utility as compared to the quasi-natural rights position which Smith espoused.

THE IMPACT OF BENTHAMISM UPON POLITICAL ECONOMY: THE EXPANSION OF THE GOVERNMENT'S ROLE IN THE ECONOMY

Before concluding this analysis of Bentham, one would be remiss if an accusation of logical inconsistency lodged against Bentham by Elie Halevy were left to stand without being contested. Lionel Robbins[70] and Shirley Letwin[71] have offered their own refutations, and therefore, what follows will be an amplification of their views. It was Halevy's contention that there was a disjunction, unperceived by Bentham, between his treatment of the principle of utility as it applied in the economic realm and as it applied in the political; that is, in adopting Smith's economics and fusing it with his own juridical conceptions, he employed two different social mechanisms for achieving the social objective of the identity of interests. In other words, while in the political realm the attainment of the end of the identity of interests required that the government impose an artificial identity through the law, because such could not be achieved spontaneously, in the economic realm the identity of interests could only be achieved spontaneously, and therefore, the government must not interfere. As Halevy wrote,

> Now, there are two possible interpretations of the principle
> of utility. Either the identity of interests, which is the aim
> of morals and legislation, is against nature, in which case if
> it is realised it must be the work of the artifices of the legis-
> lator; or else it is the spontaneous work of nature. Bentham
> applied the principle in its first form to the solution of
> juridical problems. Adam Smith and Bentham applied it in its
> second form to the solution of economic problems. Its appli-
> cation to constitutional matters may be attempted in both its
> forms.[72]

In fact, there is no such contradiction to be found in Bentham. The spontaneous identity of interests in the economic realm is dependent for its operation and the attainment of its end upon the prior existence of government and its creation of a framework of laws by which (1) property is created, defined, and guaranteed to individuals, and (2) a legal system of courts and prisons is developed. This is necessary in order to provide the security without which no property is possible, no contracts are enforceable, and hence no commerce in any but a most rudimentary form could take place. The economic system is inconceivable, on Benthamite terms, without the prior existence of a government; in Bentham's own words, property is born with and dies with the law.

Similarly, any legal system is predicated on the assumption that over a wide range of activities men will act with a certain measure of goodwill and benevolence toward each other. And it acts only by adding an "artificial" interest where this "natural" interest might prove deficient. Thus, Bentham's juridical system is not wholly comprised of "artifices" of the legislator, and his economic theory is not completely dependent upon "spontaneity."

Having denigrated contract theories and the conception of the state of nature upon which they were based, both Bentham's economic system and his political-legal framework were artificial constructs (that is, man-made), even though they were founded upon natural tendencies of men to seek the society and approval of their fellows. It will be recalled that in his exposition of his legal system, the political sanction was simply one among four sanctions, the other three—the moral, religious, and physical—not being directly under the control of the legislator. Therefore, both the political and the economic realm depend for the attainment of their common end, happiness, upon the large area of voluntary behavior on the part of individuals. It is true that Bentham thought more coercion was necessary in the legal field (for laws can act only by the infliction of punishments) than in the marketplace, but he was willing to let spontaneity reign where it was effective in the former, while he was reluctantly willing to inflict coercion where he deemed it necessary in the latter. As Robbins said, Bentham (and Smith, also) regarded the proper legal framework and the system of economic freedom "as two aspects of the same social process."

In his rejections of the nature philosophy which served as the underpinning of Adam Smith's free-market economic system, Bentham left himself open to a whole series of criticisms, the principal among which must certainly pertain to the obfuscatory nature of the principle of utility, the very principle which he sought to put in the place of the discredited natural law system. That this principle served, in Bentham's hands, to undercut laissez-faire has been abundantly illustrated. It will have even a greater effect as it passes from Bentham's hands into those of his successors. Bentham established specific general and subordinate ends for the use of wealth, to be regulated and adjudicated by government, something Smith never did. This teleological excrescence implanted on the body of Smithian economics was to prove a powerful impetus for and justification of governmental intervention in the economy, intervention which went far beyond anything of which Bentham either could or did approve. For example, his isolation of equality as one of the subordinate ends necessary for the achievement of the greatest happiness of the greatest number, combined with his contention that the greater the equality of possessions, the greater the happiness, led directly to the whole question of the equity of the free-market economic system in the distribution of its product. This question troubled J. S. Mill, who was motivated by such considerations into driving a wedge between the theory of production and the theory of distribution. And at an even later date, it bothered an economist of a socialistic bent, Wicksteed, and it spawned the school of welfare economics.

Adam Smith's various departures from strict laissez-faire were justified rather haphazardly on an ad hoc basis. When he maintained that governmental intervention was necessary to secure certain public works which would not be undertaken without such action, he invoked as a justification for such activities nothing more than common sense or a very loose "utility" claim. But his departures were few, and each seemingly derived its justification from some extreme necessity. Each such venture appeared to be a lapse from his general principles brought on by his eagerness to cover all possible objections to his system. They were, also, the result of his own failure to envision how the market would provide for these activities.

Bentham, on the contrary, placed intervention by government on a firmer philosophical foundation (leaving aside for now our criticisms of the consistency of the principle of utility). He justified all the long list of interventions in the economy of which he approved by a claim that they would lead to the maximization of happiness for society. That this is an almost infinitely broader principle than Smith's quasi-natural rights foundation needs no further substantiation.

Bentham's influence and the erosion it caused in the Smithian economic system, to which Bentham himself still largely concurred, will be quite evident when we come to examine the later Utilitarians, J. S. Mill and Henry Sidgwick. That Bentham's influence upon the development of political economy has been slighted by most economic historians, because he did not originate any new theories in pure* economics, in an error which should not be perpetuated. Indeed, his influence was quite dramatic and widespread.

---

*By pure economic theory here is meant such topics as the meaning and production of wealth, price theory, and the theory of production, etc., or the "science" of political economy.

Despite Bentham's profession of fidelity to Smithian economics, he provided the principle which was to serve as one of the primary factors behind its downfall, at least among academic economists. The changes which Bentham brought about were the result of his substitution of the moral principle of utility in place of the Smithian nature philosophy. It was not the result of any significant alterations made by him in the field of pure economics.

THOMAS ROBERT MALTHUS: POPULATION THEORY AND SAY'S LAW

In contrast to Bentham, who contributed nothing of any significance to the purely theoretical aspect of political economy, Malthus made substantial and highly influential additions and modifications upon the body of Smith's teachings. While he remained essentially an adherent of Smith's free-market and minimal-governmental-intervention approach, he questioned certain of the more optimistic tendencies of that doctrine. A complete examination of Malthus' technical alterations made upon Smith's formulations—as, for example, in his theories of value or rent—might prove interesting, but such considerations would be largely extraneous to our purposes. Malthus remained, in these matters, within the broad paths established by Smith. However, such is not the case with respect to certain other matters in which he definitely departed from his mentor in one case and elaborated on something which appeared only in inchoate form in Smith in the other: the first being Malthus' disagreement with Smith and J. B. Say concerning the possibility of a general glut or overproduction in periods of depression,[73] and the second being Malthus' population theory.

This man, who became (in 1806) the first professor of political economy in England and was later instrumental in the establishment of the Statistics Society, came to adulthood around the turn of the century, a period in which some of the ruder accompaniments of the early phases of the Industrial Revolution had become apparent. It was also a time in which the earlier agricultural prosperity of Smith's day gave way to a rise in the prices of essential foodstuffs, which only exacerbated the condition of the poor. Malthus' theory of population, which first appeared in 1798, attempted to deal with these developments.[74] At a later period, particularly after the Battle of Waterloo, Malthus became absorbed by the problems of unemployment, which he attributed to an insufficiency of effective demand, thus flouting the intellectual authority of Say's Law.

In his day he was a controversial figure, generating an entire body of literature both in opposition to and in defense of his theory of population. He counted among his most vehement and acrimonious opponents such men as the socialists William Thompson and William Cobbett. Thompson, in his *Distribution of Wealth,* went so far as to question Malthus' humanitarianism, charging that he attributed the lowly condition of the poor to their own shortcomings and not to the evils of the property system. Among his followers on this issue, however, one can count David Ricardo, both Mills, and the Philosophical Radicals. Needless to say, his population theory is still a subject of debate in our own day. Curiously enough, his account of depressions found little or no support among these followers of his population theory but was instead adopted by socialists such as Marx (who employed it to draw extreme conclusions) and later by Keynes who used it (as did Malthus to a limited extent) to justify large-scale governmental "pump priming" during periods of depression.

In his *Principles of Political Economy: Considered with a View to Their Practical Application,* which was first published in 1819, Malthus conceived of the scope of political economy and its purpose in an essentially Smithian fashion. The object of this work, Malthus wrote, was to "prepare some of the most important rules of political economy for practical application, by a frequent reference to experience, and by endeavoring to take a comprehensive view of all the causes that concur in the production of particular phenomenon."[75] Thus, he did not employ the art-science distinction which Bentham hinted at and Senior and J. S. Mill later developed. He retained a view of political economy as a discipline whose practical applicability was a critical part of its purpose. However, he did recognize that in many cases it was not possible to predict results with certainty. This was due to the complexity of the causes as they actually operate, combined with any number of unforeseen circumstances.[76] Political economy could help to delimit those instances in which predictions are likely to be accurate and those in which accuracy would be doubtful.

In general, Malthus concluded that the science of political economy bore a greater resemblance to the science of morals and politics than to that of mathematics.[77] He maintained that propositions which were dependent upon the agency of such a variable creature as man, combined with the unpredictability of nature and the soil, can not afford the same kind of proof or lead to the same degree of certainty in their conclusions as those which relate to figure and number. While there are general principles in political economy, they are more similar to those in politics or morals than to those in the stricter sciences. And he takes as evidence of this the prevalence of great differences in opinion among the practitioners of political economy. They disagree even over the most fundamental principles, such as the theory of value, wages, rent, and so on.[78] Malthus sets as the first purpose of his discipline to analyze things as they are, that is, to develop theories which are consistent with and serve to explain general experience, and only then to serve as the grounds of practical conclusions.[79] The method he employed for this purpose drew heavily upon an analysis of historical experience and whatever rudimentary statistics were available to him. From these sources he extracted general theories and then practical conclusions. As will be evident later in our treatment of Ricardo, in both his method and his delineation of the science of political economy, Malthus differed from Ricardo while remaining essentially in harmony with Smith.

MALTHUS' THEORY OF POPULATION

While it is undeniably true that there were definite hints of what was to become Malthus' population theory implicit in the *Wealth of Nations,* such indications lay dormant there until Malthus published his *Essay on the Principle of Population* in 1798. This work underwent several revisions throughout Malthus' life, with the general thrust of the doctrine remaining unchanged, although softened somewhat (in the second edition) by the elaboration of additional "preventive checks" to the growth of population, which had the effect of leaving open the possibility of mankind exercising a certain measure of control over its destiny.

The direct impetus for the writing of the *Essay* came from Malthus' desire to combat the views of William Godwin on the perfectibility of man, as expressed in his *Enquiry Concerning Political Justice.* Godwin's contention was that but for the evils engendered by government and the unequal distribution of property, mankind would enjoy an abundance of happiness. Malthus saw in this scheme for the equalization of property merely an incentive to unrestrained reproduction, for, in truth, the poten-

tial for unhappiness or happiness lies within us, and if anything, the
existence of government tends to mitigate our evil propensities.

The general outline of Malthus' population theory is well known. His
contention was that animated nature, whether animal or vegetable, had
a tendency to increase in a geometric ratio if no other obstacles are opposed to it. In actuality, however, there are always such obstacles; the
principal checks to the increase of food being found in (1) man's laziness
and unwillingness to produce beyond his consumption needs, and in the
final stages, (2) the absolute want of power to prepare land of the same
quality as the original, thus setting a natural barrier to the rate of progress.
The power of increase in the food supply is limited by the scarcity of
land and, in addition, by the law of diminishing returns which points to
the fact that additions of capital and labor to land already in cultivation
will not produce the same increase as the original capital and labor investments of the same magnitude. By studying the past—an empirical approach
to the problem of the construction of theories—Malthus draws the following conclusions: (1) that population when unchecked will increase in a
geometrical progression, a "conjecture" to be drawn from observing the
census tables from the United States, Sweden, South America, Britain,
and Ireland, while (2) when all good land has been brought into production, future increases would depend on the cultivation of increasingly
poorer land, with the result that each year the increment in the food supply would have a tendency to diminish, the effect being that even by the
most sanguine projections the food supply could at most increase by an
arithmetical progression. The point at which shortages would arise depends on such other factors as an unfavorable distribution of produce
which would diminish the demand for labor and thus curtail the increase
of food at an earlier period. Improvements in agriculture, which would
increase the demand for labor, would have the opposite effect. The general tendency would remain unaltered; that is, while population would
increase a million times in five hundred years, the food supply could
increase only twenty times, if that much.

It is apparent that in the real world such an increase in mankind's
numbers would be impossible because an expansion of that magnitude
would be severely limited by the difficulty or impossibility of procuring subsistence. Population is limited by the available food supply. Hence,
the actual increase of population over the globe must fall far short of the
potential for increase, spurred by the desire for sexual intercourse, if left

unchecked; it must obey the same law of increase as that for food. Perhaps, as many critics have suggested, Malthus' position would have been made clearer had he simply dispensed with the "arithmetical" and "geometrical" tags and just said that population, if left unchecked, had a potential for almost unlimited expansion, while the food supply had a more limited potential for expansion due to the natural limit of the availability of cultivatable land and the effects of diminishing returns. This is all he really meant, anyway.

Since man can not live without food and the food supply cannot be expanded as rapidly as can population, the former exerts limitations upon the latter. The harshest and most direct check to population, termed the "positive check" by Malthus, operated by causing the death of excess children due to malnourishment and disease. Another check operates also as the general impoverishment due to the scarcity of food discourages people from entering into early marriages, thus diminishing the birthrate. These checks resolve themselves into either moral restraint, vice, or misery. The hope is that with improved education and institutions moral restraint can be encouraged and vice and misery circumscribed. Abstinence from marriage on a permanent basis or for a period of time and strictly moral conduct towards the opposite sex constitute this "moral-restraint" check. "And this is the only mode of keeping population on a level with the means of subsistence which is perfectly consistent with virtue and happiness,"[80] Malthus contended. All other checks on population constitute either vice or misery, for example, prostitution, low morals, unnatural passions, and improper acts to prevent the consequences of sexual passion, war, pestilence, famine, unhealthy cities, unwholesome occupations, severe labor. Against this whole array of positive checks, the single hope for mankind's improvement lies in the exercise of "prudential restraint" against early marriage. It is no wonder that Carlyle termed political economy the "dismal science."

What were the conclusions to be drawn from this population theory in regard to the proper role of government? To the socialist's clamor that the conditions of the working class are directly attributable to a faulty social system, Malthus declared:

> It is to the laws of nature, therefore, and not to the conduct
> and institutions of man, that we are to attribute the necessity
> of a strong check on the natural increase of population.[81]

Even if mankind had from the beginning of time employed the most enlightened distribution and the most efficient manner of production, the
checks on population would now only be operating with greater force
and the conditions of the laboring class be worse, not better.

Furthermore, based on historical evidence and the observations of
what motivated man, "there can be no well-founded hope of obtaining
a large produce from the soil but under a system of private property."[82]
Only such a system can override man's natural indolence, and only such
a system can harness a man's desire to provide for himself and his family
and better his condition. Community of property is condemned by
Malthus as visionary, and he cites the failure of such attempts and the
insignificance of their number as providing no basis for inference as to
their feasibility. As for the future, education does not seem to provide
a means for rendering such schemes more workable. The conclusion is
the Smithian one that private property stands the best chance of securing nourishment for a large and burgeoning population.

Malthus does, however, introduce a potentially damaging addendum
to this endorsement of private property when he claims that private property
limits the actual production before it reaches the maximum point attain-
able by the physical powers of production. There is no motive for the
entrepreneur to extend cultivation unless the returns are sufficient to
pay wages plus a profit on the capital invested. Under a system of communal property all land might be brought under cultivation and all men
forced to labor on the land. Such a state of affairs is condemned by
Malthus because it would lead to the "greatest degree of distress and
depredation." It is interesting to note that Malthus conceded to his adversaries the point that communal property could provide more food than
a system of private property, even though, on the strength of his earlier
argument that only private property can fully harness man's natural motives toward self-preservation and self-improvement, such a claim would
be dubious, indeed. Malthus falls back upon a much weaker claim, that
private property, even though it might curtail cultivation, does so beneficially in that it frees part of the population to pursue the arts and sciences. He also condeded that cultivation under private property may
curtail output in a harmful manner if the original division of land was
greatly unequal and the laws had not given facility to a more beneficial
distribution. The net result is that he placed the system he was attempting
to defend under a cloud, needlessly surrendering the economic argument

as to which system would maximize production to his opponents, for on his own argument men under a system of enforced cultivation would not be as productive because their motivation would be diminished. He fell back on a Utilitarian moral argument to condemn communal property— that it would lead to depredation or a diminution of happiness and would curtail intellectual advancement.

Malthus' population theory led him to generally libertarian conclusions in regard to the function of government in the marketplace. Governments can not directly influence the way in which the various checks on population operate, but it can exercise an indirect influence. "Prudence cannot be enforced by laws without a great violation of natural liberty"— note the Smithian formulation here rather than the Utilitarian—"and a great risk of producing more evil than good"[83]—and the Utilitarian argument employed in a subordinate role as further proof. Yet a just and enlightened government can exercise some positive role by ensuring a perfect security of property which will itself engender habits of prudence among the populace. Under a despotic, oppressive regime, any increases in real wages will be offset in a short period by a rapid increase of population, whereas under an enlightened government such an increase in wages can be translated into improvements in the subsistence, conveniences, and comforts of the existing population. The latter result is attributable to the improved habits of the people, which in turn is the result of civil and political liberty and improvements in education. The "prudential check" is developed among the working class principally by the existence of civil liberty without which no one will form plans for the future because the fruits of his labor will not be guaranteed to him. Thus, the primary functions of the government in the economic realm are: (1) to secure property through the promulgation of a code of just laws and the impartial administration of them, (2) to guarantee political liberty, for without it civil liberty can not be permanently maintained.

The theory of population also led Malthus to reject the calls of his day for a "right" to poor relief, and he, along with Bentham, contributed to the rejection of Pitt's Poor Law Bill of 1797-1798. "The existence of a tendency in mankind to increase, if unchecked, beyond the possibility of adequate supply of food in a limited territory, must at once determine the question as to the natural right of the poor to full support in a state of society where the law of property is recognized."[84] The problem resolves itself, Malthus argued, into a question of the necessity of those laws which establish and protect private property. (It is interesting to observe that Malthus' ensuing argument in defense of private property bears a much stronger resemblance to Adam Smith's, or even Locke's, natural law account of the genesis of private property than to a Benthamite approach, although critics usually consider Malthus to be a satellite member of the Utilitarian School.)

The laws of nature dictate to man, a reasonable creature, the cultivation of the soil both for the support of the individual and the increase of man's numbers, and this law serves the general good and increases the mass of happiness. For the same objectives, the law of nature additionally dictates the establishment of private property and, consequently, the absolute necessity for some power capable of protecting it. The right of property, however, is the creature of positive law (and here Malthus departs from Locke and follows Smith into a most critical deviation from the Lockian natural rights formulation in which government is merely the enforcer of preexistent property rights), but the law is of such an early derivation and it presents itself so imperiously to all mankind that if it is not a natural law, it is the most natural and necessary of all positive laws. The foundation of its primacy lies in its tendency to promote the general good. Malthus' modification of the Lockian account of a natural right to property left open the possibility that property relationships could be altered by government for the Utilitarian purpose of securing a greater amount of happiness, and he claimed precisely that. His contention in regard to a "right" to relief was this—that while modification of the laws of property with a view toward increasing human happiness may be considered, the concession of a right to full support to all that might be born would be entirely incompatible with any right to property, no matter how it might be modified.

Malthus, by combining a natural law derivation of property with the Utilitarian considerations of maximizing happiness, was able to provide a principle elusive enough to validate almost any state of affairs he personally approved of, short of enthroning a "right" to relief or completely abrogating all private property. Because he found the economic arguments against communal property or equality of property conclusive—that is, they would encourage a rampant population increase while curtailing the supply of food—he opted for the granting of relief in certain cases but not as a "right." The problem became for him an empirical one of how far assistance can be rendered to the distressed poor without undermining the law of property. If the poor consider being on relief a disgraceful condition, then few would seek it out and much good can be accomplished and no harm done by granting relief. If, on the contrary, such an attitude does not prevail, many will seek aid and a general deterioration in the mass of people will result, and such aid would generate more harm than good. What it comes down to, then, is a purely Utilitarian calculation of benefits and costs.

It is evident that Smith's modifications of the Lockian property rights argument as elaborated by Malthus left open the possibility for greater discretionary powers on the part of government in its dealings with private property. And Malthus' formulation is even looser than Smith's because it explicitly validates governmental incursions into private property relationships for the purpose of increasing the general happiness. In the actual conditions which prevailed in his time, Malthus advocated that poor relief should be greatly curtailed, only given to the truly indigent, and ended completely for those born after a certain date. Thus, his pure economic theory of population led to policy conclusions that, given his Utilitarian-type accounting of the dangers to property from guaranteeing relief at that time, limited governmental incursions. The considerations which Malthus discussed concerning the dangers of population outstripping the food supply were quite influential in the formulation of the Poor Law Reform Bill of 1834, which was perceived at the time as an effort to curtail and rationalize relief even though it carried with it strong centralizing effects.

MALTHUS' OPPOSITION TO SAY'S LAW

It was the contention of Jean-Baptiste Say, a French economist of the period, that supply creates its own demand, in other words, that a general glut of goods throughout the economy due to general overproduction and insufficient effective demand is not possible. This formulation became known as Say's Law (although James Mill ought to be granted co-authorship), and it triumphed throughout the nineteenth century despite heated dissent by such figures as Sismondi, Malthus, and Marx. Counted among its adherents were Smith (who preceded Say), the Mills, and Ricardo. The controversy did not end there, as evidenced by the ascendancy of Keynesian economics in the 1930s and 1940s, and the more recent countervailing arguments of such an advocate of Say's Law as Milton Friedman.[85]

Thomas Sowell summarized the basic notions behind Say's Law in the following passage:

> The production of goods (including services) causes incomes
> to be paid to suppliers of the factors (labor, capital, land, etc.)
> used in producing the goods. The total price of the goods is the
> sum of these payments for wages, profits, rent, etc.—which is to
> say that the income generated during the production of a given
> output is equal to the value of that output. An increased supply
> of output means an increase in the income necessary to create
> demand for that output. Supply creates its own demand.[86]

Thus, while excesses can exist in certain products, corresponding deficiencies will exist, in consequence, in other goods, and a general overabundance of commodities throughout the economy is not possible. It was precisely this point which the opponents of Say's Law contested, arguing that a general glut was possible for short periods due to excessive savings. They were not contending that such a crisis would be permanent. The defenders of Say's Law found this argument of excessive savings unconvincing because they treated savings as by definition equal to investment, and consumption plus investment necessarily equal to output, which in turn would equal income.

Malthus' dissent took the following form. Both laborers and capital, he contended, may be redundant compared with the means of employing them profitably.[87] He presented the following scenario to illustrate how a general glut could spread through the entire economy due to a failure of aggregate demand. If the capital of a country were diminished by a failure of demand in some large branches of trade (by capital, here, Malthus probably meant circulating capital, that is, that portion of capital which is available to pay future laborers), and the revenue of landlords was simultaneously diminished in greater proportion owing to some peculiar circumstances, then demand would be diminished in even greater proportion than supply would be curtailed, and so commodities would be cheap, profits of stock would be low, and there would be no pressing demand for capital because there would be no pressing demand for commodities. Hence, further saving would only exacerbate the situation. In fact, Malthus claimed it was precisely this kind of development which occurred during the last two years of the Napoleonic Wars (1813-1815), the crisis being further aggravated by an increased demand for labor during the war which generated an increase in population. As the result of an unusual stagnation of effective demand and a fall in the value of raw produce brought about by large expenditures and destruction of capital in the war effort, wages and profits fell and the capital and revenue of the country fell sharply. Thus, warehouses were filled with unsold goods, and the produce, though deficient for the population, was redundant when compared to the effectual demand and the revenue available for its purchase. The last thing needed, consequently, was an increase in savings to be turned into more useless capital.

The cogency of this argument is not of direct concern for our purposes. Ricardo took heated exception to Malthus' scenario.[88] (Although critical charges might be lodged against Malthus as, for example, why would not the damage be confined to a single branch of trade which had overproduced its commodity, i.e., why would the market not be cleared by a reduction in price of those goods in oversupply, with the result that marginal producers might go out of business and their capital be invested elsewhere? Even Keynes admitted that his argument for general overproduction was dependent upon an unwillingness among laborers to take a cut in money wages—a debatable point. Thus, even if a glut were widespread throughout the economy, prices would fall and wages would fall but not in real terms; thus the situation would be self-correcting.) What is important, though, is the kind of conclusions for governmental activity which Malthus proposed as a direct result of his alteration of an economic principle which was implicit in Smith's system.

Attributing the diminution in demand for commodities compared to the available supply after the end of the war to excess savings by individuals of revenue that was readily spent by the government during wartime, Malthus concluded that what was needed was more "wasteful consumption" (as contrasted with "productive consumption"; i.e., purchases of capital goods). Expenditures by the government during wartime created a greater and more certain demand for labor and thus for commodities than was generated by individual expenditures after the war. What was needed, in Malthus' account, was an increase in the value of the national produce, and this can be done by a more effectual distribution. Little can be done by government in furtherance of this objective, but it can refrain from aggravating the situation. The government can not directly alter the distribution of land, but it can further international trade by removing barriers. Also, the government can combat the idea that by diminishing the purchasing power of unproductive consumers (the rich), the working class would be aided.

Malthus drew the iconoclastic conclusion that the government could alleviate the plight of the unemployed workers during the depression after the war by employing them in labors which would not result in the production of consumer goods. Such employments as road building and public works were considered appropriate, nonproductive occupations. In addition, he thought it would be helpful for landlords and the rich to employ workers in idle pursuits such as beautifying the employers' estates. Those employments considered helpful and desirable for the improvement of the economy were ones—like the employment of menial servants by the rich—which did not add to the capital employed in productive labor. He did not wish, however, for the government to interfere with the savings of individuals, which would be regulated by the level of profits anyway. In this he adhered to Smith's general maxim that the wealth of a nation is best secured by leaving every person free to pursue his own interests as he sees fit within the rules of justice.

For Malthus the duty of government was still one to which Smith could subscribe, that is, to avoid war and large expenditures. But to Smith's reasons for such an admonition to government, Malthus added the warning that excesses of this type would lead to a derangement of demand after the war, which would result in much suffering on the part of the working class. What is interesting for our purposes is that Malthus was led to propose an expanded role for governmental activity in the marketplace as a direct result of a change he wrought in pure economic theory. The argument was that if general gluts were possible and they resulted in depressions, then it was permissible for the government to engage in certain limited palliative measures. He went so far as to suggest that large government debts might not be so bad because they had a tendency to redistribute revenue to those sectors of the population which had a greater propensity to consume—the middle class. And he advocated the imposition of taxes to permit the government to sop up the excess capital and distribute it in ways that would augment the effectual demand.

THE ROLE OF GOVERNMENT IN THE ECONOMY

In his introduction to the *Principles of Political Economy*,[89] Malthus saw fit to admonish his readers that Smith's great principle—that the best way for the government to increase the wealth of a nation is not to interfere with the individual in his pursuit of wealth—must not be taken to exclude categorically all acts of governmental intervention. (This same

point was made by McCulloch and much later by Sidgwick and Cairnes—
that absolute laissez-faire was not the doctrine of Adam Smith and that
such a blanket condemnation of all governmental regulation makes no
sense.) The question of the government's role in the economy was more
complex than this principle would indicate. Malthus offers three classes
of interventions which are exceptions to the general rule: (1) that certain
classes of activities are "generally acknowledged" to be within the province
of government, for example, questions of the state's role in education, support of the poor, public works, military establishments; (2) that every
existing government has to maintain a whole body of laws not of its own
creation in regard to agriculture, manufacture, and commerce which were
devised by less enlightened and more heavily regulated governments; the
result of repealing all such acts might be cataclysmic; and (3) that "there
is one cause in every state which impels the government to action, and puts
an end to the possibility of letting things alone. This is the necessity of
taxation, . . ."[90] for taxation can not take place without interfering with
individual industry and wealth.

> It is obviously, therefore, impossible for a government
> strictly to let things take their natural course; and to recom-
> mend such a line of conduct, without limitations and excep-
> tions, would not fail to bring disgrace upon general principles,
> as totally inapplicable to practice.[91]

Malthus was not, in fact, drawing any distinctions which Smith had
not made before him; yet the emphasis is subtly different, placed more,
perhaps, on the exceptions than on the general applicability of the rule.
This was a phenomenon which was to increase as time went on and
economists became more defensive about being associated with an absolutist view of laissez-faire which was pinned on them by their adversaries.
But Malthus' tendency was strongly Smithian, for he emphasized that a
good statesman, just like a good physician, should be most sparing in
his use of medicine and most trusting in the healing powers of nature.
The more science a statesman possessed, the less likely will he be to interfere and the more judicious will he be when he does intervene.[92]
    It is rather ironic that Malthus, who was much more of a Smithian in
his conception of the science of political economy and its methodology
than were Ricardo and his followers, departed from the orthodox laissez-

faire position on some of the pressing policy issues of his day. We have seen how one crucial departure from Smith on the positive economic principle of Say's Law led Malthus to propose governmental interventions during depressions which took the form of endorsing government debts and large government employment of workers. From the same source came his opposition to a redemption of the public debt after the Napoleonic War and his indifference to a resumption of the gold standard after the war. As we shall see, these were all causes which his friend and frequent adversary David Ricardo vociferously championed.

Another policy prescription with which Ricardo and the laissez-fairists were continuously absorbed for over a quarter of a century was the repeal of the Corn Laws, a protectionist piece of legislation which favored the agricultural interests and injured the poor and society in general. Curiously enough, Malthus opposed the almost united voice of political economy on this question. Mathus' endorsement of the Corn Laws can be attributed to several causes: his positive doctrine that rent is a net addition to the surplus of society and not merely a transfer payment (as Ricardo thought), and thus the Corn Laws were beneficial because they raised rents; his contention that the Corn Laws actually benefited the poor by raising prices and forcing them to consume less and save more; and his greater affinity to agricultural interests than the Ricardians.

In assessing Malthus' policy tendencies, it might be a fair generalization to say that while his pure theory of general gluts led him to propose a larger role for government, his direct deductions from his theory of population led to strong laissez-faire conclusions. For example, he addressed the Commons Emigration Committee in 1827 and argued for the termination of parish relief for anyone born after a certain date to be specified by Parliament. His views on population were instrumental in shaping the climate of opinion which led to the Poor Law Reform Bill of 1834.

DAVID RICARDO: THE ASCENDANCY OF THE ABSTRACT, DEDUCTIVE METHOD

David Ricardo was certainly the dominant English economist of his generation, and although a follower of Smith, he contributed several highly influential theoretical innovations of his own. These departures from and modifications of certain aspects of Smith's economic principles did not go unchallenged in his time. Among his most zealous and persistent critics can be counted Thomas Malthus, with whom he carried on an extensive correspondence on every controversial aspect of political economy from the conception of the discipline itself to the theory and measure of value, currency, the theory of rent, profits, and the dispute over the validity of Say's Law, stagnation, and the possibility of a general glut.[93] There were, of course, many areas in which the two found themselves in agreement; for example, they both originated the principle of diminishing returns in the year 1815 (along with Torrens), and Ricardo employed Malthus' population theory in the formulation of his wage doctrine. Just as Ricardo's influence seemed to be finally waning, John Stuart Mill, in his *Principles of Political Economy,* published in 1848, gave the Ricardian system its definitive exposition and secured its dominance over yet another generation. It was not until Jevons and the Marginalist revolution of the 1870s that Ricardo's influence subsided. His contributions to economic theory included: (1) the law of diminishing returns, (2) innovations in value theory, (3) the theory of rent, (4) the "iron" law of wages (as it was later called), a result of Malthus' population theory, (5) the comparative-cost theory of international trade, and (6) the projection of a future, stationary state for the economy.

In his approach to the discipline, he was much more analytic, abstract, and deductive in his method than was either Smith or, especially, Malthus.[94] In his purely theoretical works he relied not at all upon historical or statistical observations of actual economic phenomena but rather deduced his principles from a few simple definitions and generalizations.

In a letter to Malthus written in 1820, Ricardo had this to say about their respective approaches to the discipline:

> Political Economy, you think, is an inquiry into the nature and causes of wealth; I think it should rather be called an inquiry into the laws which determine the division of the produce of industry among the classes which concur in its formulation. No laws can be laid down respecting quantity, but a tolerably correct one can be laid down respecting proportions.[95]

And so, Ricardo gave much more emphasis to a class analysis of economic society than did Smith, although he did build upon the groundwork already laid by Smith. He conceived of the produce of the earth as divided among

three distinct classes—the proprietors of land, the owners of stock or
capital necessary for cultivation, and the laborers by whose industry the
land is cultivated. In different stages of advancement in society, the proportions allotted to each class will vary, and Ricardo faults his predecessors for not adequately dealing with this problem of distribution and the
effects that growth has upon the division. For such an analysis to be undertaken, a true doctrine of rent had to be formulated (and here he gives
credit to Malthus, although he disagrees with him on many aspects of the
theory of rent), because without that, it is impossible to understand the
effects of progress on wealth, profits, and wages or the influence of taxation upon the distribution.

The taxation policies to be pursued by government were also of particular
importance to his treatment of distribution as the central core of economics, because the government in its taxation policies can not help but interfere to some extent with the distribution.

Ricardo, in his *Principles,*[96] separated political economy from any
explicit moral foundations or political considerations to a much greater
degree than did any of his predecessors, although in his letters, pamphlets,
and speeches in Parliament he exhibited a keen interest in and knowledge
of the economic policy concerns of his day. He was particularly interested
in such questions as the stability of the currency, the national debt, taxation, the gold standard, and the regulation of the banking industry.

RICARDO'S TREATMENT OF VALUE, RENT, WAGES,
AND PROFIT

Ricardo's theory of value is even more muddled than Smith's and his
various explanations of it throughout his *Principles of Political Economy
and Taxation* are often contradictory. Leaving such variations and obfusca-
tions aside, the essential features of his value theory seem to include the
following: (1) The "value of a commodity, or the quantity of any other
commodity for which it will exchange, depends on the relative quantity
of labour which is necessary for its production, and not on the greater
or less compensation which is paid for that labour."[97] Thus an increase
in the wages received by laborers does not affect exchange ratios but
merely causes a decrease in profits. The conclusion is that when wage rates
rise (since he is considering only basic labor units of time, which will be remunerated at the same rate throughout different industries), profits must

fall. (2) He is concerned with exchange value, not utility or value in use, and with only those commodities the value of which depends on scarcity and the supply of which can be increased by labor and not with those goods—such as rare works of art or precious gems—whose value depends solely on their scarcity. (3) While in the early stages of society, exchange value depends almost exclusively on comparative quantity of labor embodied in each of two commodities, as society progresses, certain other factors come into play which may alter the ratio of exchange between two commodities, such as different degrees of durability in the tools of production and different proportions of fixed capital (that is, machinery, buildings, land, etc.) to circulating capital (that is, capital available to pay the wages of labor). Thus, if business A has a large circulating and a small fixed capital, it will be affected differently by a rise in the wages of labor than business B, which has a small circulating and a large fixed capital. Relative value is influenced, then, by wages in addition to quantity of labor. But only small changes in value can be attributed to wage alterations, the most significant factor still being the quantity of labor necessary to produce the commodity. Other subsidiary factors which affect relative value are the time and distance required to bring a good to market and the differences in skill of the laborers employed in different industries.[98] On later reflection, Ricardo thought that his theory could be simplified to the following propositions:

> I sometimes think that if I were to write the chapter on value again which is in my book, I should acknowledge that the relative value of commodities was regulated by two causes instead of by one, namely, by the relative quantity of labour necessary to produce the commodities in question, and by the rate of profit for the time that the capital remained dormant, and until the commodities were brought to market.[99]

What is clear about Ricardo's theory is his rejection of utility as the determinant of value (in his rejection of Say's value theory[100]) and his insistence that cost of production alone determines value, not consumer demand (a position actively contested by Malthus[101]).

Smith considered labor to be both the determinant and measure of value, but Ricardo doubted whether any perfectly invariable measure of value could be found, although gold could be considered as such for the

purposes of his inquiry.[102] When it came to the question of price determination, Ricardo did follow Smith in distinguishing between natural
price—meaning by that the quantity of labor, both new and embodied in
machinery, necessary to produce the good, or the cost of production—
and market price—that is, the accidental and temporary deviations of the
actual price from the natural price as a result of the supply not perfectly
matching the demand.[103] If men are left free to pursue their own interests,
then these deviations will quite rapidly be corrected, as investment funds
will be directed into the production of those goods whose market price
is above their natural price and in which profits are higher than the average rate of profit. When the opposite situation exists, funds will be diverted
from the less profitable trades. Thus, this restless desire on the part of
individuals to seek the greatest profit tends to equalize the rate of profits.

> It is then the desire, which every capitalist has, of diverting
> his funds from a less to a more profitable employment, that pre-
> vents the market price of commodities from continuing for any
> length of time either much above, or much below their natural
> price.[104]

Cost of production, then, is the ultimate regulator of the price of commodities (or their exchange value), not supply and demand, which is only
a short-run factor.[105] Thus, price equals cost of production, which in
turn is apparently comprised of quantity of labor plus an average rate of
profit which is assumed to be the same for all industries. Thus:

*Exchange Value (or Market Value) = cost of production =
quantity of labor (past and present + % profit on capital
advanced*

How profit fits in the equation is not exactly clear (as was the case with
Smith), and it seems to be neglected in the treatment of market price.
This was probably due to the fact that Ricardo considered profit to be
the same for all industries in his hypothetical case of market price, and
so it would not affect the proportion in which goods would exchange.
In this passage, directed at Malthus, Ricardo includes profit as a cost of
production, something which is not at all made clear in the main body
of his discussion on value:

> Mr. Malthus appears to think that it is a part of my doctrine,
> that the cost and value of a thing should be the same;—it is, if
> he means by cost 'cost of production' including profits.[106]

It is odd, indeed, to think of profits as constituting a cost of production. This is yet another weakness of the labor theory of value and its problem with formulating a coherent view of how profits are derived.

Ricardo's theory of rent incorporated elements of Malthus' population theory, the law of diminishing returns, and his own incremental approach. "Rent is," according to Ricardo's definition, "that portion of the produce of the earth, which is paid to the landlord for the use of the original and indestructable powers of the soil."[107] He explicitly excluded from this term "rent" all interest and profit on the capital invested on the land by the landlord. (This point, alone, generated much criticism as being entirely arbitrary and contrary to common usage.) Rent payments, then, are only possible once all "abundant fertile land" has been appropriated.

> It is only, then, because land is not unlimited in quantity and
> uniform in quality, and because in the progress of population,
> land of an inferior quality, or less advantageously situated, is
> called into cultivation, that rent is ever paid for the use of it.[108]

As population expands, land of an inferior grade must be brought into cultivation, and this will be done when X increment of capital employed on land of the first quality will produce the same amount of raw produce as will the same unit of capital applied to land of the second degree, due to the law of diminishing returns. When such inferior land is brought into cultivation, then, and only then, will the land of the first quality pay rent; and that rent will be based upon the difference in productive powers of that land over the inferior land. With each progressive movement down the scale to land of the third and fourth quality, the lands of higher quality will pay more rent. The land brought into production last never pays rent.

As a result of the fact that more labor will be required to produce an equal amount of foodstuffs on land of an inferior grade, the exchangeable value of the product will rise. The exchangeable value (or price) of the entire stock of the commodity (say, all the corn produced in England) will be determined by the cost of production on the worst land which is cultivated.

When inferior land is cultivated, superior land will produce the same quantity as it did before, but the value will be greater, simply because the value is set by the cost of production on the worst land.

The landlord receives the benefit of this increase in value. Consequently, as population grows and inferior lands are forced into cultivation, the relative value of raw produce will rise. The reason for this is that more labor is employed in the production of the last portion obtained, and not because rent is paid to the landlord.[109] If the landlord did not receive rent, if he were forcibly deprived of all such receipts, the consumer would not benefit in the least, and the only ones who would benefit would be the tenant farmers on the better lands who would absorb the rent portion for themselves. The reason for this is that cost of production—and hence, exchange value—which is based on the inferior land, will not have been affected.

The result of all this is that as society becomes wealthier, the landlord will get an ever increasing share of the product. But the price of corn is not raised by the increase of rent; rather rent is increased due to the higher price of corn. Rent is not a component part of price, because price is set by cost of production on the worst land, land which pays no rent. Ricardo differs, then, from Smith, who held that rent was an additional component of price (aside from the original determinant, the quantity of labor) once all land was appropriated, and Malthus, who maintained that rent constituted an increment to the national product.

Ricardo made of his rent theory a general rule which he considered applicable to all modes of production—whether it be raw produce, manufactured commodities, or metals—that is, that value depends not on the rate of profits (which is uniform) or the rate of wages (which is also considered uniform) or the rent paid (for such was not a factor in value), but solely on the total quantity of labor necessary to obtain the good and bring it to market.[110]

It is interesting to note that Malthus, from whom Ricardo had originally gotten his basic notions on rent, dissented rather dramatically from Ricardo's conclusions. Malthus agreed with Smith and not with Ricardo in concluding that the interest of the landlord was identical to the interest of society. The landlord, Malthus said, had an interest in improvements in production, in the increase of population, in the increase of capital, and in the increase in demand for raw produce as a result of the prosperity of commerce. These interests were identical to those of society. Ricardo disagreed. Ricardo thought that improvements in production lowered rents, while Malthus came to the opposite conclusion. Malthus thought that rents had increased in the last century due to improved skills and greater capital, not simply as a result of deductions from wages and profits as Ricardo contended. The policy implications of this disagreement are reflected in Malthus' hostility to a repeal of the Corn Laws and Ricardo's approval of such a recision, arguing that no further contrived impetus was needed to the natural tendency for the enrichment of the agricultural interests.

As we turn now to Ricardo's theory of wages, we will, once again, see the influence of Malthus' population theory upon Ricardo's thinking. Labor as a commodity has a natural and a market price, the former being "that price which is necessary to enable the labourers, one with another, to subsist and to perpetuate their race, without either increase or decrease."[111] This level could be bare subsistence, but in a prosperous society it is, additionally, comprised of conveniences that have become habitual to the working class. "The natural price of labour, therefore, depends on the price of the food, necessaries, and conveniences required for the support of the labourer and his family."[112] Thus, as the price of necessaries rises, so will the natural price of labor. And since necessaries rise in price with the progress of society and the rise in population, the natural price of labor will also rise. This increase is somewhat moderated for a time only by improvements in agriculture and new imports of food. Over the long run, nevertheless, the price of labor has a tendency to conform to its natural price or cost of production. Labor and raw produce rise in their natural price as society progresses, while all other commodities tend to fall in natural price with progress, for in the latter case any increase in raw materials is offset by improvements in machinery, a better division of labor, and greater knowledge on the part of producers. The factor of supply and demand for labor will account for variations in the market price of labor. With the natural advance of society, wages would fall because population will increase at a faster rate than demand for labor. The money wages of labor would rise, but not as much as the price of commodities, and the laborers would be worse off. Profits would go down because the employer would have to pay higher wages while his goods would sell at the same price. Thus, even though both rent and wages will rise with the progress of wealth and population, only the landlord will truly benefit because he gets an increase in both money rent and real purchasing power while the laborer only gets an increase in money wages accompanied by an actual diminution in real wages. The landlord will enjoy an ever greater share of the produce as time goes on, but the worker and the capitalist will suffer a decrease.

In our discussion of Ricardo's theory of value, we saw that profits and wages bore an inverse relationship to each other, that is, when wages were high, profits were low, and conversely, when wages were low, profits were high. Now, as society progresses, wages will increase, and profits, in consequence, must necessarily fall. Eventually, with the rise in the price of necessities and in wages, an end will come when wages equal the whole receipts of the farmer. At that point, there will be an end to accumulation, capital will yield no profit, no additional labor will be demanded, and population will have reached its maximum. Long before this occurs, the low rate of profit would have ended accumulation and almost the whole produce, after wages are paid, will belong to the landlords and the receivers of taxes. This is Ricardo's stationary state.

Ricardo's projection of an eventual, static state for the economy, once labor productivity on the land had decreased to the point where profits would be squeezed out by the increase in wages to cover the increase in the price of corn, put a gloomier light upon the free-market system than Smithian economics ever had.[113] In addition, Ricardo accentuated the class-conflict analysis which was implicit in Smith's discussion of the opposing interests of landlords, capitalists, and workers. According to Ricardo's analysis, the following events are the long-range results of progress and increasing population: (1) the landlord is doubly benefited by the difficulty of production of raw produce because he obtains a greater share of the product, and the commodity in which he is paid is of greater value (it will purchase more goods in exchange); (2) the capitalist will see his profits falling as wages rise to cover the increasing cost of necessities until profits will be so low that any motive for further accumulation will have ended (In this explanation he takes exception to Smith, who attributed the fall of profits to the accumulation of capital over time and a resulting increase in competition.); (3) the worker will experience a rise in money wages, but not a great enough increase to offset increases in the cost of necessities. On Ricardo's account, then, the interest of the landlords is always opposed to that of the consumer, the worker, and the manufacturer.[114] This position is in marked contrast to that taken by Smith, in which landlords were considered to have an interest

in harmony with the interest of the society as a whole, while the interest
of the merchants and manufacturers was considered to diverge from the
general interest. Historical events may account for this difference of
opinion, with Smith focusing upon the disturbances produced by the
new, profit-seeking class and Ricardo, writing at a time when the landlords with their protectionist Corn Laws[115] were holding back improvements for the rest of society, focusing upon the reactionary legislation
promoted by the landlords. The latter's animus against the landlords was
evident in his conclusion that the landlords were the only possible bene-
ficiaries of an increase in the market price of corn, and in the following
passage he suggests that there is something inherently different (and perhaps even suspect) about the landlords' dealings with the rest of society.

> The dealings between the landlord and the public are not like
> dealings in trade, whereby both the seller and the buyer may
> equally be said to gain, but the loss is wholly on the one side,
> and the gain wholly on the other.[116]

Another perpetual source of conflict was that between capitalists and
laborers as a result of the former's profits dwindling as a direct result of
increased wage demands. But the basic conflict is that between landlords
and the rest of society.

He did, however, hold out some hope for a small, fertile country like
England to forestall the onset of the stationary state by importation of
agricultural goods from abroad, thus limiting the onset of diminishing
productivity in agriculture and its necessary result, the increase of rent.
In this case, then, the manufacturers by trading abroad would greatly
benefit the rest of society. From this source came Ricardo's vehement
opposition to the Corn Laws. Once such protectionist measures were repealed, England would prosper by free trade. She would benefit from
her advantage in manufacturing which would enable her to purchase raw
produce from abroad for less of her own value in exchange.

Thus, the potentialities inherent in Smith's class conception of economic
society were exacerbated by Ricardo. Smith's harmony-of-interest doctrine
was dealt a severe blow by Ricardo's scenario for ever worsening and totally
irreconcilable class interests.

One more element of Ricardo's treatment of political economy ought
to be given brief mention. He gradually came to question his earlier ad-

herence to the view that the introduction of machinery would benefit all
classes and came instead to view its introduction as at least temporarily
upsetting to the fortunes of the working class.[117] The employment of
machinery can not, however, safely be discouraged by the government
because if capital were not permitted to seek its greatest net return in
one country, it would be carried abroad, with the result that the regulated
country's products would suffer a relative diminution in value as compared
with the freely produced goods from abroad.

THE ROLE OF GOVERNMENT IN THE ECONOMY

It is interesting to observe that despite Ricardo's substantial theoretical
disagreements with Smith's economic principles, he did not draw conclusions from these changes which would enhance the role of government in
the economy. Despite his discernment of an antagonistic interest on the
part of the landlord to the general good of society, he did not draw any
regulationist conclusions from this analysis. The landlord would reap an
ever greater reward for producing nothing, for contributing no value at
all to the national product, and yet he must be left free to receive this
gain; nothing ought to be done by government to intervene in this natural
process. To do so would produce no benefit, he thought, because the price
of corn would still be determined by the cost of production on the least
fertile land which paid no rent. And, furthermore, any intervention would
merely serve to exacerbate the situation by disturbing the market mechanism by which capital seeks its most advantageous employment.

Thus, Ricardo's pure theory of rent and its projection of antagonistic
class interests and an eventual stationary state advantageous to only the
least productive class did not lead him to abandon laissez-faire and demand more government intervention as it quite logically could have. Why?
Perhaps because he conceived of these principles as natural laws which
could be breeched by government to be sure but only with even more
deleterious consequences, and perhaps also because of his often repeated
moral conviction that self-help, individualism, and government quietism
are goods of the highest order. While Ricardo had strong ties to Bentham,
there was still a great deal of moralistic individualism and suspicion of the
state left in him which had, seemingly, little to do with his pure economic
doctrines.

It was, then, left for others to draw different conclusions from Ricardo's rent doctrine. Most notable among these were the socialist Henry George and the later group of Fabian Socialists whom George influenced. Given Ricardo's analysis, George argued quite logically for the nationalization of all land and the payment of rent to the government.

From Ricardo's wage doctrine (that is, the principle that wages will tend toward a subsistence level, governed by custom, and based on the cost of production of the necessities and conveniences consumed by the laboring class) and Malthus' population doctrine, Ricardo drew the same conclusions about poor relief that Malthus had, that is, that the state had no business providing subsistence to the poor. Even though landlords were destined by the process of the marketplace and the progress of society to get more of the product at the expense of the laborer, all wage agreements must be left free.

> Like all other contracts, wages should be left to the fair and
> free competition of the marketplace, and should never be con-
> trolled by the interference of the legislator.[118]

The Poor Laws were condemned because they constituted such an interference, and furthermore, they had an effect opposite to that "benevolently" intended by the government: they make "the rich poor, not the poor rich." They serve only to increase the number of the poor, thus worsening their plight. Also, this fund for the maintenance of the poor has a tendency to increase progressively until it will absorb all the net revenue of the country, "or at least so much of it as the state shall leave to us after satisfying its own never failing demands for public expenditure."[119] He quotes Buchanan approvingly, to the effect that there are miseries in the social state which we can do nothing to relieve. For these reasons, Ricardo concurred with Malthus' call for a gradual abolition of the Poor Laws. The poor can be relieved, he thought, only by a regard on their part, or perhaps the legislators', for regulating their increase in numbers by discouraging early marriages. The Poor Laws run directly counter to such restraint. "They have rendered restraint superfluous, and have invited imprudence, by offering it a portion of the wages of prudence and industry."[120]

One interesting sidelight which bears comment at this point is that Bentham, Malthus, and Ricardo shared a common belief that the individuals comprising a community could all increase their wealth only if their numbers were kept down so as not to consume the entire benefits of progress in production methods. Some critics have suggested that such a viewpoint was the result of the fact that these theorists considered the beginnings of the Industrial Revolution as actually much closer to its end point. But it was also undoubtedly the product of their failure to predict the great productive potentialities of precisely the free-market system whose principles they attempted to discover and then defend. It was the result, too, of a rather static conception of the economy; that is, if one sector gets more, some other sector or class must logically get less. Thus, even though Ricardo was particularly absorbed by the question of the effects of growth upon the distribution of the produce of a country, he did not think it possible (except with the above-noted case of an England divested of the Corn Laws) that all elements of society could be benefited by progress.

Ricardo opposed the recommendations of Bentham and Malthus that the government should promote investment or employ workers in times of depression, for he concurred with Smith's assessment that stability would arise most felicitously from the free working of the competitive market system, and he concurred with Say's Law. He would have dissented from J. S. Mill's contention that distribution should be a province of government. Ricardo went along this path only as far as acknowledging that the government had a proper function in levying taxes, but such activities ought to be kept to a minimum and the distribution left unaltered.

He devoted a large segment of his *Principles* to precisely this subject of taxation. "There are no taxes which have not a tendency to lessen the power to accumulate,"[121] and Ricardo went on to admonish,". . . but the great evil of taxation is to be found, not so much in any selection of its object, as in the general amount of its effects taken collectively."[122] The government should never levy taxes which would fall on capital rather than on revenue, because such measures would impair the fund for the maintenance of labor (note the beginnings, here, of the Wages-Fund Doctrine) and diminish future production. Therefore, he rejected all schemes for the taxation of estates as contributing to the depletion of capital. This position was in marked contrast to that taken by Bentham.

In general, then, property should be easily transferable between individuals, thus ensuring that those who can employ it most productively will gain its use. Taxes should not burden any one class unfairly; rather, the "burden of the State should be borne by all in proportion to their means."[123] Security of property, Ricardo emphasized, should be held sacred and should not be subjected to unequal taxation.

Ricardo's strong animus against governmental interference, even to taxes, emerged most forcefully in his speeches and votes in Parliament. A particularly pungent example may be found in his speech on the Excise Duties Bill of 1819:

> He had a jealous distrust of raising money beyond immediate necessity, and placing it in the hands of ministers; not the present ministers only, but any ministers responsible to a House of Commons constituted like ours. . . . In fact, all taxation had a tendency to injure the labouring classes, because it either diminished the fund employed in the maintenance of labour or checked its accumulation. . . . As to the particular taxes, it was unnecessary for him to state his sentiments, seeing he was an enemy to taxation altogether.[124]

While the last statement was undoubtedly hyperbolic, Ricardo prided himself on never having voted for an increase in taxation. He voted for the repeal of such interventionist taxing measures as the House and Window Tax,[125] the tax on malt,[126] and the agricultural horse tax,[127] to name but a few. Taxation was for him an evil but regrettably a necessary evil.[128]

On the contemporary policy issues which preoccupied the legislators of his own day—how to combat the depression after the Napoleonic War, how to handle the currency problems and the inflation of the period— Ricardo was one of the strongest advocates of laissez-faire among the classical political economists.

Concerning international trade, Ricardo came down squarely on the side of free trade, speaking out quite often in Parliament against all types of protectionist measures.[129] Duties on importation or bounties on exportation were anathema to him because they diverted capital from the employment to which it would naturally flow. Such measures constituted the worst form of taxation. While the landlord has a permanent interest in gaining bounties on exportation, the manufacturer does not—an interesting reversal of Smith and another example of Ricardo's shift of allegiance to the newly emerging capitalist class. He made an important addition to Smith's doctrine of free trade through the development of a comparative-advantage analysis, which emphasized the benefits to a country of specializing in those trades in which it enjoyed a comparative advantage over its trading partner even if it did not enjoy an absolute advantage in that commodity. Both countries would benefit in the process, as each would produce that commodity which it could make most cheaply. All countries will benefit from free trade, and consequently the government should observe a hands-off policy, for anything it does would only derange the natural mechanism to the detriment of the country that engaged in such activities.

Ricardo was instrumental in arguing for the resumption of gold backing for paper currency, a practice which had been legislatively rescinded as an exigency of war in 1797. He argued that the inflation of the post-1815 peacetime economy was a direct result of the Bank of England being at liberty to issue bank notes without having the check of note holders being permitted to convert to gold on demand.[130] His plan was adopted in 1819 as Peel's Bill for the Resumption of Cash Payments. The subsequent deflation and depression was often cited by Ricardo's critics as attributable to his policy. He, in turn, placed the blame on the mismanagement of the bank directors. While Ricardo was generally sound on monetary questions from a noninterventionist perspective, he did commit one serious breach of the faith. In a posthumously published piece, "Plan for a National Bank,"[131] he advocated transferring the power of issuing paper currency from the Bank of England (and other banks) to independent commissioners appointed by the state. They would, in addition, manage the national debt, act as bankers to the government, and engage in market transactions in pursuit of these objectives. To his previous objection to J. B. Say years earlier, when he proposed a similar policy for France—that government ought not be entrusted with such powers— Ricardo now thought that independent commissioners would provide sufficient security against ministerial interference.[132] This suggestion was largely embodied in the Banking Act of 1844, the effect of which was to separate the banking from the issuing function, granting the latter to the state.

In striking contrast to Malthus, Ricardo was a vehement advocate of limiting government spending and paying off the national debt. In fact, to accomplish the latter purpose he went so far as to advocate a direct tax to pay off the debt.

Ricardo made few remarks on socialism per se, but among these scant comments was an attack upon a scheme proposed by Robert Owen for ameliorating the condition of the working class by curtailing the use of machinery. Ricardo argued that the causes of the 1819 distress could be found in other quarters. Mostly, he thought, government was to blame: for the Corn Laws, for the fetters upon trade in the form of protectionist legislation, and for the national debt, which raised taxes and drove capital from the country. Even though he acknowledged that machinery might temporarily injure the laboring class, government intervention would not relieve but exacerbate the situation. Once Owen was made aware of these principles, Ricardo felt confident that he would abandon his proposals.[133]

The truly remarkable aspect of Ricardo's position in regard to state intervention in the economy is that, despite his many and substantial disagreements with Smith on a theoretical level, he maintained an avowed faith in both the harmony-of-interest doctrine and in a limited role for government in economic matters. With the exception of taxation, which Smith also considered a proper function of the government, Ricardo held to a very minimal level of governmental activity, one that, with the exception of the proposal for a national bank, did not expand the boundaries set by Smith.

It is quite apparent that for Ricardo laissez-faire remained the general principle, virtually a natural law although he did not speak in those terms, from which departures could only be justified on an emergency basis.

There were many measures that might be adopted with propriety, even in opposition to general principles, for a time, and under the exigencies of the moment, but parliament should always provide for a return to a good system. They should go back to that system as soon and as well as they could, but at all events they should go back.[134]

For Ricardo the principal duty of government towards industry was, quite simply, to remove impediments.

Mr. Ricardo said that he conceived the duty of government to be to give the greatest possible development to industry. This they could do only by removing the obstacles which had been created.[135]

In Parliament he constantly spoke out in opposition to the preachings of interest groups for special privileges or taxes upon their competitors.[136] However anti-interventionist Ricardo himself was on policy, his theoretical innovations held out great opportunities for the opponents of his pro-capitalist position. Of particular importance in this regard are: (1) his logical projection of a future stationary state, which served to dispel optimistic projections for the potential prosperity to be generated by a freely operating market economy; (2) his labor theory of value, which was taken up by a group of socialists who largely misunderstood or ignored the intricacies of Ricardo's position by drawing the conclusion that rent and profit were deductions from the product created by the laborers, a conclusion opposite to Ricardo's; (3) his theory of rent, which was later used by socialists to urge the nationalization of all land, as rents were considered unearned deductions from the value created by labor; (4) his theory of wages, a result of Malthusian population theory, which undercut the belief that progress would automatically bring an improvement in living conditions to the workers; and (5) his class analysis of distribution which led directly to a similar approach on the part of socialists, particularly Marx, who built upon the class-conflict aspect of the doctrine while ignoring the harmony-of-interest doctrine to which Ricardo still adhered.

CONCLUSION

Bentham's introduction of a new moral principle into economics, the principle of utility, did much more to expand the role of the government in the marketplace than did any theoretical changes he may have wrought in Smith's pure economic doctrines. It is ironic that in Ricardo's, and to a lesser extent Malthus', treatment of the question of state intervention, few changes were made in Smith's minimalist approach. This is true despite the fact that they altered Smith's pure economic doctrines in several critical respects, particularly in the theories of rent, wages, population, and the stationary state. In fact, the most conspicuous change in the direction of governmental intervention was Malthus' penchant for government pump priming during depressions.

As we shall see in the following two chapters, Bentham's utility prin-

ciple was destined to survive and prosper, to the extent that it became
the dominant moral outlook of English political economists. Utilitarianism
would wreak its devastation upon the minimal-state philosophy in the
next half century, but in its first phase of influence the results were rather
mixed. Bentham, to be sure, followed his melioristic, social-engineering
proclivities down the path toward many more governmental functions
than Smith had endorsed. For Malthus, though, it was far less the principle
of utility than his overproduction-underconsumption theory of depressions
that led him to sanction an increased role in the economy for the state.
Ricardo, of the three the most Smithian in policy prescriptions and in adherence to the "be quiet" principle, departed the most from Smithian
methodology and harmony-of-interest analysis when it came to pure
economic principles.

In the end, the utility principle would defeat the general principle of
laissez-faire that Ricardo (and Malthus and Bentham to a lesser degree)
had still fervently embraced. The logical conclusion of the natural rights
position in the political realm—the laissez-faire principle—remained an
important element in Bentham's system and a great influence upon the
policy prescriptions of Ricardo and Malthus. However, as Utilitarianism
developed under the influence of J. S. Mill, this principle of nonintervention, a holdover from natural rights theory and an uneasy companion to
the principle of utility, would be subtly undermined until the general
expediency principle reigned supreme.

NOTES

1. In 1825 this measure was repealed and replaced with another
which somewhat narrowed the range of permissible workmen's associations to exclude combinations in restraint of trade and emphasized with
greater force than the 1824 act the penalties attached to the use or threat
of force or intimidation. The impact of this act was to legalize peaceful
unions but to penalize activities which threatened or coerced employers
or other workers. Benthamites championed the legalization of trade unions
as a concession to the individual freedom of the workers, but they thought
that such activities, on economic principles, could not ameliorate the conditions of the working class. A. V. Dicey, *Lectures on the Relation Between
Law and Public Opinion in England During the Nineteenth Century* (London: Macmillan and Co., 1905), pp. 190-200.

2. However, it is doubtful that any theoretical alterations wrought by Bentham in economics had any direct influence on the development of economic thought because most of his economic manuscripts remained unpublished. Presumably, his intimates had either direct or indirect knowledge of the content of these economic writings.

3. Jeremy Bentham, *An Introduction to the Principles of Morals and Legislation* (New York: Hafner, 1948), p. 4.

4. Ibid., Ch. 2; also, *Principles of Morals and Legislation*, Ch. 2.

5. Jeremy Bentham, *Theory of Legislation* (London: Kegan, Paul, Trench, Trubner and Co., 1904), Ch. 3; also *Principles of Morals and Legislation*, Ch. 2.

6. Gunnar Myrdal contends, in *The Political Element in the Development of Economic Theory* (Cambridge, Mass.: Harvard University Press, 1954), quite fallaciously, I believe, that Bentham was in fact an heir to the natural law tradition because both positions equate reason and nature, the "is" and "ought," and both present an *a priori* social philosophy. What this argument seems to ignore is the empirical component of the principle of utility; it is, for Bentham, a principle contingent upon human behavior. For example, if individuals suddenly began to avoid pleasure and pursue pain while thriving on such a regimen, Bentham would presumably abandon his first principle. On the contrary, natural law derived from *a priori* principles such as natural rights could not be disproved by comparable events. Thus, if everyone began to violate other people's rights massively, this would do nothing to invalidate natural rights theory. Also, on the level of legislation, utilitarianism had no *a priori* component as did natural law derived legal theory. For Utilitarianism, every act must be judged on its own merits, *de novo,* while for natural law theory every proposal must be judged by its coherence to immutable, *a priori* laws. For other arguments against Myrdal's interpretation see: L. J. Hume, "Myrdal on Jeremy Bentham: *Laissez-faire* and Harmony of Interests," *Economica,* August 1969, 36(143), pp. 295-303.

7. This discussion is drawn from Bentham's *Theory of Legislation* and his *Anarchial Fallacies,* in *The Works of Jeremy Bentham,* Part 8 (Edinburgh: William Tait, 1839).

8. Jeremy Bentham, "The Psychology of Economic Man," in *Jeremy Bentham's Economic Writings,* ed. W. Stark (London: The Royal Economic Society by George Allen and Unwin, 1954), Volume 3, p. 421.

9. Bentham, *Principles of Morals and Legislation*, p. 1.

10. Ibid., p. 2.

11. Ibid., p. 3.

12. Ibid., p. 1*n.*

13. Ibid., pp. 30-31.

14. Ibid., p. 42.

15. See: Bentham, *Theory of Legislation*, Part 1.

16. Bentham, "The Psychology of Economic Man," p. 424.

17. Ibid., p. 428.

18. Ibid., p. 433.

19. Bentham, *Principles of Morals and Legislation*, p. 121.

20. See: Bentham, *Theory of Legislation*, p. 16; also, *Principles of Morals and Legislation*, Ch. 17.

21. Bentham, *Principles of Morals and Legislation*, p. 322.

22. From Jeremy Bentham, *View of a Complete Code of Law*, Ch. 28, "Of Political Economy," as quoted in Lionel Robbins, *The Theory of Economic Policy in English Classical Political Economy* (London: Macmillan and Co., 1952), p. 191.

23. Jeremy Bentham, "Manual of Political Economy," in *Jeremy Bentham's Economic Writings*, Volume 1 (1793-1795), p. 234.

24. Ibid., p. 223.

25. See T. W. Hutchison, *'Positive' Economics and Policy Objectives* (Cambridge, Mass.: Harvard University Press, 1964), p. 27, for an interesting discussion of the "positive"-"normative" distinction.

26. Bentham, "Manual of Political Economy," p. 224.

27. See: Adam Smith, *An Inquiry Into the Nature and Causes of the Wealth of Nations*, ed. Wilson and Skinner (Oxford: Clarendon Press, 1976), sec. iv, ii.

28. In fact, Bentham's departures from Smithian economics and political theory are so legion that some critics have ejected him from the pantheon of "classicals" and "liberals," e.g., J. B. Brebner, *"Laissez-faire and State Intervention in Nineteenth-Century Britain," Journal of Economic History,* Supplement 8, 1948; and T. W. Hutchison, "Bentham as an Economist," *Economic Journal,* June 1956, pp. 288-306. The contrary interpretation, however, is maintained with equal enthusiasm, but I believe less cogency, by A. V. Dicey, *Lectures on the Relation Between Law and Public Opinion in England During the Nineteenth Century* (London: Macmillan and Co., 1905); and Leslie Stephen, *English Utilitarianism* (London: Duckworth, 1900).

29. Jeremy Bentham, "Methodology and Leading Features of An Institute of Political Economy" (1801-1804), in *Bentham's Economic Writings*, Volume 3, p. 307.

30. Ibid., p. 318.

31. Bentham, "Manual of Political Economy," pp. 230-231.

32. Jeremy Bentham, "In Defence of Usury" (1787), in *Bentham's Economic Writings*, Volume 1, p. 140.

33. Bentham, "Institute of Political Economy," p. 318.
34. Ibid., p. 324.
35. Bentham, *Theory of Legislation*, p. 1.
36. Bentham, *Principles of Morals and Legislation*, p. 5n.
37. Ibid., p. 70.
38. Bentham, "The Psychology of Economic Man," in *Jeremy Bentham's Economic Writings*, Volume 3, Ch. 29, p. 439.
39. Bentham, *Theory of Legislation*, p. 95.
40. Bentham, "Institute of Political Economy," p. 311.
41. Bentham, *Theory of Legislation*, Ch. 2 & 3, pp. 96-100.
42. Bentham, "Institute of Political Economy," p. 311.
43. Bentham, *Theory of Legislation*, Ch. 13, p. 66.
44. Ibid., p. 64.
45. Bentham, "Institute of Political Economy," 3, p. 311.
46. Bentham, *Principles of Morals and Legislation*, p. 170.
47. Bentham, *Theory of Legislation*, pp. 144-145.
48. Ibid., p. 63.
49. Bentham, "Defence of Usury," pp. 133-134.
50. Bentham, "Manual of Political Economy," p. 223.
51. Bentham, "Institute of Political Economy," p. 333.
52. Bentham, "Defence of a Maximum" (1801), in *Jeremy Bentham's Economic Writings*, Vol. 3, pp. 247-302.
53. Ibid., p. 311.
54. Ibid., p. 236.
55. Bentham, "Manual of Political Economy."
56. Bentham, "Institute of Political Economy," p. 336.
57. Ibid., p. 341.
58. Bentham, "Defence of a Maximum," pp. 247-302.
59. Ibid., pp. 257-258.
60. Bentham, "Institute of Political Economy," 2, p. 2.
61. Bentham, *Theory of Legislation*, p. 132.
62. Bentham, "Plan for Augmentation of the Revenue," in *Bentham's Economic Writings*, Volume 2, pp. 146-148; "Limitations of Government Traffic," p. 148.
63. Bentham, "Proposal for a (New) Species of Paper Currency," in *Jeremy Bentham's Economic Writings*, Volume 2, p. 151.
64. Bentham was particularly vehement in blaming the inflation at the turn of the century on local banks, absolving the Bank of England and the government's wartime suspension of specie backing for paper notes. He was opposed to an early resumption of convertibility of paper money to gold. See: "The True Alarm," in *Bentham's Economic Writings*, Vol. 3. Ricardo criticized Bentham's "True Alarm," particularly the view that

an increase in the circulating medium increases capital and commodities and is beneficial. Ricardo argued that any increase in the money supply can only raise the prices of commodities. See Ricardo's letter to James Mill, 1 January 1811, in Piero Sraffa (ed.), *The Works and Correspondence of David Ricardo* (Cambridge: Cambridge University Press, 1952), Vol. 6, pp. 15-16.

     65. Bentham, "Institute of Political Economy," p. 363.

     66. Bentham, "Tax with Monopoly," in *Jeremy Bentham's Economic Writings*, Volume 1, p. 369.

     67. Bentham, "Manual of Political Economy," p. 237.

     68. Bentham, "The True Alarm," Ch. 12.

     69. I am indebted to T. W. Hutchison for pointing out Bentham's departure from the Turgot-Smith position on capital and investment. See his article: "Bentham As An Economist," *Economic Journal*, June 1956, pp. 288-306.

     70. Lionel Robbins, *The Theory of Economic Policy in English Classical Political Economy* (London: Macmillan and Co., 1952), p. 191.

     71. Shirley Robin Letwin, *The Pursuit of Certainty* (Cambridge: Cambridge University Press, 1965).

     72. Elie Halevy, *The Growth of Philosophic Radicalism* (1928; rpt. London: Faber and Faber, 1952), p. 127.

     73. For a more detailed discussion of this topic, see: L. A. Dow, "Malthus on Sticky Wages, the Upper Turning Point, and General Glut," *History of Political Economy*, Fall 1977, 9(3), pp. 303-21; S. Rashid, "Malthus' Model of General Gluts," *History of Political Economy*, Fall 1977, 9(3), pp. 366-83; and A. S. Skinner, "Of Malthus, Lauderdale and Say's Law," *Scottish Journal of Political Economy*, June 1969, 16(2), pp. 177-95.

     74. Thomas Robert Malthus, *An Essay on the Principle of Population as it Affects the Future Improvement of Society* (London: Johnson, 1798; rpt. London: Macmillan and Co., 1926).

     75. The Rev. Thomas Robert Malthus, *Principles of Political Economy: Considered With a View to Their Practical Application*, 2nd ed. (London: William Pickering, 1836).

     76. Ibid., p. 11.

     77. Ibid., p. 1.

     78. For an interesting discussion of Malthus' differences with his contemporaries see: W. D. Grampp, "Malthus and his Contemporaries," *History of Political Economy*, Fall 1974, 6(3), pp. 278-304 (e.g., the determination of value and its measurement, the idea of effective demand, the place of deduction and empiricism in methodology, analytical rigor vs approximation).

79. Ibid., p. 8.
80. Thomas Malthus, "A Summary View of the Principles of Population" (1830), in *On Population: Three Essays* (New York: Mentor Books, New American Library, 1960), p. 38.
81. Ibid., p. 37.
82. Ibid., p. 33.
83. Ibid., p. 40.
84. Ibid., p. 55.
85. This brief summary of the history of Say's Law is taken from an excellent book on the subject by Thomas Sowell, *Say's Law: An Historical Analysis* (Princeton, N.J.: Princeton University Press, 1972).
86. Ibid., p. 4.
87. Malthus, *Principles,* Bk. 2, Section 10, p. 414*n.*
88. Ricardo denied that a general glut was possible, arguing that it made no sense to contend, as Malthus had, that both capital and labor could be redundant at the same time. See, for example, a letter to McCulloch dated 2 May 1820, in Piero Sraffa, *The Works and Correspondence of David Ricardo* (Cambridge: Cambridge University Press, 1952), Vol. 8, Letters, p. 181:

> It can never happen that capital and labour can be at the same time redundant; except as I said before you have arrived at the end of your resources, but Mr. Malthus talks of low profits from a want of demand, and thinks it quite possible that you may have more capital than you can employ, with a redundancy of people.
>   According to him, you produce too much and consume too little, and as you are so obstinate that you will not consume yourself he recommends that taxes should be imposed, and that government should expend for you.

See, also, the letter to Malthus dated 21 July 1821, Sraffa, Vol. 9, pp. 23-7.
89. Malthus, *Principles,* Introduction.
90. Ibid., pp. 14-15.
91. Ibid., p. 16.
92. Ibid.
93. See: Sraffa, *Works and Correspondence,* Letters, Vols. 6-9.
94. For contemporary critical discussion, see: N. B. deMarchi and R. R. Sturges, "Malthus and Ricardo's Inductivist Critics: Four Letters to William Whewell," *Economica,* Nov. 1973, N.S. 40(160), pp. 379-93.
95. Sraffa, *Works and Correspondence,* Vol. 8, 9 Oct. 1820, letter to Malthus, p. 278. Malthus replied (26 Oct. 1820, p. 286):

With regard to your new definition of the object of Political
Economy, I own it appears to me very confined; and if it be
just, I should say that political economy would be at once
converted from a science which I have always considered as
the most practically useful in the whole circle, into one which
would merely serve to gratify curiosity.

96. Sraffa, *Works and Correspondence,* Vol. 1, *On the Principles of
Political Economy and Taxation.*
    97. Ibid., Ch. 1, p. 11.
    98. For a fuller treatment of the question of interpretation of Ricardo's
theory of value, see: G. J. Stigler, "Ricardo and the 93 Percent Labour
Theory of Value," *American Economic Review,* 1958, 48, pp. 357-67.
Stigler contends that Ricardo upheld a labor theory of value as an em-
pirical, not merely an analytical, proposition. See also: H. Barkai, "The
Empirical Assumption of Ricardo's 93 Percent Labour Theory of Value,"
Economica, Nov. 1967, N.S. 34(136), pp. 418-23.
    99. Sraffa, *Works and Correspondence,* Vol. 8, letter to McCulloch,
13 June 1820, p. 194; and 2 May 1820, p. 180.
    100. Ibid., 9 Oct. 1820, letter to Malthus, p. 276-7.
    101. Ibid., p. 279.

You say demand and supply regulates value—this, I think,
is saying nothing, and for the reasons I have given in the
beginning of this letter—it is supply which regulates value—
and supply is itself controlled by comparative cost of production.

And see Malthus' response, 26 Oct. 1820, p. 286.
    102. Sraffa, *Works and Correspondence,* Vol. 9, particularly the letters
between Malthus and Ricardo during the year 1823 in which Malthus
argued the Smithian position that labor was the invariable measure of
value, and Ricardo countered that if anything could approach to such a
function, it would be gold.
    103. Ricardo, *Principles,* Ch. 4, "On Natural and Market Price."
    104. Ibid., p. 91.
    105. Ibid., Ch. 30, "On the influence of Demand and Supply on
Prices," pp. 382-6.
    106. Ibid., Ch. 1, Sect. 6, p. 47. For more on profit see: S. Hollander,
"Ricardo's Analysis of the Profit Rate, 1813-15," *Economica,* 1973, 40,
pp. 280-82; J. L. Eatwell, "The Interpretation of Ricardo's Essay on
Profits," *Economica,* May 1975, 42 (166), pp. 182-87; and Sraffa, *Works
and Correspondence,* Vol. 6, letters between Malthus and Ricardo dated
9 Oct. 1814 and 23 Oct. 1814.

107. Ricardo, *Principles,* Ch. 2, "On Rent," p. 67.

108. Ibid., p. 70.

109. Ibid., pp. 74-75.

110. Ibid., Ch. 3, "On the Rent of Mines."

111. Ibid., Ch. 5, "On Wages," p. 93.

112. Ibid. It is interesting that Ricardo's wage theory is not derived from a free-market, supply-demand process, but from the customary attitudes of workers towards necessities.

113. On the stationary state see P. R. Kolb, "The Stationary State of Ricardo and Malthus: Neither Pessimists nor Prophets," *Intermountain Economic Review,* Spring 1972, 3(1), pp. 17-30. He argues that, despite popular contentions, both theorists were optimistic about the future.

114. Ricardo, *Principles,* Ch. 24, "Doctrines of Adam Smith Concerning the Rent of Land," p. 335.

115. On Ricardo's persistent opposition to the Corn Laws, see: S. Hollander, "Ricardo and the Corn Laws: A Revision," *History of Political Economy,* Spring 1977, 9(1), pp. 1-47. Ricardo spoke out vociferously against these restrictions in Parliament, e.g., Sraffa, *Works and Correspondence,* Vol. 5, Speech of 12 May 1820, p. 47:

> There was not a more important question than that of the Corn Laws. Nothing, in his mind, was better calculated to afford capital general relief than the lowering of the price of corn.

and, 8 Feb. 1821, p. 73.

> With regard to the depression of agriculture, he believed it was a good deal owing to the laws which were enacted for the purpose of protecting it.

116. Ricardo, *Principles,* p. 335.

117. These changes were introduced in the third edition (1821) of the *Principles.* McCulloch, for one, was horrified as evidenced by his heated letters to Ricardo. See: Sraffa, *Works and Correspondence,* Vol. 8, 5 June 1821, pp. 381-6. For discussions of this topic, see: S. Marital and P. Haswell, "Why Did Ricardo (Not) Change His Mind? On Money and Machinery," *Economica,* Nov. 1977, 44(176), pp. 359-68; and S. Hollander, "The Development of Ricardo's Position on Machinery," *History of Political Economy,* Spring 1971, 3(1), pp. 105-35.

118. Ricardo, *Principles,* Ch. 5, "On Wages," p. 105.

119. Ibid.

120. Ibid., p. 107. For more on Ricardo's opposition to the Poor Laws, see Sraffa, *Works and Correspondence,* Vol. 7, letter to Mill, 12 Dec. 1818, p. 360, and 28 Dec. 1818, pp. 380-1.

121. Ricardo, *Principles*, Ch. 8, "On Taxes," p. 52.
122. Ibid.
123. Ibid., Ch. 14, "Taxes on House," p. 204.
124. Sraffa, *Works and Correspondence*, Vol. 5, *Speeches and Evidence*, 18 June 1819, pp. 25-6.
125. Ibid., 6 March 1821.
126. Ibid., 21 March 1821.
127. Ibid., 15 April 1821.
128. Ibid., Vol. 8, letter to Trower, 12 Nov. 1819, p. 133.
129. Ibid., Vol. 5, 25 May 1820, p. 47, and 30 May 1820. Ricardo did make some concessions in Parliament on the Corn Laws and bounties, arguing for a lessening of the restrictions if full abandonment was not legislatively feasible.
130. On the currency question, see: Sraffa, *Works and Correspondence*, Vol. 3, "The High Price of Bullion" (1809); Vol. 4, "Proposals for an Economical and Secure Currency" (1816). For a very complete treatment of this topic, consult: R. S. Sayers, "Ricardo's Views on Monetary Questions," in T. S. Ashton and R. S. Sayers (eds.), *Papers in English Monetary History* (Oxford: Oxford University Press, 1953).
131. Sraffa, *Works and Correspondence*, Vol. 4, "Plan for a National Currency" (1824), pp. 275-300.
132. In fact, Ricardo was thinking along these lines as early as 1815. See: Vol. 4, a letter to Malthus dated 10 Sept. 1815. For his response to Say, see: Vol. 6, 24 Dec. 1814, pp. 165-6.
133. Ibid., Vol. 5, speech of 16 Dec. 1819.
134. Ibid., speech of 30 May 1820, in the context of protectionism. See also: *Letters*, Vol. 8, 29 March 1820, pp. 172-3; and 23 March 1821, pp. 356-7.
135. Ibid., Vol. 5, speech of 29 June 1820 on the petition of the cotton weavers in which they asked for a tax on machines which competed with their hand looms.
136. E.g., ibid., Vol. 5, the speech of 7 March 1821 on the Corn Laws; 9 March 1823, arguing for the repeal of a law giving magistrates the power to fix wages of journeymen silk manufacturers; 7 May 1823, opposing a tariff on the importation of tallow; 7 May 1823, opposing a stamp and tax on linen; 30 May 1823, opposing manual weavers who blamed low wages on machinery (and so, Ricardo opposed laws to prevent the use of machinery even though by 1821 he thought that machinery could permanently injure the working class); and 11 February 1822, arguing that agricultural distress was temporary and didn't require any governmental measures for its alleviation.

Chapter 3

The Final Phase of Classical Economics: Senior, J. S. Mill, Sidgwick, and Cairnes

The period which encompasses roughly the years from 1830 to 1870 was the critical one for political economy as conceived by Adam Smith. At this juncture some of the inconsistencies in the doctrine of the Classical economists of the earlier years came to be questioned, certain tendencies in the old position which were opposed to laissez-faire came to full fruition, and the old notions of the nature of political economy as a discipline came under close scrutiny and were ultimately transformed.

In the political realm also this period was critical in deciding whether England would construct an interventionist state or proceed along individualist, minimal-state policies. While the final decision would be left to the last quarter of the century and battles were still being won by both sides, the line of march in the direction of an increased role for government in the economy and in the lives of individuals can be clearly delineated. While Tories and socialists contributed most toward the growth of collectivism at the turn of the twentieth century, during the 1830s it was primarily the Benthamite Radicals who agitated for a more activist role for the state. The principal enthusiasm of this group was, of course, the battle for a reformed Parliament which was won in 1832, with the expansion of the franchise to the middle class. But their enthusiasm was no less persistent in pursuit of social issues. Edwin Chadwick, for one, was instrumental in focusing public attention upon the plight of the poor, agitating for a reform in the Poor Laws, for state sanitary regulations, and for public provision for education. All these causes were enthusiastically backed by the Radicals in Parliament, and under their prodding the Poor Law Reform of 1834 envisioned a more centralized administration, and the first state provision for education was enacted.[1] The legacy of Bentham was particularly apparent in the agitation of the Radicals for rationalizing the state administration, erecting in the process a modern machine without which the later collectivist measures could not have been effectual.

The anti-regulationists, the free traders, won their finest battle in 1846 with the repeal of the Corn Laws under the Tory prime minister, Robert Peel, after the unremitting agitation of the Anti-Corn Law League ably led by Cobden and Bright.[2] But it is symptomatic of the cleavage in both parties between individualists and statists that in the very next year the Tory evangelical leader in Parliament, Lord Ashley (later Earl of Shaftesbury), carried a sweeping factory act, the Ten Hours Bill, which curtailed the hours of labor for children and women.[3]

Newly emerging social forces augmented the ever present paternalistic, conservative inclinations[4] of a wide body of influential men in the House of Lords and in the Commons who championed state interventionism even in this age of individualism. As Chartism waned as a lower-class movement for reform after 1848, working-class agitation turned from demonstrations for purely political reforms to a more activist trade unionism. The old Tory paternalism would eventually combine with growing socialist demands for state services to undermine the interests of the middle class and manufacturers in anti-regulationism. By 1867 Disraeli pushed through the Second Reform Bill, which extended the franchise to city artisans in an explicit attempt to forge an alliance between labor and the Conservative party. While the tactic was a short-term debacle, Gladstone being returned to office in 1868, the strategy had long-range consequences for the growth of collectivism.

Culturally, individualism, while regnant during the early Victorian period, was never without its vehement critics. Such intellectual luminaries as Carlyle, Coleridge, Southey, and Wordsworth in the earlier days, and Dickens and Ruskin later, continually flagellated the reigning ideology for its rampant materialism, vanquishing all spiritual values by a cash-nexus, and its destruction of order, rights, and duties by the turmoil of the marketplace.[5] And avowedly socialist critics leveled charges against political economy itself which went to the heart of its defense of the free-enterprise system. Initially, the main focus of attack was upon the distributional aspect of free competition, with the claim that the ideal of distributive justice was not attained in an individualistic, competitive system where some men inherited great fortunes and enjoyed most of the fruits of other men's labor. Gradually, the Smithian claim that a system based upon individual self-interest would lead to the maximization of national output fell under critical scrutiny with the charge that such an organization of industry wasted both human talents and natural resources and that it tended toward monopoly and the curtailment of output in an effort to raise prices artificially.

Orthodox political economy—the circle of those who considered themselves to be the followers of Adam Smith or Smith through Ricardo—could not remain aloof from these tremendous social forces, cultural critiques, and political challenges. John Stuart Mill, Cairnes, and Sidgwick, particularly, devoted a great deal of effort to evaluating the validity of the attacks upon Classical economics, and they themselves were instrumental in reevaluating and ultimately banishing the previous connection between political economy and the system of laissez-faire. Thus, the received doctrine suffered considerable assault both from its avowed enemies and its putative supporters.

Under the influence of both external and internal forces the connection between political economy as a science and laissez-faire as a political conclusion from it would be devastated. One of the critical internal reevaluations occurred under the twin auspices of Nassau Senior and John Stuart Mill with their analyses of the scope and method of political economy. The Smithian conception of political economy as a science whose purpose was to perceive natural laws and formulate principles which would then be of direct assistance to the legislator in his efforts to organize governmental policy in such a way as to maximize national output, came under attack. Senior and Mill divided political economy into a science and an art, following the hint offered by Bentham, with the science having nothing definitive to say to the political artist, the legislator. Senior even went so far, at one point in his life, as to deny the very possibility of an art of political economy. The general result of this discussion of scope and method was to give further impetus to the movement to disassociate political economy from the practical prescription of laissez-faire.

If political economy *qua* science could not offer practical advice with any certainty, if considerations other than economic ones must be weighed by the legislator in making policy decisions on economic matters, then the science of political economy can not definitively establish the validity of any one system of industrial organization over any other. It can not prove that laissez-faire should everywhere and at once be enacted, nor can it disprove a socialistic, regulationist organization of society. It can merely analyze the economic effects of either system, and it can only do this abstractly and hypothetically.

Another highly significant theoretical distinction was made in this period which had similar effect to the other changes previously mentioned, that is, to undermine the credibility and the belief in the individualistic economic system. This distinction was the one made by J. S. Mill, and mentioned briefly but not fully developed by Senior, that while the laws of production were inviolable and could be considered natural laws, the laws of distribution could not be so considered and must, rather, take their form from the peculiarities of time and place, and the dictates of various governments. Thus, while the laws of production were natural laws, the laws of distribution could be altered by human will. Smith and Ricardo had studied the laws of distribution in an attempt to see how in an individualistically oriented system of production each class which contributed to the process would get its share of the product. We might say, then, that they assumed that the distribution was fixed and that they were attempting only to discover the laws of distribution and the way in which the shares were divided. Ricardo, in fact, explicitly stated that the government in its taxing power should not tamper with the distribution, and the effect of Smith's four rules for taxation was the same. However, for Mill, all distributional arrangements could be altered at the will of the legislator, and all existent divisions of the national produce could be subjected to the tests of social utility and distributive justice.

As we come to examine these changes, it will become apparent that under the twin influences of the socialists' critique of political economy and the changes wrought by its defenders, political economy came to recognize ends other than the single Smithian one of the maximization of national production. The justice of the distribution effected by the free market became a question of critical importance to political economists of the orthodox school. The problems of poverty and the working class had become a much greater concern to these men than they had been to their immediate predecessors who were not indifferent to such considerations but thought that they could only be ameliorated by market processes.

THE QUESTION OF THE NATURE, SCOPE, AND METHOD
OF POLITICAL ECONOMY

In the year 1836, in works developed independently by Nassau Senior and John Stuart Mill, important changes were made in the conception of political economy as a discipline. Perhaps it was inevitable that as political economy became a respectable academic subject, its practitioners would perceive a need to narrow its scope, differentiate it from other related fields such as politics and morals, and attempt to ascertain the method proper to its development as a science. For Smith, political economy had a directly practical purpose, which was to discover the natural laws operative in man's economic relationships and then to instruct the legislator in how best to organize the government to maximize production. It was precisely this pragmatic objective for political economy which came under attack by Senior and Mill and later by their follower Henry Sidgwick. If political economy were to become an established science, then such tasks as giving definitive prescriptions to governments could be no proper part of economics *qua* science. As practitioners of an art, political economists might make suggestions to governments on economic policy matters, but they could do so more as statesmen than as scientists, and their normative judgments would have no more claim to be considered than would the opinions or value judgments of any educated man. This is but a brief description of the general thrust of the methodological alteration undertaken in this period, and a closer examination of the arguments of Senior, Mill, and Sidgwick will be helpful, as there were certain significant respects in which they differed.

Nassau Senior was appointed as the first professor of political economy at Oxford in 1826, and at that period in his intellectual development he held a view of the science which was more in tune with Smith and the early Classicists than would be his later refinements. In his *Introductory Lecture* delivered that year, he defined political economy as:

> . . . the science which teaches in what wealth consists—by what agents it is produced—and according to what laws it is distributed—and what are the institutions and customs by which production may be facilitated and distribution regulated, so as to give the largest possible amount of wealth to each individual.[6]

This definition of the discipline was in harmony with that given by McCulloch in his *Principles* or that given by Malthus in his. It considers the science to consist of a pure, theoretical aspect, a didactic function in regard to the legislator, and a teleological purpose, the maximization of wealth for each individual.

Senior's thought underwent a dramatic alteration during the ten years that intervened between the publication of his *Introductory Lecture* and his more independent and mature work, *An Outline of Political Economy*. The definition of political economy has, in this latter work, undergone a transformation in the direction of greater precision and limitation in scope. Political economy is defined now as the ". . . science which treats of the Nature, the Production and the Distribution of Wealth."[7] Banished from this definition of the science are all references to a purpose or teleology and all practical or prescriptive elements. He explicitly condemns the earlier use by economists of the term in a wider sense. Such loose definitions led these political economists to discourse on matters of government in their treatises, rather than the narrower and distinct topic of wealth. Senior elucidated his differences with his predecessors in one particularly pungent passage:

> The question, To what extent and under what circumstances
> the possession of Wealth is, on the whole, beneficial or injurious
> to its possessor, or to the society of which he is a member?
> What distribution of Wealth is most desirable in each different
> state of society? and what are the means by which any given
> country can facilitate such a distribution?—all these are questions
> of great interest and difficulty, but no more form part of the
> Science of Political Economy, in the sense in which we use the
> term, than Navigation forms part of the Science of Astronomy.[8]

While the principles supplied by the science of political economy are necessary components of any solution to these normative and practical policy questions, they are not the only or even the most important constituents of such a solution. These questions belong to the "science of legislation" which differs from political economy in its subject, its premises, and its conclusions. The subject of legislation is human welfare or happiness, not wealth as it is in economics; the premises of legislation are drawn from an "infinite variety of phenomenon"; and the expositor of legislation must urge the adoption of actual measures. On the other

hand, the premises of the economist consist of a few general propositions, the result of either observation or conscience, and scarcely requir-
ing proof or formal statement. Every man would admit their veracity
as soon as he were made aware of them. The inferences drawn from these
propositions are nearly as general and certain as the premises themselves.
Those relating to the nature and production of wealth are universally
true, and those relating to distribution are liable to be affected by peculiar
institutions of different countries.[9] But from his conclusions drawn
from these premises and inferences, the political economist is not, in
Senior's account, authorized in adding a "single syllable of advice."
This prerogative falls entirely on the political writer or statesman. "The
business of a Political Economist," Senior enjoins, "is neither to recommend nor to dissuade, but to state general principles which it is fatal to
neglect, but neither advisable, nor perhaps practicable, to use as the sole,
or even the principal guides in the actual conduct of affairs."[10]

Thus, political economy is but one of many subservient sciences to
the art of government, for that art considers motives other than the
single one of the desire for wealth, which is the motive relevant to economics, and it aims at objects of broader range to which wealth is only a
subordinate means. According to Senior at this stage in the development
of his ideas, there is in effect no art of political economy per se, and all
prescriptive functions formerly associated with that discipline are relegated
to what he alternately calls the "science" or "art" of legislation. Political
economy is limited to a pure science, the basic propositions of which can
be stated in a few sentences. The method proper to this science is, then,
one based less on observation than on reasoning from general propositions to general and certain conclusions.

Senior's methodology differed from that of his predecessors in that
he thought it was possible to deduce the science from essentially one
definition, that of wealth, and four fundamental propositions. While the
content of these propositions contained nothing novel or at odds with
previous accounts, the novelty lay in the fact that he made his assumptions much more explicit. He made the deductive method supreme, and
in this he differed from Smith and Malthus, who relied heavily upon induction, and tended more toward Ricardo.

Wealth he defined as consisting of all goods and services which possess
utility and are scarce, that is, everything that enters into the circle of exchange. The four fundamental propositions which, along with this definition of wealth, constituted the basis of the whole future deduction were

partly psychological and partly physical or natural. They consisted of the following: (1) that every person is desirous of obtaining as much wealth as possible with as little sacrifice as possible, (2) that the population of the world is limited only by moral or physical evil or by fear of a deficiency in the habitual standard of living to which each class had become accustomed, (3) that the power of labor and the other instruments of production which produce wealth may be indefinitely increased by using their products as the means to promote future production, and (4) that the law of diminishing returns applies to agricultural production.

In 1847 Senior again returned to the professorship of political economy at Oxford which he had been forced to vacate in 1831 under a rule which limited appointments to a term of five years. Once again, he reconsidered his treatment of political economy and the art-science distinction. This time, in his definition of the science, he drew attention to the distinction between physical sciences (those dealing with matter) and mental or moral sciences (those concerned with the human mind). The former are susceptible to proof by experimentation to a very much greater degree than the latter, and so economics, which falls under the category of mental science, is properly treated as a deductive science with the method of induction hardly applicable to it at all. The importance of these distinctions which Senior drew lies in his disagreements with J. S. Mill in regard to the nature of economics and the method proper to it. Senior criticizes Mill's categorization of economics as a science based upon hypothetical premises; rather he takes economics to be founded upon positive facts drawn from observation or consciousness. Instead of Mill's hypothesis of an exclusively economic man—in whom the desire for wealth is taken to be the exclusive motive, even though other motives are recognized but treated as irrelevant by the economist—Senior saw economics as a positive science based on a more realistic postulate, namely, that wealth is a universal and constant object of desire but not the sole object. They both agreed, however, in placing economics in the category of mental science.

The science of political economy, or economic science (the term "economics" was now gradually replacing the older term "political economy," the result of its demarcation from politics), as defined in Senior's *Lectures* of 1847, is "the science which states the laws regulating the production and distribution of wealth, so far as they depend on the action of the human mind."[11] All the technical terms of political economy represent either purely mental ideas—such as demand, utility, value, abstinence—or objects which are the results or causes of certain affections of the mind—such as wealth, capital, rent, wages, and profits. While political economy has to do with laws of matter, such as diminishing returns and the efficiency of machinery, they are dealt with in reference to their effects upon the human mind.

Despite this classification of political economy as a mental or moral science, Senior did not wish to enhance the scope of the science. It ought to be concerned solely with wealth, not happiness, not morals, and not virtue or honor. The political economist must be an analyst of wealth only and the effects of various measures upon production and distribution, but he must never offer a precept or advise governments to do or forbear, for then he would be a moralist, not a political economist. He can analyze the effects of governmental measures, but he can not say "do this" or "don't do that." Perhaps all this energy of Senior's and Mill's was devoted to making this distinction in order to meet the charge of opponents of Classical political economy that the whole discipline was suspect because it was merely a pretext for urging the adoption of laissez-faire social policies. Senior and Mill wanted to defend the science as a valid discipline, irrespective of and separable from any policy prescriptions.

Senior, in these later *Lectures,* does offer two definitions of a possible art of political economy, which constituted somewhat of a retreat from his position of 1836, but he is still uneasy with any "art" at this stage in the development of the science. The broader definition of the art of political economy he finds too extensive altogether and practically co-extensive with the art of government because it treats of happiness as an end. It defines the art as that

> . . . which teaches what production, distribution, accumula-
> tion and consumption of wealth is most conducive to the
> happiness of mankind, and what are the habits and institu-
> tions most favorable to the production, distribution, accumula-
> tion, and consumption.[12]

A more limited definition would be preferable because it restricts the end to wealth only, as it defines the art as that "which teaches what are the institutions and habits most favorable to the production and accumulation of wealth."[13] Senior concludes that as a political economist he must forbear such normative evaluations but that he does not wish to refuse the right to consider the practical consequences of the pure theory of wealth, but as a statesman or moralist. Bowring considered this later position of Senior's to be a weakening of his argument of 1836, but if it is, the attenuation is hardly noticeable.

In turning now to J. S. Mill's methodological efforts, certain similarities and departures from Senior's position will be apparent. Mill discusses this question in an essay entitled "Of the Definition of Political Economy; and on the Method of Investigation Proper to it," which was written in the period 1829 to 1830 but did not appear generally until it was published in 1836 in a book *Essays on Some Unsettled Questions of Political Economy*. In this essay, he makes the same criticism of Smith that Senior had, that is, that Smith failed to distinguish between an art and a science, thus contributing to the "vulgar" notion of political economy as a science which teaches how men can be made rich. If Mill did not come right out and call Smith's conception of political economy vulgar, he did the next best thing, because this so-called "vulgar" notion of the science was precisely the one held by Smith. Mill rejects this view because it confounds science—a collection of truths—with art— a body of rules or directives for conduct.[14] If political economy is to be a science, it can not be a collection of practical rules; however, practical rules must be capable of being based upon its principles, or else it would be useless. The statesman must first be a political economist in order to know how to make the nation rich. Here, Mill goes further than Senior in granting the legitimacy of a separate, yet justifiable art of political economy.

Rejecting the customary definition of political economy (and the one favored by Senior in 1836) as the science which elucidates the laws which regulate the production, distribution, and consumption of wealth, because it is too rudimentary and too broad, Mill goes on to propose one of his own. But first he makes the physical science-mental (moral) science distinction which Senior adopted from him in his *Lectures* of 1847. Political economy presupposes all the physical sciences and takes as its particular province the laws of the human mind. It takes for granted all laws of the physical sciences which pertain to production; it inquires into the phenomena of the mind which are involved in the production and distribution of these objects; and it investigates the effects which flow from the concurrence of these mental and physical laws. Mill's definition of political economy is "the science which treats of the production and distribution of wealth, so far as they depend upon the laws of human nature" or "the science relating to the moral or psychological laws of the production and distribution of wealth."[15] The first formulation was the one Senior adopted from Mill.

Mill, however, found this definition inadequate from a philosophical viewpoint, because political economy deals with production and distribution only in a social state, not in all states, and further, it only deals with a portion of the laws of human nature. On a more complete view, political economy is seen as a branch of speculative politics—that is, the science which deals with the way in which the laws of the nature of the human mind take effect in society. This branch is concerned with man solely as a being who desires to possess wealth "and who is capable of judging of the comparative efficacy of means for attaining that end."[16] (It was from this exclusive, hypothetical postulate that Senior dissented.) Its function is to predict the phenomena of the social state which result from this singular pursuit of wealth; and it abstracts all other motives except those which act as perpetually antagonistic motives to the pursuit of wealth, that is, the aversion to labor and the desire for present enjoyment of costly indulgences.

> Political Economy considers mankind as occupied solely in acquiring and consuming wealth; and aims at showing what is the course of action into which mankind, living in a state of society, would be impelled, if that motive, except in the degree in which it is checked by the two perpetual counter-motives above adverted to, were absolute ruler of all their actions.[17]

Thus, political economy investigates the following kinds of actions by men pursuing wealth: accumulating wealth, employing that wealth in the production of additional wealth, sanctioning by natural agreement the institution of property, establishing laws to forbid individuals from encroaching upon that property by force of fraud, adopting methods to increase their productivity, settling the division of the product by agreement and competition, and employing expedients such as money and credit to facilitate the exchange, and so forth. It is interesting to note that Mill includes among the strictly "scientific" concerns of the political economist questions that relate to government and the legal establishment

of property relationships and laws in the economic realm. This is a much
more expansive notion of the science than allowed by Senior. This difference may account, at least to a limited extent, for the admixture of questions of governmental policy in Mill's treatment of production, distribution, and exchange when he came (twelve years later) to write his *Principles of Political Economy.*

Senior's *Outline of Political Economy* exhibited a much greater adherence to the art-science distinction than did Mill's *Principles.* As many
critics, including Senior, have pointed out, Mill seemed to abandon completely his distinction between the art and the science of political economy
as formulated in the *Essay* when he came to compose his *Principles,* reverting in the latter to an approach much closer to Smith than to either
Senior or Ricardo. This apparent rejection of his earlier approach went
unexplained by Mill (although he did hint, in the *Preface* to the first edition of the *Principles,* that he was motivated by the desire to update the
political economy of Adam Smith, for primarily political reasons), but
perhaps these critics have not taken sufficient account of Mill's inclusion
of political elements in his definition of the science of political economy
given in the *Essay.* Leaving such considerations aside for now, let us return
to Mill's account of the science given in the *Essay.*

The aforementioned operations which political economy investigates—
those resulting from the desire for wealth—are actually the result of a
multiplicity of motives, and the political economist realizes this. He is
justified in treating man as a creature exclusively motivated by the necessity of his nature to seek wealth and to prefer a greater portion to a less,
except to the extent that the countervailing motives of laziness and enjoyment operate, because where there is a multitude of causes, they must
be studied separately. He does not suppose that men in reality are so constituted; he realizes that other motives intervene. Mill offers the analogy
of predicting the motions of the earth and planets; first, the laws of
centripetal and tangential force must be known. Political economy proceeds by treating the main and acknowledged end as the exclusive end,
even though men almost never act exclusively from this motive. By this
method, a nearer approximation to the truth is attained, Mill claims, than
would be possible by any other approach. Outside political economy,
when its conclusions are to be applied on the practical level, its results
must be corrected to account for other passions and motives. Finally Mill
offers the following definition of political economy which is, he contends, complete. It is:

The science which traces the laws of such of the phenomena of
society as arise from the combined operations of mankind for
the production of wealth, in so far as those phenomena are not
modified by the pursuit of any other object.[18]

Thus, political economy as understood by Mill is an abstract science,
a moral science rather than a natural science, a science in which experimentation is limited, and in which an *experimentum crucis* (as in the
physical sciences) is rarely possible. The method proper to it, then, is an
a priori one, "reasoning from an assumed hypothesis . . . a mixed method
of induction and ratiocination—argue upwards from particular facts to
general principles—then arguing downwards from that wider general principle to a variety of specific conclusions."[19] But in the case of political
economy, the reasoning is not based upon "particular facts" but upon
assumptions regarding man's nature, upon hypotheses, just as geometry
is built upon arbitrary definitions. It is based upon an arbitrary definition
of man's nature as wealth-maximizing, and its conclusions are, like those
of geometry, only true in the abstract. When the conclusions of the science come to be applied to the real world, the hypothetical assumptions
must be corrected to the extent that reality differs from them. And these
modifications drawn from the real world have their laws, too, and they
can be included in the science eventually. When these laws of the abstract
science are applied, an element of uncertainty arises because we can never
be sure that all circumstances have been taken into account. But such is
the fate of all the moral sciences.

One interesting sidelight to this discussion of methodology is that
here perhaps can be found one of the sources of Mill's later enthusiasm
for socialistic experimentation. Mill acknowledged that the *a posteriori*
method is applicable to the moral sciences not in discovering truth but
in verifying it. Considering the difficulty of running experiments in the
areas of concern to the moral sciences, the scientist is limited by the
actual "experiments" offered by the real world. Socialists, by experi-
menting with property relationships and distribution, would then serve
to expand the range of possibilities. If socialistic experiments provide
enough "disturbing causes," then their laws would eventually be taken
into account in the science itself, not merely in the art or practical application. This possibility opens up the question of whether the very hypothesis upon which political economy is based—that is, that man is exclusively motivated by a desire to maximize his wealth—could be brought

into question. Mill did not discuss this, but it is an interesting point for speculation, and it serves to underscore the problems inherent in a science built upon an admittedly incomplete hypothesis. In writing his *Principles*, Mill as much as conceded the point to Senior—that the possibility of other motives should not be excluded entirely from the science by absolutizing the pursuit of wealth—when he considered motives of much wider scope in his treatment of the science, much more so than even Senior himself acknowledged.

In the year 1886, Henry Sidgwick published his *The Principles of Political Economy*, a work which sounded the final notes of Classical economics. Sidgwick followed Mill in categorizing political economy as an abstract, deductive, and hypothetical science, in distinguishing between an art of political economy and a science and in asserting the need for qualifications of the general conclusions of the science when applied to actual situations. What is interesting in his admittedly derivative account of the scope and method of political economy is the extent to which he employed the art-science distinction to drive a wedge between the postulates of pure economic theory and the policy directives of laissez-faire.

He begins by denying the power of the science to decide practical economic questions. In dealing with disputes of the day "abstract economic arguments almost always come in, and are almost never by themselves decisive."[20] He goes on to argue that the scientific investigation of the laws that determine actual prices, wages, and profits, so far as they depend on free competition, is essentially distinct from any inquiry into the desirability of the system of free competition, whether it should be restrained or modified.[21] While orthodox economists have generally concluded that such a system is the most practical allocation mechanism, and therefore, they have generally concluded for noninterference on the part of the government, laymen have drawn from this the erroneous conclusion that the economic doctrines lead inexorably to the system of laissez-faire. Sidgwick goes to considerable length to show that the economist as scientist studies free competition not because he prefers it but rather because it is the simplest case to grasp. Hence, such scientific investigation does not imply the desirability of its adoption as a practical ideal or any claim for its justness. In emphasizing this separation of theory and practice, Sidgwick stands at one with Cairnes who declared in his *Lectures on the Character and Logical Method of Political Economy* that political economy has nothing to do with laissez-faire. As Cairnes wrote:

> Political economy stands neutral between competing social
> schemes, as the science of mechanics stands neutral between
> competing plans of railway construction, as chemistry stands
> neutral between competing plans of sanitary improvement.[22]

While Sidgwick allows questions of a practical nature into his treatise,
he warns that such considerations must be kept distinct from scientific
pursuits, and one must recognize the provisional nature of all such efforts.
Thus, the art-science distinction of Mill, Senior, and Sidgwick was really
something more than a pedantic, methodological debate, for it accomplished a very significant transformation of Smithian political economy.
It severed all practical policy recommendations which were advanced by
Smith from their putative foundations, the principles of the science of
political economy, and it rendered all questions of distribution, exchange,
and governmental intervention in the economy not subject to any definitive scientific resolution either for or against the laissez-faire system.

A few comments about the logical soundness of the art-science distinction advocated by Senior, Mill, and Sidgwick suggest themselves after
examining an instance of this distinction as exemplified by Sidgwick.

> . . . if a practical man affirms that it will promote the economic
> welfare of England to tax certain of the products of foreign
> industry, a mere theorist should hesitate to contradict him with-
> out a careful study of the facts of the case. But if the practical
> person gives as his reason that "one-sided free trade is not free
> trade at all," the theorist is then in a position to point out
> that the general arguments in favour of the admission of foreign
> products are mostly independent of the question whether such
> admission is or is not reciprocated.[23]

Now, it is difficult to see how the first case would fall squarely under the
category of art, in which political economy could teach nothing definitive,
while the latter falls under science, in which political economy can give a
conclusive answer. It seems that if the principles of political economy
in regard to the maximization of international and national wealth as a
result of the prevalence of free trade are scientifically true, which none
of the Classical economists denied, then its practical teachings must be
conclusive in both cases—that in the first case England can only be harmed
in the long run by the imposition of import duties, and the second case

that any single country which practices free trade will benefit despite the prohibitions enacted by other nations. The point being that such a rigid art-science distinction is rather difficult to clarify or maintain in practice. This is not to deny that these three theorists had a valid complaint against Smith and his earlier followers in that the latter group did not clarify the scope and method of political economy adequately. The Millian position had a valid point when it recognized that the free competitive assumptions of the science needed to be corrected for countervailing tendencies when examining existent situations, but Smith was not unaware of such considerations, as he often warned that the prescriptions of political economy can not be applied immediately without recognizing the claims of the parties who benefited by past regulations and who would be injured by their removal.

NASSAU SENIOR ON VALUE AND GOVERNMENTAL INTERVENTION

Senior's greatest contribution to economic theory was undoubtedly his methodological distinction between the science of political economy and the art, for that distinction was destined to become more and more important, especially toward the end of the century. In his *An Outline of the Science of Political Economy,* Senior, unlike Mill, remained true to his conception of the science, mentioning governmental activities solely as a disturbing factor through government's taxing powers and its effects upon the productivity of labor. For his political views one must turn to sources other than his economic treatise.[24] Before we examine Senior's contributions in that area, it may be useful to investigate briefly certain of his theoretical innovations in the science, because he fought a continual, internecine battle with the Ricardians over value theory, he dissented from Malthus' population theory in its extreme predictions, and he questioned the validity of the subsistence theory of wages.

While crediting Malthus with being a great benefactor of mankind, on a par with Adam Smith, for his elucidation of the connection between the means of subsistence, the extent of population, and the consequent standard of enjoyment available to people, Senior dissented from the extreme, popular notion of Malthusianism, that is, that population would tend to increase faster than the means of subsistence. Senior emphasized instead the tendency of the standard of living to rise as civilization advanced, so that with improvements in production, in knowledge, and in security and government, increasing numbers could be accommodated at ever higher levels of necessities and luxuries, with no end in sight.

Senior argued that in the absence of disturbing causes—restrictions on exchange and commerce, artificial barriers excluding the majority of people from eminence, ignorance, insecurity of person and property[25]—subsistence is likely to increase more rapidly than population.[26] These disturbing causes, the result of a rude state of civilization, are the general causes which both diminish productivity and establish a climate of improvidence in which the power of increase of mankind is unchecked by prudence, and is, in consequence, tending to surpass the means of subsistence, checked only by vice and misery. Knowledge, security of property, freedom of exchange, accessibility of rank, on the contrary, act to increase productivity and to elevate the character of the people, so that population is increased at a slower rate.

In effect, then, Senior did not reject the Malthusian analysis entirely, but rather, placed the theory's applicability to the past when men had barely surmounted the savage state. This was a significant alteration because it changed the theory from a generally pessimistic one, especially in its earliest formulations by Malthus, to an optimistic projection of a constantly rising standard of living for the masses as civilization and enlightenment progressed. Combined with the third premise of his science of political economy—that past productions can be utilized by labor to increase future production indefinitely—Senior's projections for the future were closer to the spirit of Adam Smith than to the stationary-state thinking of Ricardo, Malthus, or Mill.

Senior also dissented from the subsistence theory of wages as propounded by Ricardo. Rather than wages tending toward some arbitrary equilibrium rate as a result of population pressures at a point at which the habitual necessities of the laboring class would just be satisfied, Senior held that wages were determined largely by the productivity of labor. He gave one of the first clear expositions of the wages-fund doctrine, the theory that aggregate wages were limited by the availability of capital or, in other words, that wages were determined by the extent of the fund for the maintenance of labor, compared with the number of laborers to be maintained. The extent of the fund depended principally upon the productivity of labor which was dependent on the personal character of the laborers, the degree to which they were assisted by natural agents, the degree to which they were aided by capital, and the degree of freedom permitted by government. Another factor determining the extent of the fund for the maintenance of labor was the number of laborers employed in the production of commodities for the use of laborers, compared with the whole number of laboring families. Thus, he considered that laborers were diverted from producing goods for their own consumption to the extent that part of their labor was directed to the payment of rent, taxes, and profit. In contrast to Ricardo's position, then, rent and profit seem to be deductions from the share of the laborers, possible only because the laborers produce a "surplus value," to use Marx's term, over and above what is necessary to produce their wages.

Senior shared certain preoccupations and approaches with his contemporaries, including the division of society into three classes (laborers, landlords, and capitalists) and the attempt to ascertain the way in which the shares of these classes are distributed. It was in his theory of value, though, that Senior set himself apart from the cost-of-production theory of Ricardo and his followers. He placed an emphasis upon utility and demand which was wholly lacking in Ricardo, and he stated in general terms the principle upon which the law of diminishing marginal utility was later formulated by Jevons, that is, that each succeeding addition of the same commodity provides less satisfaction to an individual than the earlier units.

Senior begins by defining wealth, value, and susceptibility to exchange as equivalent terms. Value is determined by utility (the capacity to give pleasure, avoid pain, and in general, satisfy human wants), scarcity of supply, and transferability. In this approach Senior followed the lead of J.-B. Say, the French economist, who emphasized the utility aspect of value, a factor which was only mentioned by Smith as the necessary quality of a good which made it suitable for exchange but ignored by him as an element in the determination of value.

The result of Senior's analysis was not the abandonment of Ricardian cost of production as the determinant of value but the limitation of its applicability to a special case, that of "equal competition." In this special case of equal competition, goods would exchange for their cost of production, which is comprised of the cost of labor and the abstinence of the capitalist. Where there is equal competition, all men could become producers of a given commodity, all producers would have equal accessi-

bility to all factors of production, and capital and labor could be trans-
ferred from one employment to another without loss. It was Senior's
contention that for the vast majority of products—those in which the
appropriation of natural resources played any part or those in which
either diminishing returns (agricultural goods) or increasing returns (manufactured goods) obtained—equal competition did not apply. In other
words, the Ricardian assumptions bore little relation to the truth.[27] In
these instances, the bulk of production, cost of production played a less
and less determining role in the derivation of value as the good approached
a monopoly situation. Thus, Senior considered almost all production under
the category of "monopoly," which was a departure from general usage
and one in which he was not followed by other economists.

It seems that what he was trying to do was to reconcile cost of production with demand or utility as the causal determinants of value. What he
did was to assimilate Ricardo's rent theory to the production of almost
all goods, those produced with the aid of some scarce resource, whether it
be a natural resource, land, or a scarce talent. In these cases, the value of
the product is greater than the result of equal labor and abstinence un-
assisted by similar aids. Thus, Ricardo's assumption that most commodities
fall under the category of free competition was denied by Senior, as a direct
deduction from his rather idiosyncratic definition of equal and free competition and monopoly.

Senior criticized Ricardo for including profit as a cost of production,
certainly a legitimate criticism, but it is difficult to see how his substitution of the word "abstinence" in the place of profit really amounts to
anything substantially different. His introduction of the term "abstinence"
was about all that was taken from his discussion of value by his immediate
successors, notably Mill, as a convenient term to describe the capitalist's
function in the production process. Senior explicitly criticized Ricardo's
inclusion of profit as a cost, but he would not himself accept Colonel
Torren's derivation of profit, which was the clearest explanation of profit
to have emerged from the Classical economists. Torrens denied that profit
was a cost of production and said, rather, that it was the result of producing a greater value than the combined values of the goods consumed
in the process of production. Thus, if three hundred bushels of wheat
(on a simplified barter example) were advanced by the capitalist farmer
to cover the wages of labor and the price of implements necessary for
production for a period of one year and three hundred and sixty bushels

of wheat were produced at the end of the year, then the sixty bushels would constitute the capitalist's profit.

Although Senior made advances in clarity over the Ricardian account of profits, which seemed to be nothing more than an arbitrary percentage attached to the cost of production based on a national average of profitability, he really ended up by providing no clearer explanation of profits himself and finally reverted to the Ricardian approach of a percentage added to costs. His improvement lay in pointing out that profits were comprised of the excess of the value of the return over the value of the advance. Thus, there was no automatic guarantee of getting this return as it had sometimes appeared in Ricardo's account. Senior wrote,

> The sacrifices that have been made to produce a given com-
> modity have no effect on value. All that the purchaser con-
> siders is the amount of sacrifice that its production would
> require at the time of exchange.[28]

Thus, if the expense of producing stockings, for example, rose or fell by half, the good would rise or fall in value by half, although the labor employed on the original supply of stockings remained unaltered. This was an important point to be made in that it illustrated the arbitrariness of the labor theory of value.

What we can conclude from Senior's discussion of value and the place of profits in the determination of value is that he had a confused theory, combining elements from two theories of value—utility and cost of production—which he attempted to reconcile, a cause foredoomed to failure, as the two theories are really irreconcilable. The result of his effort was to subsume almost all production under the category of monopoly; in such a case he could find no general law for the determination of value. In regard to profit, he combined two incompatible doctrines when he said that the capitalist's and the laborer's shares were determined by the general rate of profits and the period elapsed between the advance and the receipt of profits (essentially the Ricardian doctrine), and his own theory that profits were a result of an excess of the return over the advance. Senior still suffered under a confusion common to all early economists that profit was one of the causes determining price, rather than price being the determinant of profit. Senior seemed, initially, to have seen this confusion of cause and effect, but in the end he succumbed to it also. In general, then, Senior's contribution to value theory consisted of his emphasis upon demand or utility (he equated the two terms) as a constituent of value and his more subjective cost theory of value, providing a more psychological explanation of cost as consisting of the abstinence of the capitalist and the sacrifice of the laborer. His notion of profit as the remuneration of abstinence provided J. S. Mill with the key to a justification of profit.

Senior is remembered less for his innovative departures from Ricardian economic theory—which is a regrettable oversight—than for his efforts on several government commissions which investigated some of the seminal issues of his day. As an adviser to the Whig party on economic matters, Senior served as a member of the Poor Law Inquiry Commission of 1832, and he was its guiding force and the formulator of the bill which reformed the Poor Law in 1834. He also served as a member of the commission investigating factory conditions in 1827, the Royal Commission on the Distress of the Hand-Loom Weavers of 1841, and the Royal Commission on Popular Education in 1857. Whether he engaged in these activities as a statesman or as a political economist, to employ his own distinction, is a debatable point to be sure, but it is undoubtedly true that he deployed principles drawn from the science of political economy to lend authority to his arguments in this field of art, an art whose existence he had denied in his treatise.

Before we discuss Senior's opinion on the Poor Law, which was his most influential venture into the political affairs of England, his general views on laissez-faire and governmental intervention deserve scrutiny because they constituted the most radical position taken by any of the Classical economists. This is not to say that on the practical level Senior was a rabid interventionist or that he proposed interventions into the economic realm which went far beyond those advocated by his fellow political economists, for this was not the case. In fact, in his *Outline of Political Economy* his scant references to government came only when pointing to the restrictive measures, the burdensome taxation and the insecurity of possessions imposed on industry by government, the effects of which were to diminish production and curtail men's incentive to invent, invest, and labor for distant objectives. He considered these interventions to be disturbing factors to the natural state of unfettered production. Rather, the uniqueness of his approach lay in his unequivocal disavowal of laissez-faire as the general principle, departures from which must be justified by claims of overriding public need or emergency or at least a claim stronger in particular instances than the one to individual liberty. The first formulation was the one implicitly adopted by Smith when he enumerated the minimal state functions of government and the second by Bentham. Senior's departure, then, was on the level of theory, not practice, as can be seen most clearly from the following passage taken from his *Lectures* given at Oxford in 1847 and 1848.

> The only rational foundation of government, the only founda-
> tion of a right to govern and of a correlative duty to obey, is
> expediency—the general benefit of the community. It is the
> duty of a government to do whatever is conducive to the wel-
> fare of the governed. The only limit to this duty is its *power*.
> And as the supreme government of an independent state is
> necessarily absolute, the only limit to its power is physical or
> moral inability. And whatever it is its duty to do it must
> necessarily have a right to do. . . . it appears to me that the most
> fatal of all errors would be the general admission of the proposi-
> tion that a government had no right to interfere for any purpose
> except for that of affording protection, for such an admission
> would prevent our profiting by experience, and even from ac-
> quiring it.[29]

Now, the interesting feature of this argument is that it wholly over-
turns laissez-faire as the general principle, replacing it by expediency (a term equivalent to Bentham's utility, as it instructs that any measure which is conducive to the general welfare falls within the proper province of government). From the assessment that a particular activity would be expedient is derived the government's duty to perform that function and its right to perform it. Senior never proved that expediency ought to be the regnant principle, just as Bentham did not prove utility and the natural-rights theorists did not prove the validity of their first principles. He assumes that expediency is the only valid basis of government and the only feasible test of any particular proposed measure. That this argument offers much greater potential scope to governmental intervention than the principle of laissez-faire, whether grounded on natural rights (as in Smith) or on the utility principle (as in Bentham and J. S. Mill), is obvious. The government is only limited, once the expediency of a proposed measure is established, by its power. Where the government can claim expedi-

ency for an act, it has the duty and the right to proceed, so that the only remaining question is whether it has the power to accomplish its objective. The deduction of a right from a duty is an odd argument, even odder coming from an Englishman and not a German.

The laissez-faire argument—that government should be limited to affording protection against force and fraud and people should be left free to pursue their ends by all other means—gained its ascendancy over opinion, Senior thought, from the fact that the *expediency* of certain measures is more readily apparent than others. Protecting against force and fraud is simply the most easily proved activity of government in terms of expediency. But, he claimed, when the expediency of other measures has been established, then the government has a duty and a right to perform them, and they carry the same legitimacy and status as the force and fraud cases. These other measures of governmental intervention are not justified, then, as exceptions of only limited applicability, as with Smith, Bentham, or Mill, but as legitimate functions of government, carrying the same degree of duty and right as in the force and fraud cases. Governments may make mistakes, perhaps more in their interventions in areas other than protecting people from force and fraud, but to refuse to interfere once proof of expediency has been given is also to fall into error.

Senior's test of expediency had great potential for expanding governmental intervention, but as we will see, his judgments of when expediency was actually proved in particular cases was colored by the Classical inclination in favor of individual initiative and against restrictive regulations by government. Immediately after asserting that laissez-faire was illegitimate as a general principle, for example, he went on to declare that the greatest objection to governmental interference is its tendency to keep the people in "leading strings,"[30] to deprive them of the power to manage their own common affairs. This is straight out of Bentham.

If the purpose of Senior's disavowal of laissez-faire was not an immediately practical one, then why did he make such a point of it? There was certainly much room for the justification of particular acts of intervention based on expediency in Bentham's scheme, which established "be quiet" as the general rule and judged all departures according to their utility. In practice, Senior did nothing more. No, the reason behind his disavowal must be sought elsewhere. By the middle of the century, considerable criticism had been leveled against political economy as not properly a science at all, but merely a set of supposed principles whose purpose was to provide a pretext for restricting intervention by government in the economy. Such attacks were forthcoming from the socialists, the German Historical School of economists, and certain liberals who saw a need for greater government activity to redress social ills. For the later defenders of the Classical doctrines of political economy—for Senior, J. S. Mill, Sidgwick, and Cairnes—it became increasingly important to salvage the science of political economy and to distinguish it from any particular social philosophy or position on state intervention in the economy. They themselves wanted to recognize certain social claims which would have had to be rejected on the laissez-faire principle. Although this was less true for Senior than for the others, it was an important component leading to their attempt to disassociate themselves from the absolutist principle. While Senior went further in his philosophical rejection of the principle than did Mill or Sidgwick—they still held rather shakily to the Benthamite doctrine of laissez-faire as the general rule, departures from which need to be justified by a claim of overriding utility or expediency— he remained on the practical policy level much more wary of government activity than they did although not nearly as skeptical as had been Smith, Bentham, Malthus, and Ricardo.

The potential for government expansion inherent in Senior's principle of expediency was kept in check by his perception of the current malaise of government as being paternalism or the tendency on the part of civilized governments to spoil their subjects by "overcare and ill-regulated indulgence."[31] In contrast to barbaric governments, which impoverish their peoples by oppression and despoliation, modern governments aggravate and perpetuate poverty or misery "by controlling and misdirecting industry and abstinence; by abolishing the punishments which the laws of nature inflict on idleness, improvidence and vice; and by weakening the checks by which she keeps population within the means of subsistence."[32] These regulations and follies result from ignorance, Senior says, ignorance of the laws of political economy concerning the production of wealth—namely, that production depends on capital, capital on abstinence, and abstinence on security.[33] The main thrusts of the reformer must still be launched against ill-advised regulations, holdovers from Mercantilist economic misconceptions. However, Senior did see many areas in which governmental intervention would be expedient.

A large number of these interventions sanctioned by Senior were in the general field of governmental efforts to redress the evils of poverty.

On the question of sanitation and housing legislation, he held that it was within the power of government to alleviate the menace of defective habitation and its consequences, filth and disease.[34] The government can regulate construction, drainage, and streets, but it can not legislate by fiat that everyone should have a house of a certain size. Even though these cases fall under the general category of proscribing activities which injure only the individual engaging in them and not others, Senior sanctions them because the state actually does know better in these affairs; the poor were found to be generally indifferent to their unsanitary habitations, according to the Committee on the Health of Towns.

Also, in regard to the efforts to place limitations on the hours of labor for adults and children, the Factory Acts of 1833, 1844, and 1847, Senior disputed the two major objections to them. He denied Smith's argument that a man's labor is his sacred and inviolable property to be used as he sees fit without injury to others. On this view all regulations would be a violation of the workers' and employers' liberty. Against this, Senior claimed to have proved that the government has a duty and a right to "take any measures, however they may interfere with the will of individuals, which are conducive to the general welfare of the community."[35] He rejects the principle that the government can act only to prevent injury to others. Similarly, he denied the weaker objection that admits government regulation in acts that might only indirectly injure others, although it may not act to prevent the individual from injuring himself. Proponents of this objection would argue that governments usually act wrongly when they presume to know better than the individual what is in his own interest; this is the position taken by Utilitarians. Senior concluded that these early Factory Acts, which regulated the hours of labor for children and women, were legitimate in the case of children because their interests could not safely be left to parents who benefited from their labor and illegitimate with respect to females because it treated them as perpetual children unable to handle their own affairs at any age. In the case of adults, both male and female, Senior concluded that on the basis of expediency alone the government should not restrict the hours of labor, for it is likely to err and act mischievously where it has incomplete knowledge of the likely effects of its actions on production. If this objection were overcome by proofs of its salutary consequences, then Senior would, presumably, have gone along with the Ten Hour Bill or other similar measures. But barring such proofs, he concluded that

the government should act circumspectly, since its power is absolute
and there is no recourse against it should it act wrongly. His position,
then, went the Utilitarians one better in applying expediency as the sole
criterion without recourse to any preconceived notions about limiting
government regulations to those which harmed others only, whether
directly or indirectly. To a third objection which simply denied that government interference could be useful in these matters, Senior reserved
judgment, citing the fact that such regulations were in their infancy.

Thus, applying his standard of expediency, and considering the effects
of these acts on productivity and upon England's commercial standing,
Senior favored the following kinds of government activity: compulsory
state education for children provided free to the poor by the state; regulation of the hours of labor for children and factory safety regulations;
and government regulation of housing. The government can also provide
the poor with amusements—parks, art exhibitions, and theaters. In the
opposite vein, he opposed the Corn Laws and restrictive trade union efforts
to limit their numbers by legislative action. His positions, then, were not
unlike those of the other political economists of his day, although he
founded them upon a more expansive principle, that of expediency alone.

The potential for expansion implicit in this principle can be vividly
illustrated by an examination of Senior's views on the question of Ireland,[36]
which he wrote about in 1831 in a *Letter to Lord Howick on a Legal
Division for the Irish Poor*. Here, he advocated much more government
intervention to alleviate Ireland's poverty; he suggested that the government should increase the size of the wage fund, decrease the number of
workers by encouraging emigration, engage in public works which would
benefit future production, influence the distribution of capital between
classes and districts, and encourage the formation of larger, more productive capitalist farms.

Senior, as we mentioned previously, was the guiding force behind the
Poor Law Reform Act of 1834 which went partway toward removing
the old Settlement Laws (which confined workers to their parishes, thus
preventing recipients of relief from seeking better jobs in other districts)
and curtailing the system of paying outdoor relief in the form of supple-
ments to the laborer's pay based on the size of his family and the amount
of his wages. What Senior urged in the place of these local, chaotic regulations which served only to destroy incentive was a national system of
relief, operating on the principle that the indigent should be offered
assistance only in workhouses and only to the extent that their position

would be worse off than the poorest independent laborer and their work harder. He was only partially successful in getting his views adopted, but the general spirit of the legislation was in the direction he proposed, as it acknowledged a standard of "less eligibility" but left the adoption of the workhouse scheme up to the local authorities.

In his later Oxford *Lectures,* Senior wrote that in a certain state of society, that achieved by England but not Ireland, the government could remove the dread of destitution. It is within its *power,* and it can be accomplished without destroying the incentive, industry, or providence of the poor, so therefore, it is *expedient* and the government had a *duty* and a *right* to perform this function. Such is the case, however, only in a society possessing "superfluous wealth."[37] But it must be accomplished in a way that will not engender more evil than it removes—a delicate balancing act indeed. In contrast to Malthus' opposition to a right to relief, Senior argued that: "To be effectual the law must give a *right* [emphasis his] to relief."[38] To inhibit the natural tendency of such a right to impair industry and providence, the two great moral principles according to Senior, the aid must be given in a form that none but the truly destitute would tolerate; the situation of the recipient must be rendered less eligible than that of the independent poor.[39]

In his writings on the French Revolution of 1848, Senior expressed a much more critical attitude towards socialism than that taken by J. S. Mill. Aware of the impossibility of creating a wealthy class out of the masses of the poor by government fiat and the ease with which wealth can be destroyed by the same means, Senior was skeptical on economic grounds and on feasibility or expediency grounds of socialistic ventures. It is not within the power of government, he contended, to correct the inequalities of fortune.[40]

> It requires a long train of reasoning to show, that the capital of which the miracles of civilization depend, is the slow and painful creation of the economy and enterprise of the few, and of the industry of the many; and is destroyed, or driven away, or prevented from arising, by any causes which diminish or render insecure the profits of the capitalist, or deaden the activity of the laborer.[41]

Thus, the state can readily destroy wealth by relieving idleness from its just punishment and depriving abstinence and foresight of their natural reward, but it will only succeed in aggravating the plight of the poor.

Senior was, in many ways, a unique and an idiosyncratic theorist. He criticized the Ricardians' theory of value based on cost of production and seemed to be on the threshold of offering a utility theory of value; yet he ended by compromising the two theories in a logically unsatisfactory fashion. He distinguished between political economy as an art and as a science, denying that an art could legitimately exist; yet he was one of the most active of the Classical political economists in the world of practical politics. He categorically rejected laissez-faire as a first principle; yet he was far more skeptical of governmental interference in upholding restrictive trade unions, in sanctioning socialistic experimentation, and in alleviating poverty through redistributive schemes than was J. S. Mill, who still avowed his belief in laissez-faire as the general principle.

Despite these paradoxes, Senior's work was to prove quite influential. His art-science distinction inaugurated the wave of the future in economics as it came to replace political economy, and his proclamation of expediency as the general criterion to judge governmental intervention and the desirability of social legislation was to have far-reaching impact in the last quarter of the century. On the latter point, he was more utilitarian than the Utilitarians, throwing off the notion that the individual is the best judge of his own affairs and should be left free in all areas that harm only himself, a holdover from Smithian natural rights doctrine, which was still a large part of orthodox Utilitarianism. Thus, unlike Malthus, for example, who denied a "right to relief," Senior accepted such a "right" on expediency grounds when he concluded that such could be granted without undermining productivity and incentive. This is another rather compelling illustration of the tendency towards greater governmental intervention inherent in the utility or expediency principle, as opposed to the inflexibility, one might even say rigidity, of the natural rights position.

JOHN STUART MILL: 1806-1873

John Stuart Mill was the subject of one of the most interesting, demanding, and rigid educational experiments ever documented in modern times. Under the constant tutelage of his father, James Mill, he mastered Greek, Latin, and mathematics at the tender age in life when normal toddlers attempt to grasp the rudiments of their native language, and at

a mere seven or eight years old he was privy to the intellectual conversations that his father conducted with the leading Utilitarians of the era.
As he wrote in his *Autobiography* half a century later, this unique and
peculiar education elevated his mind, taught him how to think critically
and independently, placed him perhaps a quarter century ahead of his
peers in intellectual development, and by starving his emotional and
spiritual development, led ultimately to his intellectual crisis, his "mental
breakdown" at the age of twenty.

From his father, he absorbed the seminal doctrines of the Utilitarian
School: a belief in representative government, complete freedom of discussion, and democracy as the security for good government; an opposition to aristocratic rule and a detestation of established religions; an
interpretation of human psychology which viewed man's character as
formed by circumstances through the universal principle of association
as expounded by Hartley; and, consequently, a faith in the influence of
reason and universal education as providing the greatest possibilities for
unlimited progress. These doctrines of the elder Mill were adopted by the
youth when he founded a discussion club of young Philosophical Radicals,
the purpose of which was to analyze the great works of this school.
Benthamism, Ricardian political economy, Hartleian metaphysics, and
Malthusian population theory (as a positive means of securing the improvement of the laboring population) provided Mill and his companions with
what seemed to Mill at the time to be a complete and coherent world
view.

But for Mill, at least, this harmony in intellectual outlook was to undergo a dramatic and shattering scrutiny when, at the onset of young adulthood, his previously emotionally starved nature began to emerge from his
father's domination. Coleridgian poetry and Germanic philosophy of
institutional development and progress provided the catalyst which shook
Mill's convictions to their foundation. During this period, he experienced
new inspirations from Continental thinkers, particularly Comte, and his
own countryman Carlyle.[42] What impressed him were their notions of
progress as unfolding in stages with institutions being suited to the particular stage and not greatly modifiable by human discretion, their conception of political institutions as relative and not absolute, subject to the
control of the strongest element in society, and their principle that an
understanding of politics depends upon a prior philosophy of history or
progress. Socialist ideas also served to reawaken his critical faculties and

provide a challenge to his youthful beliefs, a challenge with which he was
to grapple for the remainder of his life. The St. Simonians in particular
held much fascination for him. In their doctrines of a natural order of
human progress through organic periods and critical periods and in their
social schemes in which labor and capital would be managed for the general advantage of the community and each individual would be required
to take a share of the labors in accordance with his capacity and be remunerated on the basis of the quality of his work, Mill found much of
merit, declaring their aims to be both rational and desirable. However,
he did question the efficacy of the means they proposed for securing
these objectives.[43] Their criticisms of the accepted doctrines of Liberalism appealed to Mill and provoked him into a reexamination of the doctrines of the political economists:

> . . . it was partially by their writings that my eyes were opened
> to the very limited and temporary value of the old political
> economy, which assumes private property and inheritance as
> indefeasible facts and freedom of production and exchange
> as the *dernier mot* of social improvement.[44]

At this stage in his odyssey, Mill shrank back from endorsing the practica-
bility of socialism. He commended socialists for projecting such an expansive ideal for human society, for the proclamation of such an ideal could
not but be helpful to others, perhaps less extreme in their attempts at
social amelioration within the framework of the present society.

During this "breakdown" period, which ended about 1830, Mill, as
he related in the *Autobiography,* had acquired almost all the basic conceptions which he would employ throughout the remainder of his life
in his various attempts at reappraising his Benthamite heritage.[45] After
that period his only avowed changes in his political position lay in his
greater appreciation and acceptance of a "qualified socialism" as the
ultimate prospect for humanity, and a transformation of his political
ideal from one of pure democracy to a modified system of weighted
voting based on ability and a scheme for the representation of minorities
(as outlined in his *Considerations on Representative Government*).[46]

But throughout these intellectual transformations, Mill retained a certain body of beliefs from his early days. Among these were his beliefs in
freedom of expression and the sanctity of the individual in his mental
development. Although he tempered his adherence to pure democracy,

he retained his conviction that the greatest threat to the individual lay in oppression, whether from an aristocracy, as Bentham and James Mill feared, or from a newly emerging democratic majority, as J. S. Mill feared from his reading of de Tocqueville and his observations on the power of public opinion to tyrannize over the vanquished minority and the independent thinkers. The power of reason and education to ennoble men, both morally and intellectually, was another belief that he retained throughout his life, never losing hope that with advancement in learning, progress would inevitably follow.

As he emerged from his years of self-doubt and despair, he did not reject Benthamism completely but rather, attempted to reconstruct the central core of Utilitarianism, the principle of utility, in a way that would allow for more emotionality, more spirituality, more aesthetic appreciation, and more sympathy in the judgment of men's actions. What he criticized Bentham for was incompleteness and one-sidedness in neglecting these elements by dealing only with an overly egotistic "man," a strictly calculating machine.[47] In his essay on Bentham, published in the *Fortnightly Review* of 1838, he analogized Bentham to a one-eyed man, for whom Mill found much tolerance, provided that the one eye was a penetrating one.[48] Mill faulted Bentham for excluding from his pleasure-pain, self-interest motivational mechanism all attempts by men to pursue spiritual perfection as an end in itself or to dedicate their lives to some external ideal of excellence. Bentham's ethical system failed to take account of the element of conscience or to mention self-respect or to provide inspiration for men to seek an elevation of their character through self-culture. For the instruction of men in how best to conduct the *business* aspects of life, Bentham's teachings are sufficient, but they are deficient whenever the spiritual aspect of man's nature comes into play. Bentham erred in thinking that the business part of life constituted life in its entirety. On the political level, Mill found Bentham's removal of all checks to the will of the majority excessive, in that it ignored entirely the threat to society from the tyranny of public opinion, and the tyranny of the majority. Bentham, then, was not to be rejected, Mill argued, but to be corrected for his tendencies toward myopia.

In the ensuing discussion of Mill's contribution to the expansion of the theoretical justification for governmental intervention in the economy, we will focus upon the importance of the "production-distribution" distinction which he advanced and the way in which it allowed him to bring into question the very foundation of all previous Classical political

economy—the institution of private property. However, before we examine
Mill's political economy, it will be necessary to scrutinize his departures
from and proposed improvements on Bentham's moral system.

MILL'S UTILITARIANISM

Mill was far less of a political egalitarian than Bentham, who came in
his later years, when disillusioned with the lack of enthusiasm accorded
his reformist schemes by an aristocratic government, to endorse fully
the doctrine of pure democracy. In his moral system, too, Mill was much
more of an elitist than Bentham, as he criticized Bentham for placing all
pleasures, intellectual and banal, upon an equal footing, discriminating
between them, not on the basis of their quality but merely on their intensity and duration and their tendency to produce subsequent pleasures
unalloyed with pains. Mill attempted to place pleasures in a hierarchical
order based upon their "intrinsic" quality, not their "circumstantial advantages" as he implied Bentham had done.[49] In order to accomplish this
ranking of pleasures, Mill had to invoke the Platonic notion of the wise
man capable of judging between pleasure of the flesh and that of the
mind. Having experienced both, he can be the only one capable of judging between them. This *deux ex machina* affixed to the Benthamite
principle of utility changed it essentially from a principle which in its
application gave equal weight to everyone's pleasures regardless of their
nature as judged personally by the legislator to a principle which required
some elite, omniscient authority to declare which pleasures are to be preferred, which are to be discouraged by legislative policy, and who is going
to be encouraged in his mental pleasure and who discouraged in his venal
delights.

While Mill insisted that each man is to be treated as one and his pleasures given equal consideration, it is quite evident that his principle, by
leaving much greater room for individual value judgments by a moral
legislator, permits and necessitates an ever greater measure of discretion
on the part of civil authorities given the task of evaluating policy recommendations in the light of their tendency to promote the greatest happiness of the greatest number.

It will be recalled that, in the last chapter, Bentham's principle of
utility was criticized on the grounds that it left too much room for arbitrary

decisions on the part of government officials in applying the principle to concrete cases. The reason given was the elusiveness of the principle itself. We found that the principle was really two principles—one dictating that the individual pursue the greatest happiness for himself and the other directing that the general good of society as a whole ought to be the end—and that, furthermore, the principle was not decisive as to whether a policy affording a greater total happiness with great inequality is to be preferred to one offering fewer units of happiness but with a more equal distribution. The relevant question at this point is—did Mill provide an explanation of the principle of utility which could overcome these objections, or did he succeed only in muddying the waters a bit more?

Mill follows Bentham's example in declaring that, like all ultimate ends or first principles, the principle of utility does not admit of proof in the ordinary meaning of the term.[50] The sole evidence that anything is desirable is the fact that people do actually desire it. Mill claims, then, that no reason can be offered why the general happiness is desirable except that each person desires his own happiness. Each person's happiness is a good to that person; therefore, the general happiness is a good to the aggregate of all persons. Thus, Mill commits the same logical fallacy, the fallacy of composition, that Bentham committed before him. Given that:

> Frederick desires Frederick's happiness.
> and Albert desires Albert's happiness.
> Therefore Frederick and Albert desire the happiness
> of Frederick plus Albert.

This is simply not a logically legitimate deduction; for it to be legitimate one would have to assume the following additional premises: that

> Frederick desires Albert's happiness.
> and Albert desires Frederick's happiness.

The point is that one can not deduce from the statement that each individual prefers his own happiness over his own pain, that therefore the happiness of the aggregate of all persons is an object of desire for each one of them or desirable for them, or even say exactly what that would mean. Mill has not improved on Bentham's argument at all in this respect, which is rather curious considering Mill's otherwise acute logical faculties.

Mill underscored the importance of the moralist and legislator placing the happiness of all people upon an equal footing. It is important to take note of his phrasing because it differs from Bentham's. What he says is that this equal claim of everyone to happiness involves an equal claim to *the means* of happiness, except to the degree that the inevitable conditions of human life and the general interest set limits to this maxim.[51] The conclusion is that all social inequalities which have ceased to be considered expedient assume the character not of simple inexpediency, Mill maintains, but of injustice—they appear tyrannical. One may conjecture, then, that if private property, for example, were to cease being considered expedient, then it would be just to abolish the institution and its inherent inequality. Actually, one need not engage in speculation on this score, for this is precisely Mill's argument in the *Principles of Political Economy* and the "Chapters on Socialism." If it were proved that socialism would provide a feasible alternative to capitalism and, in addition, overcome Mill's concern over its possibly deleterious effects upon individual independence and creativity, then it would be acceptable.

It is quite evident that Mill's moral foundation is much more radical than Bentham's, for Mill says that each individual has a claim to equality in the *means* of happiness, something Bentham did not maintain. The implication of Mill's foundation is, clearly, that each individual, as far as possible considering the demands of general happiness and the conditions of development of the society, has a claim to be supported.

Mill improved upon Bentham's doctrine in one respect, that of clarity, when he declared that the Utilitarian standard is not the agent's own greatest happiness but the greatest amount of happiness altogether. He chose the collective formulation of the principle explicitly, while Bentham shuttled from the individualist to the aggregative formulation depending on the occasion. The result of this choice on Mill's part was that the principle became much more social in orientation, more sympathetic, and more concerned with unselfish beneficence. Noble characters are necessary to the fulfillment of the Utilitarian ideal. Between his own happiness and that of others, Utilitarianism, Mill enjoins, requires one to be as strictly impartial as a disinterested and benevolent spectator. The Christian moral injunction of Jesus is quoted with approval as personifying the ideal of Utilitarian moralists—to do as you would be done by, and to love your neighbor as yourself.[52] This summons up memories of Smith and his "impartial spectator" much more than it does Bentham. Although

Bentham did say that beneficence was a virtue, his man was beneficent for the rewards it would bring to him and not for some abstract ideal of sympathy with mankind.

In order to promote this ideal, Mill proposed two means: the first contends that the laws and social arrangements should place the happiness or the interest of every individual as nearly as possible in harmony with the interest of the whole; and the second urges that education and public opinion should use their power over human character to establish in the minds of each individual an indisoluble association between his happiness and the good of the whole:[53]

> . . . so that not only he may be unable to conceive the possibility of happiness to himself, consistently with conduct opposed to the general good, but also that a direct impulse to promote the general good may be in every individual one of the habitual motives of action.[54]

This passage is far closer to Rousseau's thinking than to anything in Bentham. Mill appears to have resolved Bentham's uncertainty concerning the boundary between individualism and the need for collective action to achieve the greatest happiness of the greatest number by moving the line over in the direction of the collective.

However, Mill's lifelong distrust of the tyranny of the majority made him, in the end, back off from an ultimate vision of social unification in which each would identify his happiness completely with the whole. A vision of such oneness awakened his fears of an unbearable interference with human individuality once society had reached this ultimate and distant state in which the happiness morality would be ingested as a religion. But short of this end, Mill went much further than Bentham had in extolling the virtues of human fellow feeling and benevolence and in emphasizing men's powerful natural sentiments directing them toward a social state in which a collective, not an individual, interest would be the end of their actions as civilization advances.

For Mill, the Platonic wise man is more than a philosophical construct designed solely to provide a theoretical tool by which to judge between pleasures. Bentham's famous epigram—that a Utilitarian is indifferent as between poetry and pushpin—is categorically rejected by Mill. It is better to be a human being dissatisfied, he triumphantly declared in contravention of Bentham, than a pig satisfied, better to be Socrates dissatisfied than a fool satisfied. The final judge between pleasures must be the one who knows both the mental and physical pleasures or a majority of such men if they disagree. That this doctrine had more cogency when it was buttressed by the Platonic teleology of the realm of the Ideas is abundantly apparent. The Platonic man of wisdom was in touch with the Forms, with an existent hierarchy which had more reality than the flux of the natural world. When he claimed that the study of mathematics was, say, superior to the life of a farmer, he had an entire eschatology to back him up. Mill's wise man has no such claim. Where does he get his authority; who designates him as the authority for a particular society; and how does one know that he truly knows all pleasures and is unbiased and a perceptive observer? An infinite regress seems to be involved here. One would need wise men to designate the wise men, and other wise men to select the first group. . . . These are all problems raised by Mill's innovation, but he does not answer them.

It is interesting to note the parallel between Mill's introduction of the wise man in the *Utilitarianism* essay and the proposals which he advanced in his *Considerations on Representative Government.* In the latter work he introduced a scheme for giving multiple votes to the intellectual and success elite. In addition, he suggested that Parliament should be limited in its functions to approving or rejecting bills devised by a panel of experts who would have sole authority to propose all legislation—the wise men of the moral theory busy at work in the political realm. This elitist tendency is not a late aberration of Mill's but can be traced back to his earlier infatuation with Comte and the St. Simonians. In "The Spirit of the Age," published in 1831, for example, Mill traced the malaise of England to the enervation of its ruling class. Every age needs a natural aristocracy of intellect to rule, he argued, and England's problems could only be resolved by disestablishing the old, eviscerated elite, and infusing the newly emerging, vital elements with power.[55]

Mill's explication of the principle of utility left much greater room for discretion, for what we have seen to be arbitrary determinations of what constitutes the greatest happiness of society on the part of legislators and moralists than did Bentham's already loose formulation. It is also quite evident that Mill's greater emphasis upon man's social nature and his identification of his own interest with that of the whole left the way open for a much more favorable attitude towards governmental intervention in the economy and even socialism, should the expediency of the latter prove evident. The tension between individualism and the aggregative implications of the principle of utility were still apparent in Mill, but, except in the extreme case of total social homogeneity, Mill seemed less troubled than Bentham by the need for social unification and harmonization of interests.

THE IMPORTANCE OF THE "PRODUCTION-DISTRIBUTION" DISTINCTION IN THE POLITICAL ECONOMY OF J. S. MILL

When Mill came to discuss the methodology behind his *Principles of Political Economy* in his *Autobiography*, he admitted that the treatise was not a work of merely abstract science, as would seemingly have been expected from the writer of the *Essay*, but an effort at application, a revision of Smithian economics. Without ever renouncing the art-science distinction of the earlier *Essay*, or even mentioning it, he appears to have concluded that political economy can not be studied or applied without considering a whole range of ethical and social considerations which fall outside its narrow boundaries. Political economy, Mill concludes, can not be treated as a thing by itself but must be viewed as a fragment of a greater whole—as a branch of social philosophy. In the following passage, Mill has gone full circle and returned to a Smithian conception of political economy as inextricably bound up with normative ethical and political questions. Political economy, he writes, is:

> . . . so interlinked with all other branches that its conclusions,
> even in its own peculiar province, are only true conditionally,
> subject to interference and counteraction from causes not
> directly within its scope; while to the character of a practical
> guide it has no pretension, apart from other classes of considera-
> tions. Political economy, in truth, has never pretended to give
> advice to mankind with no lights but its own.[56]

Adam Smith insisted upon political economy's instructive powers for legislators. Mill's conception of the science went back in the direction of Smith's concern for practical applicability, and away from Senior's efforts to extricate the science from all pragmatic considerations and make of it a purely abstract, deductive discipline. It is interesting to speculate on Mill's motives for abandoning his distinction from the *Essay*, but certainly one intention was to present a political economy with as broad a sweep as Smith's but without his predecessor's natural law affinity and, most assuredly, without his laissez-faire conclusions.[57]

Mill retained from the *Essay* the categorization of political economy as a mental science. What he says in the *Principles* is that to the extent that the economic conditions of a nation depend upon the state of physical knowledge, it is the proper subject for the physical sciences, but insofar as the conditions are moral, psychological, and dependent upon man-made institutions and social relations or upon the principles of human nature, they fall under the province of the moral and social sciences, and are, hence, the proper object of political economy.[58] Truths discoverable by political economy have the certainty but not the precision of the exact sciences.[59] Economic theorems can not be so constructed as to encompass all the complicating circumstances which may affect the result in any particular case. For example, a man may agree to accept less compensation for his labor, or agree to pay a higher rent rather than move, out of considerations of custom or ease. The laws regulating rent, profits, and wages are true only insofar as men are actually in any given case influenced solely by motives relevant to the case and governed by the overall motive of an "ordinary mercantile motive of profit and loss."[60] The subject matter of political economy is wealth, which Mill defines as:

> . . . all useful or agreeable things which possess exchangeable value; or, in other words, all useful or agreeable things except those which can be obtained, in the quantity desired, without labour or sacrifice.[61]

In his *Autobiography*,[62] Mill characterized the original element in his political economy as consisting of the distinction he drew between the laws of production, which he said had the properties of natural laws, and the laws of distribution, which were subject to human intervention and man-made conventions and institutions. He claimed to have been awakened to this distinction, which he said was overlooked by previous political economists, by his reading of the St. Simonians and the promptings of his wife, Harriet Taylor Mill. However, Senior had made the same distinction in his *Outline of Political Economy* in 1836, although he was not prompted by this observation into questioning the validity of private property and the general framework of the competitive system as Mill eventually did. Mill is justified, then, in crediting himself with the thorough application, if not the original formulation, of the production-distribution distinction.

Let us now examine Mill's argument rather closely and critically, because it is the basis of all his subsequent endeavors at disassociating political economy as a science from any *a priori* association with or justification for a particular economic system or method of property distribution, that is, of his efforts to purge political economy of any identification with the laissez-faire system exclusively. What Mill maintained was that the laws pertaining to the production of wealth are "real laws of nature," dependent on the properties of objects, the "unchangeable conditions of our earthly existence," and the knowledge we possess of these properties at any given time. The laws of distribution, on the contrary, are dependent on the human will and merely the necessary results of particular social arrangements, although the consequences of such laws are not arbitrary. Mill's predecessors, he argued, failed to distinguish between the two kinds of laws and assumed that the existent social arrangements— as the causes of the determination of wages, prices, and rent, for example— are inherent necessities, impervious to human intervention and will. The existent institutions and customs of a particular society, which constitute the conditions and presuppositions upon which deductions about the shares of distribution must be made, are treated by Mill as transitory, as not "final." With progress and social improvement, these presuppositions (for example, the existence of private property) are liable to be altered, and hence, the laws of distribution, which depend partly on necessities of nature and partly on social arrangements, will be correspondingly transformed.

Mill's contention that there is nothing optional about the natural laws of production[63]—which depend upon antecedent accumulation, the ultimate properties of the human mind, and the nature of matter, while the distribution of wealth is conducted at the discretion of society—is superficially quite appealing. "The things once there, mankind, individually or collectively, can do with them as they like,"[64] he argued, and any disposition takes place at the "consent of society." Men are permitted to keep what they produce at the option of those in authority, and the rules consequently differ at different times and in different places. However, the consequences of these rules of distribution are not arbitrary and are as much like the character of physical or natural laws as are the laws of production.

Now, if these laws of distribution have consequences which are not arbitrary but necessary and uncontrollable by human will, then in what manner do they differ from the laws of production? The latter, too, can be altered by human intervention—we can attempt to construct better-organized assembly lines employing more sophisticated technology, but we can also in our ignorance utilize methods inappropriate to the desired end. Similarly, in the case of distribution, we could redistribute property with the objective of achieving equality or greater production, only to find that we have instead created chaos and the reemergence of inequality by the back door of black markets. In the former case, production has been curtailed by the application of counterproductive means; in the latter case, intervention in the distribution of productive resources has led to the consequence that less is available for distribution. In what way do these cases differ? Mill admits that production depends on more than the properties of matter, that its extent and sophistication is attributable to an additional cause, which is the extent of human knowledge concerning the physical universe and its laws. The breadth of this knowledge is, then, dependent upon human volition, character, motivation, and so forth. If we are ignorant, apply inappropriate means, or lack diligence at our labors, our steel will crumble, plaster will crack, and our tractors will lie broken and idle in the fields. Production can be further affected by human intervention to the extent that government regulatory agencies dictate the minutiae of industrial processes to industry.

Mill does not deny all this; yet he fails to see that, just as the laws of distribution of goods can be affected by government activities, so can the laws of production. In the case of distribution, private property can be proscribed or income can be progressively taxed, while in the case of production, featherbedding or minimum wage laws or environmental codes or other actions may be legislated. Furthermore, when the laws of distribution are altered, production is affected, a consequence of which Mill was well aware when it came to analyzing the effects of socialism upon production but a truth of which he apparently lost sight in the process of drawing this theoretical distinction between the laws of production and distribution. If authorities intervene in the productive process and alter the "laws" or rules of production in an unenlightened manner, then less will be produced—this would constitute a breach of natural law under

Mill's terminology. And if the same authorities intervened to abolish private property or confiscate incomes above the subsistence level, then less would be produced (due to lack of incentive, maladministration, etc., according to Mill himself) and less could be distributed—this, too, seems to carry the causal necessity of a natural law. Mill's distinction appears to have collapsed. Men can intervene foolishly to alter the rules of production, the laws which approximate most nearly to reality and, hence, secure the greatest output, and they will pay the necessary and inevitable consequences. In a similar fashion, they can alter the rules of distribution, but they will suffer the inevitable consequences if their intervention is of a kind which goes against man's nature, his motivational mechanism, and his natural desires. Men can "violate" the "laws of production" as well as the "laws of distribution," and they will pay the consequences in both instances.

Mill's purpose in drawing this distinction, as he stated it in the *Autobiography,* was to underscore the point that social arrangements regarding distribution—such as private property—could not be assumed to be inevitable or immune to human intervention as he said previous economists implicitly held. To the extent that any of the earlier political economists suffered from such a misapprehension, his distinction, though invalid if our previous argument was correct, may have hinted at an important truth: that economists should not assume the permanence of existing economic relationships. But it is difficult to point to any of the English Classical economists, with their attention to other systems, such as Mercantilism, agriculturalism, and socialism, who suffered under that particular error.

The *Principles of Political Economy* represented another significant departure from previous treatments of the subject in that its format reversed the order of the subtopics of exchange, distribution, and production, as the subject matter had been presented by Adam Smith and his followers. The format of the *Principles* appears, on first inspection, to be logically organized, proceeding from production to distribution and then to exchange. However, it is actually inverted, because production is not the primary constituent or the proper starting point of economic investigation. Men's needs, desires, and expectations comprise the fundamental constituent in political economy, for it is these aspects of volition which govern what is to be produced, how much is to be produced, and in what manner production is to be carried forth. Production, then, is a derivative, not a causative agent in the economic process. Mill categorized political economy as a mental science, heavily dependent upon an analysis of man's nature and his motivations. Thus, it appears that for a science so conceived, the order employed by Adam Smith in the *Wealth of Nations*—beginning with man's inclination to truck and barter and its consequence, the division of labor, and then proceeding to a discussion of exchange and exchange value—is far more logical.

Thus, Mill lost sight of an important element in Smith's political economy, its consumer orientation. For Smith, all production had as its end the satisfaction of human needs. Consumption was the end of production. By placing production first in his treatise, Mill undercut the very purpose behind the whole process, which was, in Smith, the effort by each individual to secure the means of his own survival and enjoyment. By treating production as a primary, almost a given, Mill was able later in his discussion of distribution to treat the products of industrial society as almost preexisting entities, there to be distributed by those in authority. While Mill was careful to analyze the effects of changes in distribution on production—he is not being accused here of having committed any sins in that regard—his order of discussion of production and distribution served the same purpose as the production-distribution distinction: to sever the connection between the laws of economics and the political prescriptions associated with the laissez-faire doctrine. In pointing this out, we are not imputing a particular motivation to Mill; rather that was his stated purpose, admitted quite freely in the *Autobiography*, although not in the *Principles*. But we are questioning the validity and cogency of the means he employed for effecting this objective, that is, the production-distribution distinction and the order production-distribution-exchange followed in the *Principles*.

MILL'S TREATMENT OF THE LAWS OF PRODUCTION

Mill's rendition of the laws of production followed the traditional Smithian model in distinguishing between the three requisites of production: labor, natural agents, and in every society above the primitive level the previously accumulated stock called capital. The owners of capital—who are such as a result of their restraint, their abstinence, to use Senior's term which Mill adopted—have a claim to profit arising from the fact that they have advanced wages to productive laborers rather than employing their funds on idle consumption. They have acquired a claim to repayment and an extra return, for without this incentive there would be no encouragement to accumulation beyond what was necessary to satisfy one's immediate needs.[65] These advances of capital provide the laborers with food to maintain them until their efforts are productive; in addition, the capital provides them with the shelter, buildings, tools, protection, and materials which the work requires.

On the question of rent, Mill followed Ricardo's lead in denominating such payments as unproductive expenditures when paid for the use of the land itself and not for improvements made on the land by labor. The use of such natural agents is indispensible, but the payment for them is not, because the payment is not the necessary condition for bringing land into existence, as it would be for the production of man-made implements. The payment for land, Mill thought, was not one of the expenses of production, although it necessitated a larger accumulated capital. In this attempt to rationalize Ricardo, Mill does not succeed in clarifying the argument; it is difficult to understand how something can both be and not be a cost of production. What Mill was driving at, one can speculate, was the point that rent was not a *necessary* constituent of cost of production and could, under a different economic system, be dispensed with or modified. It is merely an unproductive expenditure attendant upon the existence of private appropriation. Thus, Mill drew the consequences from Ricardo's doctrine of rent which the latter had abstained from concluding. In fact, Mill was instrumental in the founding of the Land Tenure Reform Association, whose immediate program was the advocacy of a tax upon landlords to appropriate the unearned income that they received as the result of progress. Their philosophical position was that land as a value not created by men should be controlled, if not owned outright, by the community. Here we have a clear case of a change in pure economic theory, the substitution of a Ricardian theory of rent for the Smithian theory, which finally had its affect upon the theory of governmental policy. But even here, it could be contended, the abstract doctrine was only driven to its logical limits as a result of Mill's moral principles. Indeed, Ricardo held the same pure theory of rent, but it did not lead him to call for collectivization—quite the contrary. The following passage from a letter to Charles Eliot Norton reinforces the interpretation that it was a utilitarian moral judgment and not a pure economic principle which governed Mill's attitude toward state control over property, movable as well as landed. What he is explicitly saying is that the state has the same right over all kinds of property and the extent to which it chooses to exercise that authority is only a question of expediency.

> There is, however, this great *practical* difference between the case of moveable wealth and that of land, that, so long as land is allowed to be private property (and I cannot regard its private appropriation as a permanent institution) society seems to me bound to provide that the proprietor shall only make uses of it as shall not essentially interfere with the utility to the public: while in the case of capital, and moveable property generally, though *society has the same right,* yet the interests of society would in general be better consulted by laws restrictive of the acquisition of too great masses of property, than by attempting to regulate its use.[66]

In regard to the productive factor of labor, Mill distinguished between productive labor, which was either fixed and embodied in external objects or in persons as a result of education, and unproductive labor, by which he meant utilities not fixed in objects but consisting in the mere service rendered. Thus, all labor expended by government when maintaining peace and security and all labor involved in providing services was not productive labor; it produced utility but not wealth. Smith also made this distinction, and it was adopted by his followers, although Senior, who held a theory of value which gave greater prominence to utility, included services among wealth. By adopting this distinction, Mill was led into several confusions and errors, which were endemic to a "real-cost" theory of value, one which looked not to a good's or service's tendency to produce satisfaction in the consumer as the standard of value, but rather to some ultimate standard of permanence or accumulativeness. Thus, Mill was led by this distinction to conclude that all labor which had immediate enjoyment for its end was unproductive because it does not add to the accumulated stock or the national wealth of the nation. Unproductive labor may be useful, but society grows poorer by it, because those employed in such ways consume goods, but they do not produce.

In fact, this view is more primitive than Smith's because he categorized only government activities as unproductive, while Mill, who lost sight of Smith's consumer orientation, could see *wealth* only in something that could be touched and accumulated. That "unproductive laborers" could produce utilities, meet human needs and desires, was a view which Mill acknowledged as an advocate of culture and progress but not when he came to make this distinction. But what Mill was driving at with this distinction was another one, that between unproductive consumption and productive consumption. The point was that, while the former is not to be regretted in an opulent society, its maldistribution, its unequal distribution, is to be regretted and possibly remedied.[67] If this unproductive consumption is a surplus, which it is in Mill's account—because it goes beyond what is required to supply a worker with his subsistence, even in the most favorable use of such luxury when it goes to the workers—then it can be regulated by society.

Just one peculiar result of this—the abandonment of Smith's consumer orientation and the productive-unproductive labor distinction—was Mill's assertion that:

> What supports and employs productive labour, is the capital
> expended in setting it to work, and not the demand of pur-
> chasers for the produce of the labour when completed. De-
> mand for commodities is not demand for labour.[68]

Demand determines the direction of labor but not its extent which depends on the amount of capital. It is apparent that there is a conceptual problem here. While it is true that labor is employed by the owners of accumulated capital, it is so employed, and the extent of its employment is based upon the capitalists' assessments of what future demand will be. Demand for goods is demand for labor, despite Mill's assertion to the contrary.[69] Mill declared that:

> . . . a person who buys commodities and consumes them him-
> self, does no good to the labouring classes: and that it is only
> by what he abstains from consuming, and expends in direct
> payments to labourers in exchange for labour, that he benefits
> the labouring classes, or adds any thing to the amount of their
> employment.[70]

Undoubtedly, current labor is employed by previously accumulated capital, but this capital is called into existence only by the anticipation of a future demand for the products which can be produced by its application. Consumption is the end of production. Thus, by consuming goods a person indirectly employs those individuals involved in the production of the commodity. If he failed to consume, there would be no reason for further production, and unemployment would result. Mill's failure to appreciate this causal connection between consumer demand and employment was a direct result of the general underemphasis upon demand found in all the Classical writers. His statement that demand is significant only in exchange and not in production has been shown to be mistaken.

Mill concluded from all this that a demand for the labor of bricklayers by the rich is beneficial to the laboring class, while a demand for the products of velvet makers is not beneficial; and a shift from the former to the latter would curtail the production of necessities for the laboring class. This seems to be entirely erroneous, being founded upon a prejudice against production of luxury goods. Furthermore, it contains a fallacy which seems to lie in his hidden assumption that there is a fixed amount of production for the whole economy—that if A consumes goods with his money rather than employing laborers directly, those laborers will not be employed.[71] But, in fact, they would simply be employed by the producer of the goods which A purchases.

Mill is led by this fallacious reasoning to conclude that an income tax which falls on the luxuries of the rich will not curtail the employment of labor.[72] This is incorrect. If the rich have less money to expend on luxuries as the result of an income tax, less labor will be employed in the production of such goods. Will the capital of these luxury industries be, then, employed in other productions? Not if the demand for these other goods is not augmented, as it would not be with less money to be expended by all consumers as a result of the tax. (It would also depend on what activities the tax revenue was expended on.)

In general, Mill adopted the view of Smith and Bentham that industry is limited by capital, but he argued that in instances in which all available capital is not productively employed—when there are insufficient numbers of laborers, unsold goods, and funds that have not found investment—the government can bring capital nearer to its limit by importing laborers, laying on taxes, and employing the amount collected productively, or by applying taxes to pay off the national debt. He disagreed with Ricardo's gloomy projection that the introduction of machinery would harm the laboring class, arguing instead that the process went on so gradually and its benefits were so out of proportion to its temporary dislocations, that adjustments could be made quite naturally, and improve-

ments could be financed out of the increased product and not from circulating capital, that is, the fund for the employment of laborers.[73] Although dismissing Ricardo's argument against machinery, Mill was quick
to remind the reader of the implicit expediency criterion which he applied
throughout the work:

> But this does not discharge government from the obligation of
> alleviating, and if possible, preventing the evils of which this
> source of ultimate benefit is or may be productive to an ex-
> isting generation. If the sinking, or fixing of capital in machinery
> or useful works were ever to proceed at such a pace as to impair
> materially the funds for the maintenance of labour it would be
> incumbent on legislators to take measures for moderating its
> rapidity: and since improvements which do not diminish em-
> ployment on the whole, almost always throw some particular
> class of labourers out of it, *there cannot be a more legitimate
> object of the legislator's cure than the interest of those who are
> sacrificed to the gains of their fellow-citizens and of posterity.*[74]

The remainder of Mill's discussion of the laws of production was devoted
to the following topics: first, an examination of the causes behind the
variations in the productivity of productive labor in different times and
places, which he attributed more to the quality of the human agents involved than to their material surroundings and also to the security from
government rapacity which exists at any given time, government engendered insecurity being the most pervasive and paralyzing deterrent to
individual initiative. In the course of this discussion he condemns all
laws which favor one class at the expense of another, which "chain up"
the efforts of any part of the community in pursuit of their own good,
or which intervene between those efforts and their natural fruits. Such
measures are condemned as "violations of the fundamental principle of
economical policy," because they tend to diminish the aggregate productive powers of the community.[75] Second, he analyzes the advantages and
disadvantages of large- and small-scale production and of joint-stock
companies, arguing that the competition of the marketplace presents an
unfailing test of which scale of production is best suited to each particular
industry. While generally suspicious of the efficiency of government-run
businesses, he concluded that when, as in the case of gas or water companies, the market is such that only one or two companies are likely to

survive, it is better to have one, because the two would collude and not compete anyway, and the duplication would only represent a waste of resources. His recommendation was that such industries should be treated "at once as a public function; and if it be not such as the government itself could beneficially undertake, it should be made over entire to the company or association which will perform it on the best terms for the public."[76] Thus, the government may properly forbid a second railroad from serving the same route as an already existing line on the grounds that such a replication of services would constitute a waste of capital and land. Mill's solution to monopolistically inclined trades was either to nationalize them, or if that were not feasible, to keep regulatory control in the hands of the government which could grant temporary concessions but never divest itself of ultimate control. So spoke the lifelong employee of the East India Company. The existing companies have a right to compensation only as holders of a proprietary right which is now conceived by Parliament to be opposed to public utility.[77]

Finally, Mill adopted the Malthusian population theory, Ricardo's argument for diminishing returns in agricultural production, and the Ricardian notion of the eventual stationary state. The latter, Mill thought, would occur when a country had carried production as far as the existing state of knowledge could take it, given the current strength of the effective desire of accumulation. Further advances, then, would depend upon an increase of one or the other of these. The stationary state, Mill projected, would be for Europe at least a thing of the far-distant future, as these two restrictions have little effect there. Rather, it seemed as though knowledge and the desire to accumulate proceed unabated, despite low interest rates. The obstacles to an increase in production, then, come from the limitation of land only and not of capital, labor (population), knowledge, or the desire to accumulate. But even this obstacle is counteracted to a certain extent by inventions which increase the productivity of industry.

On the whole, then, Mill was much more sanguine about the prospects for progress aiding the working class than was Ricardo. Improvements in government, in the moral and social realm, and in the removal of government restrictions and taxes would counteract the law of diminishing returns. However, he did not abandon the Malthusian principle; he claimed that even if wealth were equally distributed and all productive implements were jointly controlled, a doubling of population would have a disastrous effect.[78]

In drawing this analysis of Mill's treatment of production to a close, one should emphasize once again that his isolation of production as the fundamental, primary starting point of economics has been found wanting. Also, his insistence that demand constitutes a demand for goods only and not labor has been challenged. The productive-unproductive-consumption distinction was seen to be based merely upon a prejudice, one against expenditures on consumer goods and luxuries and in favor of expenditures on the necessities of laborers. In addition, the productive-unproductive-labor distinction appeared entirely arbitrary and devised with little regard for consumer utility.

THE LAWS OF DISTRIBUTION AND MILL'S EVALUATION OF SOCIALISM

Mill's treatment of the laws of distribution, which included his controversial and famous analysis of the leading socialist movements of his day, was the outcome of the production-distribution distinction. If all laws of distribution were, indeed, man-made and men held their products only at the sufferance of society, then all existing property relations can be brought into question. Is the present distribution of property just? Is it expedient? Does it provide for the weak and the poor? Questions of this type become a crucial part of the political economists' task.

As Mill revised his *Principles of Political Economy,* his attitude towards socialism underwent subtle changes of both tone and substance. In the first edition of 1848, he appeared to be more critical than he would become in the third edition of 1852,[79] and, finally, in his posthumously published "Chapters on Socialism," he partially reverted to his earlier skepticism, putting greater emphasis upon the measures by which the private-property system could be improved and perfected, rather than upon the vision of a far-distant socialistic future which had seemed to hold considerable attraction for him in 1852. The extent to which Mill's views were substantially modified between 1848 and 1852 is open to doubt, for in the "Preface" to the third edition, he lamented that critics had misinterpreted his position from the first edition, considering him to have been hostile to socialism when, in fact, he had been receptive to its possibilities for a future society. Also in the *Autobiography* he implied that he had modified his views in writing the 1848 edition, fearing that the public was not yet ready to absorb such relatively extreme ideas. In that work of the 1860s he declared that in the 1840s he had considered himself to be a socialist.[80] After the French Revolution of 1848[81] and more study on his part of the best socialist writers, the negative tone of the 1848 edition was replaced by a "more advanced opinion."[82]

During his earlier days as a Benthamite, Mill had looked for social remediation in the institution of universal education, leading to voluntary redistribution of property and eventually the improvement of the conditions of the laboring class. He did not question private property and inheritance at this stage, and he thought that the inequalities engendered by the property system could only be mitigated by the comparatively mild measures of abolishing primogeniture and entails. Inequality of property and the injustice of some being born to riches and others to poverty drove him and his wife, Harriet Taylor, toward socialism and away from democracy, abandoning pure democracy out of fear of the ignorance and brutality of the as yet uneducated masses. Their socialist vision encompassed the following elements: a society which would be divided no longer into the idle and the industrious, in which the rule that those who do not work will not eat should be applied impartially to all, in which the division of the produce will be made in concert on an acknowledged principle and not a mere accident of birth as at present, and in which individuals will strive to procure benefits for society as a whole and not merely for themselves. Education, habit, and the cultivation of the sentiments must operate first to change men's characters or rather to develop the inherent social feelings which have been discouraged under the present system. Generations will have to pass before men will achieve this state, but man's constitution does not prohibit such an interest in the common good. Existing institutions serve to accentuate the self-interest motivation which men have, but through small, communal experiments, other institutions which would bring out the communal tendencies of man could be developed and perfected. Private property can not be dispensed with before these other, selfless motives have been cultivated, but its continued existence should be considered as "merely provisional."

Mill did not, however, entirely desert the vestiges of his Benthamite individualism or concern for individual liberty, as evidenced in the following passage from the *Autobiography*, which mirrored a similar statement in the "Preface" to the third edition of the *Principles:*

> The social problem of the future we considered to be, how to unite the greatest individual liberty of action, with a common ownership in the raw material of the globe, and an equal participation of all in the benefits of combined labour.[83]

What form such a combination would take, Mill was willing to let the future inhabitants of the globe decide. Nothing definitive could be concluded now, anyway.

Mill's opinions on socialism underwent several reevaluations as has been indicated previously, and it will be instructive to examine these positions more closely, beginning with the 1848 edition of the *Principles*. The difficulties of effecting socialism were stressed in this original version, with particular skepticism expressed regarding the problems of fairly apportioning labor among the members of a community who differ in abilities and tolerance for labor, of stimulating the desire to produce and labor beyond the minimal levels required by society, of regulating population, and of achieving perfect equality which, even if possible, would produce a monstrous conformity. The general tone of the discussion was taken to be more critical, apparently, than Mill had intended, for in the second, and even more explicitly in the third, edition (which is the form in which the argument remained through the final edition, with changes being limited to stylistic rather than substantive alterations), he stressed the possibilities which some futuristic form of socialism might hold for surmounting these problems. In this edition, the St. Simonian and Fourierist systems, which admit a measure of inequality on some principle of expediency or justice, are considered with more favor than the extreme positions of Owen, Blanc, and Cabet who advocated absolute equality in distribution.

It was now Mill's contention that one can not say that such schemes of common ownership are impracticable. His former objection—that under socialism men would shirk their fair share of labor with the result that productivity would be curtailed and new inventions and methods would be less likely to be tried by bureaucratic personalities—is deflated with the claim that in our modern businesses each man does not reap the rewards of his own labor directly anyway, so that the same objection can be lodged against the existing system. Men, he thinks, are capable of a much larger public spirit than they are ever called upon to display in our competitive system, and even if such were not the case, they would under socialism prove no lazier than men on a fixed salary are today. Thus, the extent to which energy would be either depleted or enhanced is an open question, one that can not be decided *a priori* but rather must await the onset of socialistic experiments.

To another of his former criticisms—that the assurance of subsistence would increase population—Mill now felt that public opinion, which would constitute a much greater force under socialism, would prevail against the instinct toward selfish intemperance. Finally, the problem of the difficulty of fairly apportioning labor is dismissed as a not insurmountable objection. Anyway, such a system, no matter how imperfect it might be or how far it missed the ideal of perfect justice, must be less unjust than what we have at the present time. Thus, Mill asserts that if the choice were between the current state of affairs as of 1852, in which the harshest labor is the least remunerated and those who labor not at all get the most reward, or communism, he would choose communism.[84]

However, the possibilities were more extensive than that. First, less extreme schemes of a socialist nature could be devised, on the order, perhaps, of the St. Simonian or Fourierist variety. By apportioning more benefits to those who work more, they would approach a less perfect ideal of justice than the absolute equality of the communist system, but they would be more just than what exists currently. While praising both these movements, Mill criticized the St. Simonians for their select, scientific boards to apportion work, suspecting that such control would not be tolerated. Fourierism is praised for adapting the motive to exertion which exists in society as presently constituted to a more just system of ownership and control. And second, communism must be compared to the private-property system as it could be at its best, when it would be freed from its origins in usurpation, conquest, and violence, and made truly the system which rewards men on the basis of their labor and not the labor of others, unfairly acquired. "The laws of property," Mill argued, "have never yet conformed to the principles on which the justification of private property rests."[85]

If the law had taken as many pains to ameliorate the inequalities arising from the workings of the individualistic principle as it had in aggravating them, if legislation had favored the diffusion of wealth rather than its concentration, then the principle of private property would have no necessary connection with the physical and social evils which socialist writers attributed to it as its inherent properties.[86] Comparing capitalism at its best, that is, as the system which guarantees to each individual the fruits of his own labor and abstinence, and all that is opposed to this principle expunged, with communism at its best, Mill concludes that we are too ignorant to judge which of the two systems will be the ultimate form of human society. The choice will probably depend, Mill hopes, on which system allows for the greatest amount of human liberty and spontaneity.

This last consideration was closest to Mill's heart, and he once again warned that liberty, which stands next in order of priority to subsistence, must never be sacrificed to the desire for affluence or equality. Socialism, however, could be so arranged that it would not fall victim to such a mistaken hierarchy. "The restraints of Communism would be freedom in comparison with the present condition of the majority of the human race,"[87] he wrote. Most workers under capitalism have little more freedom than slaves, and women are subject to domestic tyranny. Despite his inclinations towards socialism as offering a more just ideal for mankind, Mill could not remove from his mind that nagging worry that the uniformity in thought which he saw spreading and eventually engulfing society would be accentuated under such a system, for it would present an education even less diverse than that in his time. The perils to individuality presented the most troubling aspect of socialism or communism.

This is as far as Mill ever went in the direction of socialism. It is, indeed, much further than any of his predecessors among the Classical economists had gone. They condemned socialism as totally impractical and economically disastrous, if they considered it at all. Mill's approach was friendly, yet cautious and irresolute. His attempt to analyze socialism and the attacks upon the private-property system advanced by its proponents was enlightening and long overdue from the Ricardian economists. What Mill concluded, then, was that the future would hold the answer, that the decision between private property at its best and communism perfected would be made by future generations. In the meantime, all forms of socialism deserve a trial on a small scale, with only willing participants, and at no peril to the rest of society.[88]

Without in any way attempting to circumscribe the future options of mankind, he concluded that economists in the near future will, nevertheless, be primarily occupied with analyzing a society based upon private property and individual competition:

> . . . and that the object to be principally aimed at, in the present stage of human improvement, is not the subversion of the system of individual property—, but the improvement of it, and the full participation of every member of the community in its benefits.[89]

Consequently, in his chapter on the "Probable Future of the Labouring Class," Mill was enthusiastic about the spread of cooperative societies as vehicles to overcome both the selfishness bred by capitalism and the economic weakness of the working class. It is interesting to observe that in his discussion of the laws of distribution in Book 1 of the *Principles*, Mill placed greater emphasis upon the importance of cooperation in production than he did on the Smithian division of labor.

Finally, when he came in 1870 to reject the wages-fund doctrine in a review of Thornton's critique of it, his instincts toward identification with the poor and the downtrodden could be given freer reign.[90] That doctrine—by insisting that the available capital to employ labor was at any given time a fixed sum composed of the savings of capitalists, and the laborers' shares were determined solely by dividing the fund by the number of laborers to be employed—doomed all trade union activity, since one group of laborers by organizing and demanding higher wages could benefit themselves only by injuring other, usually less skilled laborers.[91] But once this doctrine was overthrown and the fund was seen as expandable or contractable depending upon the price at which labor was purchasable, trade unions were seen to be beneficial; they could actually expand the laborers' share without injuring other workers if by combining workers could hold out for higher wages which the market could bear.[92] Mill never revised his *Principles* to incorporate this change, writing in the "Preface" to the seventh edition that the whole question was still too undetermined to warrant inclusion.

Mill's outlook on socialism underwent a subtle reorientation again in 1869 with the beginning of a work on the subject which remained incomplete at his death. These posthumous "Chapters on Socialism" were published in the *Fortnightly Review*[93] in 1879 by Mill's stepdaughter, Helen Taylor. Once again, the tone of the piece shifts back to that of 1848 rather than the more sympathetic 1852 version. Communism in its revolutionary form is now unambiguously condemned as a total violation of liberty and self-determination and what's more impractical and disastrous. The socialists Fourier and St. Simon are given a more hospitable treatment, but more emphasis is placed upon a criticism of the socialists' attacks upon private property and the errors they committed on that score than was displayed in the 1852 version. Control of an entire society by a central authority is categorically rejected, and the danger to liberty, even from a small socialist community, is given considerable weight as an objection to socialism. The economic objections to socialism are similarly given a much more friendly treatment than they were in 1852. Once again, the incentive problem and the difficulty of equitably apportioning work and rewards is rehearsed.

Mill still grants to the socialists their case against the injustice, inequality, and waste of the private-property system as presently constituted, and he remains hopeful about socialism as a future ideal, but some of his practicality and cautiousness of 1848 seem to have reemerged in his old age, perhaps as a result of the waning of revolutionary movements in Europe. The change may also be attributable to his lifelong concern for the creeping uniformity of opinion which would be accelerated even more, he feared, by the advancement of socialism.

He expended considerable effort on exploding the fallacies in the socialists' case against capital. For example, he denied that wages have a tendency to fall under capitalism and suggested, rather, that wages are increasing as society advances and the press of population on subsistence had actually diminished as a result of both progress in production and emigration. He criticized the socialists for their imperfect conception of competition, claiming that they failed to credit the competitive system with keeping down prices. They also erred in attributing monopolistic tendencies to previously dispersed industries. He accused them of being mistaken regarding the proportion in which the produce of society is really divided when they spoke as if the capitalist had the use of both his capital and the profit; in fact, the capitalist gives the first to the laborers for their support and only has the second for his own use.

He gives credit to the socialists' critique of competition in conceding that the present, widely dispersed market gives no guarantee of quality. However, cooperative stores can solve this problem without the necessity of overturning the private-property system. And he argues that profit constitutes but a small part of the circulating capital of the country, and even if it were dispersed among all the workers, they would be benefited less than by a single technological improvement.

These economic issues, however, he considered to be of less importance for the evaluation of private property than the moral and intellectual considerations.[94] On these counts, he found socialism impossible for man as presently constituted, although as a scheme for a future society he still considered it to be desirable and, perhaps, feasible. But its real benefit lay in its projection of an ideal of equality and justice toward which the private-property system could move without altering its guiding principle. Private property could be altered to approach the ideal. Society determines what it considers to be individual property, and it can alter that determination without violating anyone's rights as long as it pays compensation. If it were proved of general benefit, then landed property could be abolished and taken over by the state, and monopolistic industries, such as railroads, could become state property.

His conclusion, however, remained unchanged. Socialistic experiments deserved a trial, and their feasibility cannot be determined by *a priori* reasoning or condemned on economic principles. Thus, Mill did not abandon his potentially revolutionary investigation, for he argued that the working class, now enfranchised, was entitled to a wholesale re-examination of social institutions. Such rights and privileges which could not stand this test would eventually have to be abandoned. His objective was to determine which "institutions of property would be established by an unprejudiced legislator, absolutely impartial between the possessors of property and the non-possessors."[95] There is no doubt that this was a radical approach—in the true sense of radical, as going to the root—even though his conclusions were tentative and unresolved. While in the *Principles* he argued that private property is the proper subject matter of the economist for the immediate future simply because it is what we are presented with, he takes a much more positive attitude towards individual property in the "Chapters." Here, he argues that one must evaluate the challenges made by the socialists, so that what is valid in their ideas can be absorbed peacefully, without abandoning the old system. Those ideas can be combined into a "renovated social system."[96]

Thus, private property, under the impetus to reevaluation provided by the emerging working-class movement, must be subjected to the test of general welfare. The poor have little left to gain by political rights, but they have far to go to be liberated from their economic dependence, an evil equal to any that mankind has ever suffered.[97] Mill's genuine sympathy with the poor is quite evident. His aim was to aid them by discovering, without preconceived notions, which system would actually secure their improvement.

Certain features of Mill's analysis of socialism remained unaltered throughout these various reappraisals which changed the tone more than the substance of his analysis. Principal among these was Mill's receptivity to socialism should it prove its feasibility in small, experimental communities. He was by no means wedded to the private-property system, conceding at all times the moral case against capitalism advanced by the socialists. Socialism for Mill always remained more of a distant ideal to be realized by future generations. Private property and its motivation of individual self-interest remained the regnant social system, at least for the foreseeable future. Socialism provided a moral goal towards which the private-property system could be steered by improving its inheritance laws, its bankruptcy laws, its legal definitions of property, and its distributional system. Mill's disciple Henry Sidgwick, as we shall see, seemed to fear socialism while accepting it as the almost inevitable wave of the future. Mill's attitude was far more positive, although as Harriet's influence faded after her death, his inherent cautiousness reemerged. This was quite evident in the "Chapters" with his much greater skepticism in regard to the feasibility of a socialistic organization of production and distribution and his diminished faith in the socialists' capacity to remake men to suit their social schemes.

Let us return now to Mill's treatment of the laws of distribution in the *Principles.* He resumes his analysis with the assumption that the private-property system will be the one with which the political economist must contend for the foreseeable future. His discussion of the genesis of the institution of private property is fascinating, for it departs from Locke's argument in just one critical respect, and that is sufficient to change the complexion of the conclusion in regard to landed property completely. Mill begins by isolating the essential elements of the concept of private property:

> The institution of private property when limited to its essential elements, consists in the recognition, in each person, of a *right* to the exclusive disposal of what he or she have produced by their own exertions, or received either by gift or by fair agreement without force or fraud, from those who produced it. The formulation of the whole is the right of producers to what they have produced.[98]

From these attributes of individual property, Mill goes on to examine what in society are the "necessary consequences or reasoned conclusions" from them. He disputes the notion that the laborer should receive the total product of his exertions, claiming that since capital is a necessary prerequisite to any production, those who provide the capital must be repaid for their saving and abstinence. There is nothing revolutionary in that, but it is exceptional in that it is one of the few (along with Senior's) clearly expressed rationalizations of the justifiability of profit offered by the Classical economists.

In his treatment of the questions of inheritance and landed property Mill is innovative. While not denying that laborers, too, benefit from previous savings, he argues that inheritance can be justifiably curtailed and regulated by government for the public interest. The concept of property implies only the following consequences: (1) the right of each to his own faculties, (2) the right to what he can produce by them, (3) the right to whatever he can get for those products in a fair market, and (4) the right to give this to any other person at his discretion and the corresponding right of that other to receive and enjoy it.[99] Mill contended that the right of bequest after death forms part of private property, but the right of inheritance does not. Thus, he follows Bentham in asserting that when someone dies intestate, the state should provide funds for his dependents on a minimal level of comfort from the estate, but beyond that the funds should devolve upon the state. But Mill went even further than Bentham when he argued that the state should limit the amount that any individual could receive as the beneficiary of a bequest to some designated level of moderate comfort. While it belongs to the idea of owning property to be able to bestow it, property is a means only and not an end, Mill argued, and so when the power of bequest is used in conflict with the "permanent interests" of mankind—for example, in the institution of primogeniture or the establishment of a public trust the disposition of which is directed toward a certain objective in perpetuity—the government can justifiably intervene, limiting the right of bequest on grounds of expediency.

Now, what are we to make of this argument? To begin with, it is difficult to see how if right number 4—the right to receive property as a gift—is an essential element of the concept of private property, as Mill claimed, the government can intervene to limit the amount any individual can receive. This would be to alter one of the characteristics of private property. This was, clearly, Mill's intention, but his argument was too facile. He wanted to have it both ways: to uphold private property in principle and to show how it can be curtailed to achieve certain ends which are not an essential part of its nature. Here Mill's Utilitarianism came into play. But he did not want to avow explicitly that his inheritance scheme was a violation of this traditional notion of private property. By arguing that A has a right to dispose of his property but B has a right to receive only as much of what A wants to give him as society deems desirable, the concept of private property has been circumscribed. Mill admitted this, but he did not admit that a violation of anyone's property rights had occurred. If

A can not give B all that he wishes, then clearly A's property rights have been truncated. He does not enjoy the full benefits of the use and disposition of his property.

Mill recognized that he was altering the freedom of bequest—that was his avowed intent—but he claimed to have done so without altering an essential attribute or consequence of property. Evidently, on his own exposition of the essentials of property he did make such an alteration. The problem was that his exposition of the essential characteristics of property came straight out of the natural-rights, Lockian conception of a right to the use and disposition of what one has produced, while his inclusion of a Utilitarian, expediency standard as the ultimate determinant of the extent to which free disposition is to be permitted by society introduced an entirely different standard. His argument was more confused than Bentham's because it conflated the two divergent strains. Bentham must be credited with having made a clear choice. Mill's argument would have served his purpose better if he had simply avowed utility as the standard to begin with, and then derived a definition of the essentials of private property from this criterion.

The heart of Mill's undermining of the traditional, Lockian principle of property came in his analysis of landed property. Finally, in Mill, Smith's and Bentham's denial of property as a natural right (with Smith considering it to be almost a natural right, but not quite of the same priority as the rights to life and liberty and Bentham denying all natural rights) bore its full fruit. Locke contended that private property in land could be legitimately acquired as a result of one's right to one's own body, the products of one's labor, and eventually the right to that land with which one has mixed one's labor. The sole proviso was that enough and as good must be left for the rest of mankind. Locke's argument was weak as a result of that last stipulation, and Mill drove his wedge in at that point. Because property in land was exclusive—by my acquisition I have deprived others of an equal benefit—it fell into a different category, Mill argued, than property in movables which are reproducible to an almost unlimited extent.

Let us examine Mill's argument more closely. The purpose of granting exclusive property is to secure to producers the product of their effort and abstinence. (Notice the implicitly Utilitarian formulation right at the outset. For Locke property was not "granted," which implies some entity to do the granting, but existed prior to the organization of government.) Thus, this principle can not apply to what is not produced by labor, that is, the raw materials and land of the earth. The only valid claim to landed property is derived from the fact that most of its benefits are reaped as a result of labor and time, and therefore, only those people who have actually labored towards its improvement have a claim to property. Political economy has nothing to say in defense of landed property where this is not the case. Because "no man made the land"[100] and it is the original inheritance of the whole species (which is Locke's argument, also), its appropriation is wholly a matter of general expediency. "When private property in land is not expedient it is unjust."[101]

> The claim of the landlord to the land is altogether subordinate
> to the general policy of the state. The principle of property gives
> them no right to the land, but only a right to compensation for
> what ever portion of their interest in the land it may be the policy
> of the state to deprive them of. . . . But subject to this proviso
> the state is at liberty to deal with landed property as the general
> interest of the community may require, even to the extent,
> if it so happens, of doing with the whole, what is done with a
> part whenever a bill is passed for a railroad or a new street.[102]

The community has too much at stake in proper cultivation to leave such matters to the discretion of landlords when they have proved themselves unfit. Thus, in the case of Ireland, the tenants should be made proprietors and the landlords divested of their property with adequate compensation. Generally, then, in all questions of doubt, the balance should incline *against* the proprietor. (A definite reversal of the Smithian or Benthamite presumption in favor of property owners.) No exclusive right should be recognized unless it is productive of some positive, public good. Ownership of land is a monopoly defensible only as a necessary evil—when its utility has been disproved, it becomes an injustice.

Mill's argument begins with cultivation creating a right to property, as in Locke, but once again, Mill's expediency or utility standard intervened on an ad hoc basis. Therefore, he ended his argument with the claim that even those individuals who cultivate the land, not just the absentee landlords, hold their property at the sufferance of society and for the good of society, for they hold an exclusive monopoly which bars the rest from such possession. Even the cultivator is "morally bound, and should whenever the case admits be legally compelled, to make his interest and pleasure consistent with the public good."[103]

Perhaps what is objectionable in Mill's presentation is the unshakable-impression that he has pulled a rabbit out of a hat, that he has ravaged Locke while putatively only rationalizing and making him more consistent. Bentham's honesty about the principle of utility is, in comparison, quite refreshing. He avowed, openly and defiantly, that property is born with and dies with government. Mill's argument was too facile, too elusive. If he wanted utility as the standard, why didn't he begin with it, openly declaring it to be the regnant principle? Why begin with the Lockian baggage? According to his initial argument, the cultivator's right to the land should have been secure; yet, thanks to what appears to be an arbitrary introduction of the utility standard, his claim was also subject to the test of public expediency. Mill's argument, then, was confused, unnecessarily so, as Bentham had proved.

It is conceivable that Mill's motivation for including a Lockian derivation of property was to show that its defect—the claim that enough and as good must be left for the rest of humanity when land is taken from the common inheritance of all mankind—could be legitimately used to undermine an indefeasible right to property. If so, he was not explicit about that intention. He ended by supplanting a right to property over reproducible objects, with the claim that even here the public good could be an overriding claim. This clearly went beyond his initial argument, which acknowledged the Lockian derivation of a right to the fruits of one's own labor as a consequence of property in one's own body. It is an intriguing question, this one of why Mill did not explicitly acknowledge the principle of utility when it came to writing his *Principles*. In fact, when he does invoke it he refers to it as a criterion of expediency. A work is not made more scientific by refusing to avow openly one's moral principles.

The remainder of Book II of Mill's *Principles* is devoted to a discussion of the way in which the products of society are divided. In typically Ricardian fashion, Mill attempted to isolate the causes which determine the shares going to laborers, capitalists, and landlords. He improved on the Ricardian model in the exposition of a theory of profit which is the most refined and sophisticated explanation offered by any of the Classical economists. Other than that, there was nothing really novel here, so it will suffice to do little more than enumerate Mill's positions. On one count, however, Mill did diverge slightly from his predecessors in that he considered custom to be a contributing factor in the determination of the division of the produce under a private-property system. Thus, competition alone could not be considered the determining factor, although its

dominance is gradually secured as civilization advances. Competition is
still the basic assumption upon which economic reasoning ought to proceed, but correction must be made for the effects of custom as a disturbing cause.

In regard to wages, then, Mill advanced the strict wages-fund doctrine
in the *Principles,* the same doctrine which he was later to abandon. The
idea was that wages depend mainly on the demand and supply of labor
or on the proportion between the laboring population and the available
capital fund for the employment of labor. His conclusion was that nothing
can permanently alter the general level of wages except an increase or a
diminution of capital as compared with the quantity of labor available for
employment.[104] Efforts to improve the conditions of the laboring class
can only be successful if they either increase the fund of capital—as a
direct result of progress—or diminish the number of laborers. Thus, Mill
accepted the Malthusian population theory. And he rejected such schemes
as a minimum wage law or councils of workers and capitalists to determine
wages on the basis of equity and not just demand or the efforts of philan-
thropists to shame the employers into paying higher wages. All of these
efforts were doomed to failure on purely economic grounds as a result
of the wages-fund argument:

> Since, therefore, the rate of wages which results from com-
> petition distributes the whole existing *wages-fund* among
> the whole labouring population: if law or opinion succeeds
> in fixing wages above the rate, some labourers are kept out
> of employment.[105]

If such an artificial increase of wages were enforced by law, then either
public relief through taxation or a legally compelled increase of the capital
fund would have to be undertaken by the government. The ultimate consequence would be, Mill feared, that taxation for the relief of the poor
would engross the whole income of the country. Those who wish to benefit the laboring class should leave them in the condition in which their
wages depend directly on their numbers.

However, Mill declared that time had disproved Malthus' objections
to a Poor Law and a right to relief. It was Mill's contention that an absolute right to life, to relief, could be granted, that experience had demonstrated that laws could be constructed in such a way that they would

not be injurious to prudence, self-restraint, and industry.[106] Thus, he
adopted the position of Nassau Senior, that relief could be made ample
in respect to necessities but accompanied by conditions which would be
disagreeable, including restraints on the recipients' freedom and privation
of indulgences. One of these freedoms which it would be necessary for
the state to restrict would be that of procreation, because without such
a limitation upon the recipients of public alms, future dependent popula-
tions would eat away the substance of society.

The best way of aiding the poor, then, was still the Malthusian way
of changing the minds and habits of the people with the result that their
numbers would be curtailed through the exercise of the prudential check.
But Mill does recognize an absolute right to public support in an advanced
society, although he looked to the limitation of population, through legal
regulations on marriage and public opinion exercised against large families,
as the only long-range solution for the problem of poverty.[107] To accomplish the latter, a program of effective national education would have to
be enacted, but such a measure could only be effective if the conditions
of the poor were improved for a whole generation. To accomplish this
he suggested either a national plan for colonization (which would limit
the number of workers and thus raise their wages) or a plan by which
all common lands would be divided among a new class of small proprietors.
Comfort must be made habitual to a generation before education can
really work its effects upon the limitation of population. By 1865 Mill
saw these requisites coming to pass spontaneously through the cheapness
of emigration and the increase of knowledge.

It is interesting to observe that Mill disagreed with Smith's pleasant
assumption that the most nasty and onerous labors would be remunerated
at the highest level. Rather, Mill contended, such disagreeable labors are
the worst paid because, in a labor market oversupplied with labor, people
are willing to take such unskilled jobs at low wages. Also, wages are kept
artificially high for skilled labor which requires education, as a result of
the impossibility of the mass of people obtaining the necessary education
to fill these jobs. To a certain extent, these inequities are corrected as
civilization advances and education becomes more evenly dispersed.

Mill's analysis of the constituent elements of profit was quite sophisticated.[108] It proceeded along the lines proposed by Senior. The profits of
the capitalist are the remuneration for his abstinence. But this is only
part of profit, the part that is equivalent to what someone would be will-

ing to pay for the use of the capital—that is, interest. The capitalist who is also the employer of his capital expects to receive a return for: (1) an equivalent for his abstinence (the extent of this depends upon the strength of the effective desire of accumulation), (2) an indemnity for risk (insurance), and (3) a remuneration for his labor and skill of superintendence. The lowest general rate of profits which can exist in society as a whole is that which is barely sufficient to compensate these forces. Although on the average various employments hold out not equal profits, Mill says, but equal expectations of profits, differences in the rates of profit in different industries are accounted for by differences in risk, agreeableness of employment, and natural or artificial monopolies.

When it came to pinpointing the derivation or the cause of profit, Mill adopted the Ricardian (and that ultimately held by Senior) notion that labor is the root cause of profit, producing more than it consumes in wages, not exchange—selling for more than a product cost to produce—but the fact that labor produces more than is required for its support. This is the "surplus-value" analysis of profit, which went no further than Ricardo or Senior. If the laborers of a country produce 20 percent more than their wages, the rage of profit will stand at 20 percent. In the final analysis, then, Mill arrived at the same unsatisfactory solution as we have criticized in Senior. Mill ended his discussion by adopting the Ricardian formulation that the rate of profit depends upon the level of wages, and the two stand in inverse relationship to each other. Thus, there was an incompatibility between his analyses of the constituents of profit and the causes of profit; they were essentially two different arguments.

Mill adopted the Ricardian rent doctrine—that land of a better sort only pays rent when worse land is brought into production—and he accepted the Ricardian conclusion that rent does not form a part of cost of production or the advances of the capitalist.

We have seen in this section how Mill, through his distinction between the laws of production as natural laws and the laws of distribution as subject to human intervention, was drawn into a revolutionary analysis— revolutionary for Classical economics—of socialist systems. This argument shook to the very foundations the Classical political economists' assumption of private property and free competition as the regnant social system. Mill opened up large areas of speculation in this regard. However, as a result of his own conclusion that private property was the system which would continue to exist for the immediate future, he was led to

a consideration of the shares of distribution along the lines laid down by
his predecessors, particularly Ricardo. Mill's admixture of a Lockian derivation of property with a utility or expediency standard was found to be
suspect on grounds of logical inconsistency.

THE THEORY OF EXCHANGE AND THE PROSPECTS
FOR THE FUTURE

It seems odd, indeed, to come to a discussion of value after production
and distribution have been treated, but that was Mill's design. Without
intending to disparage Mill's perspicuity as a prognosticator of intellectual
trends, it is intriguing to reflect upon his statement that as of 1848 the
theory of value was complete.[109] It was precisely this aspect of political
economy which was to undergo nothing short of a revolution in approach
a mere twenty-three years after Mill first made this declaration.

This theory of value of which Mill spoke as firmly established was the
cost-of-production theory which he adopted intact from Ricardo. He
made the same distinction between goods of which there was an absolute
limitation of supply, such as art works, in which supply and demand set
the value; and goods capable of indefinite increase, such as manufactured
goods; and goods capable of increase but at increased cost, such as agricultural goods, in which the value is set by cost of production. The natural
value of goods of the latter type is set by the cost of production—that is,
mainly, by labor expended on their production, both past and present
labor—around which the market value fluctuates as an equilibrium point.
Supply adjusts itself in time and the market value is equivalent to cost
of production, that is, the minimum price or value necessary for the product
to be continued in production. The cost of production, then, determines
the extent of the demand, and the supply conforms to that value. This is
straight out of Smith, through the filter of Ricardo.

Mill explored no new ground, then, in his value theory, adopting Ricardo's
analysis ready-made. He followed Ricardo in declaring that general profits
and general wages do not enter into value, only the relative differences
in the two between different industries. He also agreed with Ricardo that
rent does not enter into cost of production. There is no point, therefore,
in going into a lengthy critical evaluation of Mill's theory, as this has already been done with Ricardo's theory from which Mill did not depart
in any essential respects.

Mill agreed with his fellow Classical political economists in upholding a gold standard and a paper currency convertible into gold. He condemned an inconvertible paper currency as providing too great a temptation to governments to inflate the currency in order to pay off the public debt. On another significant issue which we have previously discussed, that of Say's Law, Mill argued against Malthus' contention that a general over-supply of commodities could spread throughout a nation, resulting in a paucity of demand, unemployment, and depression. Mill agreed with Say that as the means of paying for commodities is provided by other com-modities, supply creates its own demand.[110] In criticizing Malthus and Sismondi, Mill advanced a theory of commercial crises based upon over-speculation resulting in a sudden and dramatic annihilation of a great mass of credit. (This account, by the way, was endorsed by the Margin-alists and the Neo-Classical economists of a later period.) Speculators have no money to meet their debts, because the commodities they spec-ulated on have not risen in price as they expected, and a general decline in prices is the result as people are reluctant to part with their money.

Mill's explanation was a bit vague, but he seemed to be aiming in the right direction. What is important for our purposes is that his theory denied Malthus' solution of creating an artificial demand by make-work government projects. Mill claimed that a restoration of confidence was all that was necessary and that no diminution of supply or addition in demand was required.

And on the issue of international exchange, Mill adopted Ricardo's relative-advantage analysis, with the consequence that comparative cost determines the interchange of goods between different nations, not the absolute cost of production. He agreed with his fellow Classical economists in extolling the advantages of international trade as a means of lowering prices to consumers, enjoying the benefits of novel imported goods, and improving the methods of production. Commerce was additionally advan-tageous as an intellectual and moral stimulus and as a vehicle for render-ing war obsolete. As commerce advanced, so the argument went, people would view the wealth of other countries as an advantage, not a threat to their own country's wealth.[111]

Curiously enough, then, Mill's iconoclastic approach to the laws of distribution did not cause him to reevaluate the theory of exchange. He did not depart in any significant way from the general Ricardian doctrines derived from Smith: of the cost of production-labor theory of value, of the notion that the level of wages, profits, and rent does not affect value, and of the theory of rent. Neither did he depart from Ricardo's analysis of comparative cost and supply and demand as the regulating factors in international trade, nor did he disagree with the Classical endorsement of the benefits of free trade between nations, both on economic grounds and as an insurance policy against future wars.

When he came to discuss the dynamic element (as contrasted to the previous static treatment of economics), the effect of progress on production, Mill remained within the general framework developed by Ricardo. As a direct disciple of Ricardo and the Malthusian population theory, he held that as economic progress advances, landlords will tend to be greatly enriched while the cost of the laborers' subsistence tends to increase and profits fall.[112] As society improves, profits tend to a minimum at which point society is on the verge of the stationary state. From the latter view, Mill concluded that in a wealthy and industrious society this tendency of profits to a minimum as capital accumulates greatly mitigates the economic argument against the expenditure of public money for valuable although industrially unproductive purposes.[113] His reasoning, evidently, was that if the level of profit were so low that people had little or no incentive to invest their money in productive ventures, no harm could be caused by the government's absorbing this excess money and spending it on social programs.

This notion of the stationary state was a curious one, as we have previously observed in relation to Ricardo, and it was brought about, Mill thought, because the increase of wealth was not boundless. As far as one can decipher, he thought that profits would fall because there would be a constantly diminishing field for new investments and not as a result of increased capital intensifying competition and driving prices, and hence, profits, down, as Smith contended. Mill thought that eventually the progressive state must end in the stationary state and that society was always on the verge of it. To counteract the effects of such stagnation upon the poor, he urged that restraints on population must be recommended to the laboring class and they must be impressed with the desire to keep up their standard of living by limiting their numbers.

That is just about as far as Ricardo went, but Mill carried the argument a step further. He actually embraced the stationary state, which had previously been viewed as casting a dismal pall over Classical economics. The stationary state, Mill declared, would be an improvement over our present condition of competition and self-aggrandizement:

> But the best state for human nature is that in which, while no one is poor, no one desires to be richer, nor has any reason to fear being thrust back by the efforts of others to push themselves forward.[114]

The present economic stage is but an early phase of human improvement, and what is needed now is better distribution to be achieved by a restraint on population. In embracing the stationary state—in which population would be moderated, produce better distributed, and inheritance limited—as an improvement over our present condition and as an arena in which man can devote himself to mental improvement, Mill went far beyond Ricardo, while still employing Ricardo's economic argument.

In the first chapter of the book on exchange, "Of the Probable Futurity of the Labouring Classes," the inclusion of which Mill attributed to his wife's inspiration, we can see the change wrought by Mill in Smith's conception of political economy as a vehicle for increasing production only. An improved distribution and a larger remuneration for labor is preferable, Mill declared, to a mere increase of production. That single sentence epitomizes the intellectual movement wrought by Mill's generation. Questions of distribution and the alleviation of poverty became of paramount importance, and it was no longer implicitly assumed that by increasing production the political economist or the statesman had fulfilled his function or that poverty would be automatically ameliorated without any special concern on the statesman's part.

Mill's hope for the future was that through education, self-government, and the cultivation of the virtue of independence, the laboring class could be elevated into a position of equal partnership with capitalists. Perhaps, finally, an association of laborers themselves could be achieved. Cooperative movements ought to be encouraged to exist side by side with capitalist industries in order that each might develop in those areas in which it had an advantage. The capitalists, for example, would employ their superiority in having a single management to take on new and risky ventures. However, the workers would accept this only in a transitionary state. Eventually, they would have to be admitted to a share in the profits of the capitalist, who might then give up the struggle and lend his capital to the associations. Thus, capital might spontaneously become the property of all those who participate in production. This "would be the nearest approach to social justice, and the most beneficial ordering of industrial affairs for the universal good which it is possible at present to foresee."[115]

A movement in this direction should commence; the time is ripe, Mill agrees with the socialists; yet he is unwilling to join in their condemnation of competition. It is still the best insurance against monopoly, and in the present state of society its expansion is always a good.

Here we have seen Mill start from orthodox Ricardian doctrine concerning the stationary state and reason from that to socialistic conclusions about the future state of society. Even though he was unwilling to jettison competition entirely, as his final statement seems to retract some of his earlier enthusiasm for cooperation and animus against competition, Mill, nevertheless, went much further than any of the other Classical economists before him would have ever dreamed possible in the direction of socialism, given their shared doctrines on value, rent, profits, wages, and so on.

Mill's imagination, his fervor, and his desire for social amelioration and justice made him impatient with a competitive system which appeared to be a great engine for the increase of production, but a laggard in the area of distributive justice. Never impatient enough to demand a violent revolution, fearful of the consequences of untried doctrines upon a captive population, and concerned about the individual and his claims to independence, Mill's prospects for the future lay in the hope that within the private-property system subtle changes could be effected which would prove both economically feasible and socially just in the distribution of the national product.

GOVERNMENTAL INTERVENTION IN THE ECONOMY: SUBJECT TO THE STANDARD OF GENERAL EXPEDIENCY

Mill began the final book of the *Principles* by displaying the inadequacy of the political principle which would restrict government intervention to the protection of the individual and his property from force and fraud. He argued that such a restrictive principle would not permit acts of governmental interference which every reasonable man and every existing government does and must acknowledge as a legitimate function of the state. The nearest one can come, Mill admonished, to laying down a universally

applicable principle in regard to the proper limits of government activity
is to say that any action which is *generally expedient* for the government
to perform, any action which men want the government to take, it has a
right to execute. However, he did acknowledge the noninterference principle—that is, laissez-faire—as the general principle, departures from which
must be justified by a claim of overriding expediency.

In appearance, then, this was a very Benthamite formulation. But as
Mill's argument unfolds and the circumstances in which governments
interfere legitimately are recounted, the principle of laissez-faire, even as
a guideline, is almost completely negated. Finally, he declared that in
particular circumstances there is not anything important to the general
interest which the government may not do if individuals are not doing
it or can not do it.[116]

Mill found the laissez-faire doctrine—that government should be limited
to protecting people against force and fraud—entirely too arbitrary and
restrictive. Other functions of government which command almost universal agreement are eliminated by this principle, including establishing
and enforcing laws of inheritance, defining property, obliging people to
perform their contracts, and deciding what contracts are fit to be enforced. All these are proper governmental functions, universally acknowledged to be valid. Also, governments perform a whole range of services
simply because they "conduce to general convenience";[117] examples are
coining money; prescribing a set of standard weights and measures; paving,
lighting, and cleaning streets; raising dikes and embankments for controlling rivers. In addition, there are limits to the doctrine that individuals
are the best judges of their own interests in that such a principle is applicable
only to those people who are capable of acting on their own behalf. The
exceptions are children, lunatics, and those fallen into imbecility, over
whom the government may act as protectors of their interests. All these
functions—the necessary functions of government, inseparable from the
very idea of government, or exercised habitually and without objection
by all governments—are fundamental to government, and they constitute
the minimum that any government performs.

But enough has been said to show that the admitted functions of government embrace a much wider field than can
easily be included within the ring-fence of any restricted
definition, and that it is hardly possible to find any ground

of justification common to them all, except the comprehensive
one of *general expediency;* nor to limit the interference of
government by any universal rule, save the simple vague one,
that it should never be admitted but when the case of expediency is strong.[118]

Mill distinguished these kinds of activities from the optional functions
of government, about which there could be disagreement concerning their
efficacy or desirability. The distinction between the two classes of activities
is, apparently, not a rigid one, for the two classes of functions are not to
be determined on different principles—both are to be subjected to the
test of expediency—but the former are distinguishable from the latter
only by the fact that the former comprise functions which are universally
undertaken by all governments, while the latter embrace activities sometimes judged expedient and sometimes not.

Mill first considers the economic effects arising from the manner in
which governments perform their necessary and acknowledged functions.
These include raising taxes, enacting laws regulating property and contracts, and enforcing the laws through a judicial apparatus and a police
force. On the subject of taxation, Mill endorsed Smith's four maxims—
that (1) the subjects should contribute in proportion to their respective
abilities, (2) the tax paid by each should be certain and not arbitrary,
(3) it should be levied in a convenient manner, and (4) it should take
from the people as little as possible over what it deposits in the treasury.
However, he thought that equality of taxation, the first of Smith's propositions, warranted further elaboration. His conclusion was that while a
graduated income tax would be unacceptable as a penalty on the prudent
to relieve the prodigal, a graduated tax on estates would be acceptable as
a means of diminishing inequalities of wealth. (He did, however, endorse
an income tax which would exempt from taxation all incomes below the
level sufficient for the provision of necessities. It would levy a fixed percentage on all incomes above that level; such a tax would be the least
objectionable of all taxes, he claimed.) Such a graduated estate tax would
be justifiable on the grounds that it would only affect unearned fortunes.
On the same grounds, it would be advisable to tax any kind of income that
would have a tendency to increase steadily without effort on the part of
the recipient. For the state to appropriate unearned incomes of this type
would be no violation of the principle on which private property is

grounded (here, Mill is referring back to his previous argument concerning the genesis of landed property). Thus, the "unearned income" of land-lords could be legitimately appropriated by the state; by the standard of the "general principle of social justice" they have no claim to this income. Mill drew this conclusion as a direct result of Ricardo's theory of rent, which he adopted, combined with his own theory of property which excluded land from the category of things over which men can have a fixed and unchallengeable claim.

Concerning the economic effects of ordinary government activities in the other two areas, regulating property and enforcing the laws, Mill emphasized the point that oppression by government was worse than insecurity of property or anarchy. And he described, in typical Smithian and Benthamite fashion, the various erroneous theories upon which acts of governmental intervention had been justified. (He did, however, acknowledge that government had a legitimate right to regulate joint-stock companies and partnerships and to enact insolvency and bankruptcy laws.) Included under the false grounds of interference were: (1) protectionism— the fruit of the false Mercantilist system was condemned by Mill and the free-trade position upheld, with the proviso that infant industries could be protected temporarily if they were of a kind that would be naturally suited to the country; (2) interference with contracts, particularly of the type of usury laws, were rejected as spurious on Bentham's economic arguments that they were counterproductive, they achieved the opposite of their intended purpose, and they were unnecessary because the individual was the best judge of his own interests in this particular case; (3) attempts by governments either to cheapen or to make more costly certain commodities were rejected because they operate to discourage production, and, in the case of food, to make the working class dependent on the rest of society by making them a present of subsistence at the cost of increased taxes for everyone else; (4) government grants of monopolies were challenged as equivalent to a tax on the people because such grants raised the cost of goods and encouraged laziness and backwardness in the protected industries; (5) laws against workers' efforts to raise wages were condemned as an example of the survival of the spirit of the slave master; trade unions should be tolerated as long as they are voluntary, because they have an educative effect, even if their prospects for gaining higher wages are limited by the availability of capital; and, finally, (6) government attempts to control opinion were roundly anathematized by Mill on the same grounds as he took in his essay "On Liberty," that is, that such excesses are antithetical to progress and in addition even hostile to economic prosperity.

When Mill passed from these generally admitted functions of government and their perversions to an evaluation of the optional functions of government, he once again adverted to the laissez-faire principle. Although he rejected the conclusions of the advocates of the laissez-faire principle— that the government should be limited to the minimal-state, night-watchman functions—he did envision a role for the principle in representing a starting point for debate and a criterion, departures from which must be justified by an overriding claim of general, public expediency. In pursuing this approach, Mill mirrored Bentham very closely.

Attempting to take a middle ground between the advocates of wholesale interference on the one hand and the extreme noninterventionists on the other, Mill argued that the question of governmental interference does not admit of any *a priori,* universal solution but requires instead an endeavor to draw the line in particular cases between too much and too little governmental activity. Both extremes represent excesses and errors in certain circumstances, and an attempt must be made to mediate between the two polar positions. Mill derives a commonsensical solution by taking the principles of each and combining them together, with the expediency standard serving as a corrective to the inflexibility of the laissez-faire principle.

There are two categories of governmental interference, argues Mill, and in the first—that of "authoritative interference," that is, controlling the free agency of individuals—the government's role should be more circumspect and hesitant than in the second—that of giving advice and promulgating information or establishing agencies to do what can not be entrusted solely to private interest. This is the familiar distinction previously drawn by Bentham. But Mill's second category is more expansive than Bentham's. Falling under the latter category would be such activities as church establishment, schools, colleges, a national bank, government industries (without monopolies against private banks or industries), post office, corps of engineers, and public hospitals.

Authoritative interference, which involves direct curtailment of the freedom of individuals, must be subjected to much more stringent standards. In all civilized governments, no matter what their constitutions may be, there must be a recognition of a circle around every individual from which government should be excluded. Where should this limit be placed, and how large a province shall this reserved part embrace? It should, Mill contends, include all that which concerns only the inward or outward life of the individual and does not affect the interests of others or affects them only through moral example. Thus, Mill concludes that opinion should be left free, and so should actions not injurious to others. Even in the portion of our conduct which does affect others, the onus of making out a case to restrict such activity always lies with the defenders of a legal prohibition.[119] (This is the same argument which Mill later advanced in the essay "On Liberty.") To be prevented from doing what one is inclined to do is irksome, and it also starves the creative faculties of man. "It is not merely a constructive or presumptive injury to others which will justify the interference of law with individual freedom."[120] Mill, in one telling passage, steps back from the extreme tendencies of this exposition when he says that

> Scarcely any degree of utility, short of absolute necessity, will justify a prohibitory regulation, unless it can also be made to recommend itself to the general conscience; unless persons of ordinary good intentions either believe already, or can be induced to believe, that the thing prohibited is a thing which they ought not to do.[121]

Despite the severity of the language in the critical phrase of this quotation, Mill clearly expanded the scope of government intervention in the sphere of individual activity when he allowed that any regulation could be warranted if some nebulous entity called the "general conscience" were judged, by the legislator presumably, to have consented to such an abridgment of their liberty.

With respect to government activity of the second type, the case for rejection is a far weaker one, since Mill maintains that such activities do not directly interfere with an individual's free agency. Even in these cases, however, there is still a *prima facie* argument against intervention because it must be supported by compulsory taxation.

Mill then goes on to adduce several other instrumental objections to governmental intervention. Every increase of the government's functions necessarily increases its power, and that power is to be feared even in a democratic state. The independence of the individual must be jealously

guarded from the overweaning force of the mass. Also, every increase of
the functions of government presents an additional problem in management and organization. Things tend to be done worse by government
than by private agencies. Here, Mill endorses the typical Classical argument that the individual is the best judge of how his business should be
conducted because he has the greatest interest in its outcome. Where this
"interest" argument holds true, it should condemn all governmental intervention, for example, in the common operations of industry or commerce.
Even if government could do a better job in a particular instance, it should,
in general, forbear from acting, because individual initiative has an educative
function and, furthermore, it would be extremely dangerous to human
welfare if most intelligence and talent were coopted by the government.

On the basis of the foregoing instrumental arguments, Mill concluded
that "*Laissez-faire,* in short, should be the general practice: every departure from it, *unless required by some great good,* is a certain evil."[122]
Although not explicitly advocating a utilitarian standard, this is what
Mill's statement actually amounts to. If a greater good can be proved for
any particular act of governmental intervention, then the laissez-faire
objection is surmounted, and the government is justified in proceeding.
This is a completely different standard, with utterly different conclusions
for practical governmental action, than the one advocated by the natural
rights proponents of the nonintervention principle. For such theorists—
the Frenchman Bastiat is a convenient example—the laissez-faire principle
absolutely forbids governmental activity of Mill's second type, and it limits
the first category to government acts which protect people and their
property from force and fraud. No overriding reasons, such as general
expediency or general utility, are acknowledged as warranting any contravention of the noninterference principle; for such acts would constitute
a violation of the natural rights to life, liberty, or property. But it was precisely this Bastiat-type notion of laissez-faire which Mill in his letters, in
which he is often much more explicit about his true convictions, condemned. In a letter to Cairnes on his article criticizing Bastiat,[123] Mill
suggested that Cairnes might pursue a further assault upon Bastiat's system to

> show how far from the truth it is that the economic
> phenomena of society as at presently constituted
> always arrange themselves spontaneously in the way

which is most for the common good or that the interests of all classes are fundamentally the same.[124]

Laissez-faire, for theorists of Bastiat's type, is a principle derived from
the natural rights of individuals. The reasoning is that if individuals do not
have a right to compel their neighbors, to violate their property, to tax
them, to conscript them, and so on, then the aggregate of individuals—
the government— can not possibly have such rights. Thus, the government
is limited to defending individuals from encroachment of their rights by
other individuals. But for Mill, the laissez-faire principle is of an entirely
different order. It is not based upon any prior foundation, such as natural
rights, but is, rather, the conclusion of induction based on experience
only. It is, then, based upon expediency, upon a series of instrumental
assessments that government activity is to be rejected over a certain broad
range of issues because it produces certain undesirable effects. Hence, it
is merely a general conclusion, to be dispensed with when this same
standard—general expediency—dictates that some greater good will be
served by governmental intervention. In the final analysis, Mill really
has one standard, expediency, not two as would appear from the way in
which his argument unfolded. By the end of his argument, the expediency
standard reigns supreme, and the laissez-faire principle is almost completely discarded. Mill declared, finally, that the government can do anything important to the general interest.[125]

Mill next considered precisely those cases in which the general objections against governmental intervention do not obtain, that is, the cases
in which the nonintervention principle is overridden by counterconsidera-
tions of greater importance. The assumption upon which the laissez-faire
principle was based in Utilitarian treatment was the psychological observation that the individual is the best judge of his own affairs because his
interest is the most intimately connected with the outcome. Mill's contention was that in certain cases this general principle did not hold true—
that, in fact, the individual was not the best judge of his own interest in
all cases. While in most instances the individual is the best judge of commodities for his physical needs, he feels the want of mental "commodities" in inverse proportion to his need. When the need is greatest for
these cultural, character-building goods, the lack of them is hardly felt
at all. The voluntary, market system can not fulfill these cultural needs
because the demand is not there. What Mill is saying, in effect, is that he

is willing to supplant the judgments of individuals in the marketplace
when he feels that those judgments are misdirected—an elitist, authoritarian
assertion, to be sure, but one in which he was joined by Bentham and when
it came to education, even Smith. As Mill wrote:

> Education, therefore, is one of those things which it is admissable
> in principle that a government should provide for the people. The
> case is one in which the reasons of the non-interference principle
> do not necessarily or universally extend.[126]

On the Utilitarian ground that all members of a community suffer from
the ignorance of some, Mill maintained that the government can compel
parents to give their children an elementary education and also make
available such an education at public expense. He preferred that the funds
for such an enterprise come from public charity rather than taxation and
that education ought not be a government monopoly.

Other instances in which the individual is not the best judge of his own
interest would include the following cases: (1) Those individuals—lunatics,
idiots, and infants—who are incapable of judging or acting for themselves
should be superintended by the government. In the case of children, the
government is justified in compelling parents to do everything in the
interests of the children which it can be proved desirable for parents to
do for their offspring. The government may prevent children from being
overworked; thus, Mill endorsed the Factory Acts. This is, quite evidently,
a widely expansible concession—that the government can make parents
do anything which it is decided that parents ought to do for their children. An Orwellian theorist, without Mill's obvious concern for individual
liberty, could take this proposition and run with it.

(2) The laissez-faire principle only obtains when grounded on present,
personal experience, he contends, and so when the individual attempts,
irrevocably, to decide what will be best for his interests at some future
date, the state is justified in intervening. What Mill had in mind, here,
were marriage contracts and contracts in perpetuity.

(3) Mill argued that whatever can only be done by joint-stock companies is often better done by the government. The point was that since
individuals can only manage their affairs by delegated authority in such
circumstances, it is better to opt for public control. Even if the government can perform these functions better, however, it is often of greater

general benefit that such functions be left in private hands but under government regulation. In monopolized industries, the government should either take them over, regulate them, and make concessions for a limited time, or confiscate profits if they are mismanaged, depending on the particular circumstances of the industry involved.

(4) The laissez-faire principle is also overriden in cases where individuals alone can not give effect to their own judgments and their joint ventures can only have effect when they are sanctioned by law. Examples of this would include limiting the hours of work by government edict, and cases in which something would be advantageous to a class, but to the immediate interests of every individual to violate. Thus, if a large class of competitors, say laborers, could only limit their hours of work by legal means, even though it would be in the interest of all as a class to limit their hours of labor, Mill would sanction such a law. He would prefer that such a state of affairs could be reached through voluntary means, but he doubted that such could be accomplished in this case because it would be to each individual's interest to work more hours at a higher rate than that freely agreed upon by everyone, and eventually, everyone would be forced to work longer hours at the old, lower rate.

(5) The nonintervention principle, based on the individual being the best judge of his own interest, does not obtain where an individual is acting in the interest of another. Thus, public charity, in the form of the Poor Laws, is to be preferred to private charity.

(6) Also, the principle does not hold in those cases where an individual, acting solely from his own interest, acts in such a way as to effect the interests of the nation or posterity. Government regulation of colonial policy is warranted, then, on the ground that such activities affect the permanent interest of civilization.

(7) And, finally, the government ought to act when no individual has an interest in performing an important public service because no adequate remuneration would accompany such a performance. This last exception comes straight from Smith. What Mill had in mind here are such activities as scientific exploration, lighthouses, and endowments and salaries for the maintenance of a scholarly class. But Mill went much further under this heading than did Smith, who envisioned little more than roads, canals, and sewers. It will be instructive to quote Mill at length on this point, since it illustrates so perfectly the extent to which the expediency standard rendered the laissez-faire principle nugatory.

It may be said generally, that *anything* which it is desirable
should be done for the general interest of mankind or of future
generations, or for the present interests of those members of
the community who require external aid, but which is not of
a nature to remunerate individuals or associations for undertaking it, is in itself a suitable thing to be undertaken by government: though, before making the work their own, governments
ought always to consider if there be a rational probability of its
being done on what is called the voluntary principle, and if so,
whether it is likely to be done in a better and more effectual
manner by government agency, than by the zeal and liberality
of individuals.[127]

Thus, Mill concluded that the government can do anything which is
for the public good, if it would not be done but for its agency. The determination of what constitutes this "general interest" is left to the discretion of government officials, with the admonition that liberty should be
restricted only in those instances in which the "general conscience" will
go along with the circumscription. In a sense, then, Mill took Bentham's
"be quiet" principle of governmental intervention, justified on instrumental,
Utilitarian grounds, and proved precisely what we said of the potentiality
for ever expanding government activity which lay dormant, yet implicit
in Bentham's formulation. Mill's final discussion of governmental intervention was along Benthamite lines; yet it was not incompatible with
his earlier treatment of socialism in Book II of the *Principles.* If individual
interest failed to secure automatically either the individual's own benefit
or the benefit of society (the latter was implicit in most of Mill's analysis
of the cases in which the individual was not the best judge of his own
interest), then the government was justified in stepping in to remedy the
deficiency. Clearly, there was nothing in the final book which would
provide a *prima facie* case against redistribution or government ownership
of the means of production, provided only that such activities were determined actually to conduce to "general expediency." Thus, while socialism
here and now was further than Mill wanted to go, the principle of government intervention judged solely or predominantly by the standard of
"general expediency" was almost infinitely expansible, as Mill himself
realized.

What restrained Mill personally from advising such extreme, socialistic
ventures was not his principle of governmental intervention but, rather,

economic arguments concerning the possibility of a curtailment of production under a socialistic organization of industry and his own *personal*
preference for individual liberty and his desire to be assured that such
will not be irreparably damaged by socialistic conformity and regulation.

Mill moved the boundaries of governmental intervention far beyond
his predecessors, even though he himself backed away from some of the
more extreme consequences of his method, relegating socialism to a distant
future. However, he was quite willing to incorporate some of its fervor
for distributive justice and greater equality within the present organization
of the private-property, competitive system. He accomplished this expansion by the introduction of the production-distribution distinction,
which rendered all laws of distribution subject to the intervention of
government; by the utilization of the "general expediency" or utility
principle which, in effect, undercut the laissez-faire principle; by drawing
the consequences of Ricardo's rent doctrine, when he declared that the
government may rightfully confiscate unearned incomes; by making a
critical alteration in the Lockian argument for private property, which
made ownership subject to the discretion of the community; and by exploding, in important instances, the conviction of the Classical School
that the individual is the best judge of his own interest. And he did *not*
affect this expansion by advancing any essentially new theories in the
field of pure economics—his theories of value, rent, labor, and wages
came straight from Ricardo.

He accomplished what can be considered nothing less than a demolition
job on the connection between pure economic doctrines and the question
of government intervention which had existed in Classical economics.
The Classical system had been based upon individual interests leading to
the general interest and the individual as the best judge of his own interest,
and this was precisely what Mill challenged in critical cases. This was to
have far-reaching effects, as our subsequent investigation will relate.

However, we do not have to wait for the future to perceive the effects
of Mill's work, for even in the acts of governmental intervention which he
unequivocally endorsed we can see an expansion much beyond that advocated by his predecessors, yet not that much beyond the acts of intervention endorsed by Bentham. Thus, Mill sanctioned, at one time or another, the following governmental acts of intervention in the economy:
the state ownership of land in the case of Ireland;[128] the aiding of workers
thrown out of work by the introduction of machinery;[129] the curtailment

of inheritance;[130] the granting of a right to relief;[131] the enforcement of
a legal restraint against those who brought children into the world who
were a burden on society;[132] the regulation of marriage;[133] the introduction
of an income tax;[134] the regulation of joint-stock companies;[135] the regulation or nationalization of monopolistic industries;[136] the provision of compulsory education;[137] the regulation of colonies;[138] the provision of funds
for scientific discoveries, universities, and scholars;[139] the regulation of
the hours of work of children;[140] and the Laboring Classes Dwelling Bill
which proposed government loans to improve private homes.[141]

It was primarily on the philosophical level, in his rendering of the principle of utility as a less rigid and more elitist doctrine, and his production-
distribution distinction that Mill really set himself apart from the rest of
the Classical School, although this is not meant to deny that his advocacy
of government regulation or nationalization of monopolistic or large
industries went beyond anything advocated by his fellow political economists.

One Classical principle which was entirely absent in Mill was the Smithian
notion of the harmony of interests—that each individual by pursuing his
own interests will be led by an invisible hand to take that course which
will be most beneficial to society. For Mill, who questioned in so many
important cases whether the individual could even be the best judge of
his own interests, the disharmony of interests as a result of the existence
of poor and rich classes seemed the overwhelming social reality, so much
so in fact that he never even discussed the harmony-of-interest doctrine
explicitly. He argued, instead, that in many cases, such as monopolies,
joint-stock companies, or landownership, the general good will not be
served by the free play of individuals pursuing their own interests. Thus,
Mill built upon the class-conflict aspect which was an element in Smith's
economics but a subordinate one to the harmony-of-interest contention
by following the lead of Ricardo's rent doctrine and the socialists' critique
of the capitalistic distribution system.

CAIRNES AND SIDGWICK: THE FINAL ASSAULT
UPON THE LAISSEZ-FAIRE PRINCIPLE

In the 1870s and 1880s two disciples of J. S. Mill, J. E. Cairnes and
Henry Sidgwick, proceeded to complete the task that their mentor had
begun. They attacked with great vehemence the popular notion of the
time, which they saw as the factor discrediting economic science among

the intellectuals of the day, that economics as a science was inextricably
bound up with the laissez-faire doctrine. Neither man was of any out-
standing importance to the history of economic thought. No new pure
economic theories can be credited to them, for despite Sidgwick's rather
fumbling attempt to reconcile the Ricardo-Mill cost-of-production theory
of value with the new, Jevonian marginal utility theory, nothing really
came of the attempt, as the two theories were incompatible. While Sidgwick's *The Principles of Political Economy* is little more than a rephrasing
of Mill's *Principles* (following Mill in the production-distribution distinction and in the order of the treatise), Cairnes's sometimes fractious criticism of some of the leading doctrines of Classical economics still did not
place him at any great distance from his close friend, Mill. Our interest in
them, consequently, is confined to their vigorous attacks upon the nonintervention principle and Sidgwick's endorsement of Mill's discussion of
the circumstances in which the principle that the individual is the best
judge of his own interests breaks down. Also, Sidgwick's analysis of the
extent to which natural liberty would lead to the greatest benefit for the
individual or society will be treated.

Cairnes, in an essay entitled "Political Economy and Laissez-Faire"[142]
delivered at University College in 1870, attributed the then current dis-
enchantment with political economy to the identification of it in the
public mind with the doctrine of laissez-faire, with the result that economics
was looked upon as a hindrance to reform. While the doctrine may have been
useful in Europe eighty years ago when trade and industry were contained
by artificial restrictions, it is antiquated, and the main line of advance now
depends upon concerted action by society as a whole—precisely the kind
of activity proscribed by the noninterference principle. Such was the contention of the opponents of laissez-faire. Cairnes met their objections not
by a defense of the principle but by a denial that this dictum had any
intrinsic connection with the science of political economy. It was his contention that the maxim of laissez-faire has no scientific basis at all, that
it is at best merely a handy rule of practice, "useful, perhaps, as a reminder
to statesmen on which side the presumption lies in questions of industrial
legislation, but totally destitute of all scientific authority."[143]

For laissez-faire to be considered a scientific principle, the following
two assumptions would have to hold, Cairnes argued. First, the interests
of human beings are fundamentally the same, and consequently what is
most for my interest is also most for the interest of other people. Second,

individuals know their interests in the sense in which they are coincident with the interests of others, and in the absence of coercion, they would follow them. The first assumption Cairnes was willing to concede, except for the reservation that class interests are not harmonious, even if individual interests of man *qua* man are one. But the second assertion he found irreparably flawed.

> Nothing is easier than to show that people follow their interest, in the sense in which they understand their interest. But between this and following their interest in the sense in which it is coincident with that of other people a chasm yawns. This chasm in the argument of the *laissez-faire* school has never been bridged. The advocates of the doctrine leap over it.[144]

It seems as though Cairnes has constructed here a straw man to be demolished by him with impunity. Advocates of the noninterference principle, such as Smith, did not contend that men's interests are fundamentally the same in the sense that what is in my interest is also in yours. Rather, they claimed that by each man pursuing his own interest, without exercising force or fraud over others, he will be led by his own selfish motives to invest his resources and energies in the production of those commodities which are most wanted by other people. The desire for profit—and a greater gain over a lesser—will provide the incentive to satisfy other people's desires. Similarly, Cairnes's second stipulation—that men know their interests as coincident with others and do, in fact, pursue those mutually compatible interests—was no part of the laissez-faire principle. Was it not considered as the virtue of the free competition system that a mutually beneficial result would occur spontaneously without men having to be motivated by beneficent intentions towards their fellows? In Smith's system, for example, it was demonstrated that men could live happily and prosperously together without it being necessary, although it might be desirable, for them to exercise the higher virtues. All that was required was that men pursue their own commercial interests without exercising compulsion over their compatriots.

Leaving such reservations aside, let us return to Cairnes's argument. What he was really striking out against was the Smithian notion of a harmony of interests, the notion that by pursuing one's own interest one will act in a way that will be beneficial to the whole society. Cairnes argued that while laissez-faire had been steadily progressing for half a century, there had resulted no substantial mitigation of the disparity of incomes, that class legislation had been pursued by the three classes of society, and that the abolition of the Corn Laws had not secured the elimination of poverty. In short, laissez-faire had not proved itself to be the panacea for society's ills. There is no guarantee that society will spontaneously organize itself in a manner most beneficial to the common good. "In other words, *laissez-faire* falls to the ground as a scientific doctrine."[145]

However, to overthrow the scientific authority of the nonintervention principle was not to enshrine the opposite principle of paternalistic, state control. Cairnes was suspicious of such overweaning authority, and he argued that while laissez-faire was discredited as a scientific principle, it was an incomparably safer practical rule for statesmen than its adversary. It should not be enshrined as an absolutist dogma; exceptions must be permitted, and it must not stand in the way of salutary proposals for social and industrial remediation.

What Cairnes wanted from laissez-faire was something more than Smith, for example, claimed for it. Smith had simply contended that the unfettered market system would maximize production. Cairnes and his fellow economists of the third or fourth generation wanted the economic system to affect a "just" distribution, and for this reason they found laissez-faire defective. Political economy as a science, Cairnes said in attempting to salvage its reputation, is simply concerned with wealth—discovering the natural laws of its production, analyzing economic phenomena that are found together, and determining cause-and-effect relationships—and it does not aim at any practical end. Thus, he endorses the Mill-Senior position of the 1830s. As a science it stands absolutely neutral between competing social systems; it can simply analyze the probable results of certain economic causes and the effects of various methods of organizing industrial production and distribution. He does not deny, however, that the "knowledge which it gives may . . . be employed to recommend some and discredit"[146] other social systems. But it is neutral in the sense that it can not pronounce judgment on the worthiness or desirableness of the ends aimed at by such systems.

In practical politics, other considerations must be introduced to provide the objectives to be sought. Economic science can merely tell us what the probable effects of various measures will be. It can provide data toward a sound opinion, but that is all. Political, moral, educational, and

aesthetic considerations must provide the teleology, the ends to be aimed
at by the legislator, and such objectives can outweigh the purely economic
solutions. "Economic science has no more connection with our present
industrial system than the science of mechanics has with our present system of railways,"[147] Cairnes declared, echoing the early position of J. S.
Mill. Economic science has a supremely important function because ignorance of the likely results of governmental action can bring forth "calamitous
blows from nature." Curiously enough, Cairnes ends his assault upon the
assumed connection between laissez-faire and political economy with a
particularly caustic attack upon socialism. "Thus economic ignorance,"
he declared, "when it has conceived, brings forth socialism, and socialism
breeds despotism, and despotism, when it is finished, issues in war, misery,
and ruin."[148]

Without intending to caricature Cairnes's position, it appears that what
he was saying was that while economics *qua* science can tell you that war,
misery, and ruin will be the effect of a socialistic organization of society,
it can not tell you whether such results are good or bad, desirable or undesirable. But he did have a valid point against some of the more extreme
advocates of laissez-faire. Political economy as a science may indicate that
the effects of unfettered, free competition will be a maximization of production, but it can not tell you that such a result is morally right or that
it should be pursued in practice by the statesman. Some moral principle—
be it natural rights or the greatest good of the greatest number or whatever—would be necessary in order to make such a value judgment. To the
extent that Smith and Bentham confused normative and positive considerations, the art and science of political economy, such a point was well
taken.

Henry Sidgwick made some of the same points as Cairnes had against
the identification of political economy with the political system of laissez-
faire. He did not, however, share Cairnes's animus against socialism. Writing
in the last two decades of the nineteenth century, he apparently felt that
while sociological prediction was by no means a refined art, he was, nevertheless, resigned to the spread of socialism and governmental interference.
The expanding scope of intervention in the economy, which had been
apparent for the two decades preceding his writings, appeared to him to
be the wave of the future.[149] Far from sharing J. S. Mill's enthusiasm for
such an occurrence, he worried about the deleterious effects on production from a socialistic distribution and a public ownership of the means

of production. "I object to socialism," wrote Sidgwick, "not because it would divide the produce of industry badly, but because it would have so much less to divide."[150] Thus, his opposition to socialism is not based, he says, on a standard of absolute justice but rather on a utilitarian or "economic" consideration, that is, a cost-benefit analysis.

On the same grounds, he is opposed to the reification of the laissez-faire principle. Rather, each act of governmental intervention must be judged on its merits, on the utility standard, judging the extent to which it furthers or inhibits general happiness or "social utility." Sidgwick was concerned about the same problem that had bothered Mill, which was the absence of a motivation equivalent to individual self-interest by which a socialistic system could be made to produce as prodigiously as the free-enterprise system. He worried about the extent to which governmental intervention in behalf of the poor, for the purpose of achieving greater equality of distribution, would undercut the motive toward self-help and industry which propelled the private-property system. Taking the Millian approach, he was amenable to small-scale socialistic experiments, to a gradual expansion of the government's role in the economy, to government nationalization of oligopolistic industries, and to protectionist legislation. Concerning the latter, he went further than Mill in granting the protectionists' argument that in some cases such legislation can actually benefit the protecting nation and the world. This, of course, was a complete reversal of the Classical free-trade position. However, he did not advocate protectionism in practice because he thought that by granting it in legitimate cases, there would be an irresistible public demand to do likewise in illegitimate cases.

On the question of laissez-faire, Sidgwick argued that a confusion had resulted from the fact that the assumption by political economists of free competition as the hypothetical model for their investigations had been taken for the conclusion aimed at by such reasoning. In general, he conceded, English political economists have been advocates of nonintervention as a vehicle for the production of wealth but with no claim that such will lead to the most equitable distribution of wealth. They have usually held the view that any intervention by government would impair production more than it would increase the utility of the produce by a better distribution. Sidgwick grants that laissez-faire contains a large amount of truth in that self-interest is a potent motivation. Nevertheless, there are many cases in which its optimistic conclusions do not obtain. Natural

liberty fails to affect the general good in the following circumstances:
(1) when wealth is not maximized because other ways of employing time
are valued more highly by individuals than engaging in production; (2)
when one challenges the assumption that utilities valued highly by the
rich are useful to the community in proportion to their market value;
(3) when a waste of social resources occurs, for example when two railroads are built right beside each other; (4) when bequests are made and
there is no guarantee that the money will be used for the most socially
useful purpose; (5) when the individual can not receive adequate remuneration for the benefit he gives to society, for example, lighthouse keepers,
conservationists, discoverers of scientific truths; (6) when there is a
shortage of skilled laborers as a result of the expense of education; then
the government can profitably provide such education even though it
could not be remuneratively undertaken by private agencies; (7) when
there is a loss of productivity to the community as a result of low wages
to workers; it is then in the public interest to pay them more, even if it
is not in the interest of particular employers to do so; (8) when monopoly
exists and there is a divergence between public and private interests; (9)
when combinations are necessary for some social purpose, since they can
be destructive if not regulated by government; (10) when the fluctuations
of supply and demand lead to unemployment or half-employment; and
(11) when waste results from advertising or the imperfect matching of
supply to an unknown demand.

Thus, Sidgwick concluded that even if the assumption were granted
that the individual is the best judge of his own interest, the "scientific"
ideal of economics—free competition—cannot be taken as the practical
ideal of the art of political economy.[151] Wherever free enterprise fails,
governmental intervention is a possible remedy, but a Utilitarian, cost-
benefit analysis must be run, because such interference has its drawbacks
and disadvantages. However, as moral and political progress advances,
the disadvantages of interference will be mitigated. Sidgwick resolves this
discussion by supplanting Mill's general rule of laissez-faire with a general
rule more hospitable to governmental intervention.

> To sum up: the general presumption derived from abstract
> economic reasoning is not in favour of leaving industry altogether
> to private enterprise, in any community that can usefully be taken
> as an ideal for the guidance of practical statesmanship; but is on

the contrary in favour of supplementing and controlling such
enterprise in various ways by the collective action of the community.[152]

And so, Sidgwick did not hesitate to draw the conclusion from Mill's arguments displaying the exceptions to laissez-faire, conclusions from which Mill
shrank in the end. Sidgwick declared that laissez-faire should be abandoned
as the general rule and that where government activity can meet the Utilitarian, cost-benefit standard, there should be no taint or presumption against
intervention. Thus, Sidgwick completed the work of Mill, Senior, and
Cairnes of separating political economy from any identification with a
particular social or economic system.

The utility principle, in Sidgwick's hands, finally fulfilled its inherent
potentialities, which were evident as far back as Bentham. The laissez-
faire principle was, finally, overthrown. It had originally gained its plausi-
bility from the natural-rights moral position, and it survived for a while
in uneasy cohabitation with the principle of utility. When social considerations which were excluded on a natural rights foundation—such as achieving greater equality by other than market means or realizing some standard
of distributive justice—became of great importance, the utility standard
could accommodate these claims only by jettisoning its connection with
the laissez-faire principle. There was nothing in the utility principle itself
to oppose the moral claims of the socialists, provided only that these
schemes for social improvement could be achieved by the proposed
means and without burdensome costs overriding the benefits.

Thus, Sidgwick concluded that the extent of paternalistic legislation
should be decided on empirical grounds and on other than economic
(wealth) considerations; and he questioned the premise of laissez-faire
that the individual is the best judge of his own interests. Where this
maxim does not hold, the government may legitimately intervene. The
ethical standard which he preferred the statesman to apply in deciding
between individualism and socialism was the utilitarian one of greatest
happiness, so far as that depends on the production and distribution of
material goods.[153] However, he acknowledged that other ethical standards
could be employed to decide the question.

Sidgwick argued that in the case of distribution there is a *prima facie*
ground for interference by government based on the great inequalities
of income to which the individual organization of property leads. He
cites Bentham's contention that when an individual's wealth increases,

his happiness increases but not in the same proportion. His conclusion was that the greater the equality of distribution throughout society, the greater will be the satisfaction of society from the wealth it possesses. But such would be true only if production were not unduly curtailed and population did not increase. It was precisely these considerations which kept Sidgwick from enthusiastically embracing redistributive schemes. However, if socialism could be demonstrated experimentally to have solved the problem of hampering production, there would be no Utilitarian, or economic, objections to its enactment.

Sidgwick contended, then, that there are both *a posteriori*, economic arguments against laissez-faire as providing the most economical production of wealth (the eleven cases recounted above) and also legitimate moral arguments against the laissez-faire system's tendency to distribute its products in a grossly unequal, even unjust fashion. He had personal, utilitarian reservations against a too zealous government effort toward relieving the latter because he worried about the cost in terms of diminished production. His general position is summed up rather neatly in the following passage from an essay entitled "Economic Socialism":

> If, however, we can find a mode of intervention which will reduce inequality of distribution without materially diminishing motives to self-help, this kind of intervention is not, I conceive essentially opposed to the tradition even of orthodox political economy—according to the English standard of orthodoxy. . . .[154]

While one can concur with his assessment of the English political economists' willingness to accept governmental intervention if it was shown to be not injurious to production in the case of the Utilitarian economists (which includes the Classical School economists after Bentham), it would be false as applied to Smith to the extent that he was a consistent advocate of the "nature philosophy." Thus, it would be false of Smith to a very large extent but not completely, for as Sidgwick wrote, Smith was no dogmatic theorist of natural rights.[155]

CONCLUSION

We have seen in this period the fruition of the movement, originated by Senior and Mill and carried to completion by Sidgwick, to separate

the science of political economy from the art of government and to disassociate the science from any connection with a particular economic and
social system—namely, laissez-faire. This development was prompted by
a general scholarly desire to make economics into a respected academic
discipline, a science with an identifiable and separable domain with a
method proper to it and with all extraneous moral and political considerations expunged. This was definitely an advance in scientific precision,
for it recognized, where Smith and Bentham had not, the separation of
normative considerations from pure economics. And it dramatized the
effect of such value determinations upon the question of the proper scope
of governmental intervention in the economy. This bifurcation was also
prompted by a desire on the part of these economists to disassociate themselves and the science from any connection with an absolutist doctrine of
laissez-faire.

As Sidgwick pointed out and as Mill demonstrated in his own enthusiasm for socialism, they were bombarded with socialistic arguments which
condemned the distribution effected by the free market as inequitable,
challenged the private ownership of land as usurpation, and denied the
capitalists' claim to profit and a share of the workers' products. They
largely conceded the "distributive justice" complaint to the socialists
and acknowledged that if production would not be cataclysmically dis-
rupted and if population would not multiply egregiously, then they
would have no objection to a government-managed or -owned economy
along socialistic lines.

Mill was the central figure of this era: it was he who first drew (along
with Senior) the art-science distinction and the production-distribution
distinction, and he was the first English orthodox political economist to
answer the challenge of the socialists and acknowledge their case as being
not, *a priori*, in opposition to the teachings of political economy. The
utility principle finally came, under Mill's guidance, to supplant all vestiges
of the laissez-faire principle as grounded on the moral system of natural
rights. And it was Mill's disciple Sidgwick who finally overthrew, on
utilitarian grounds, the noninterference principle as even a general rule
or inductively derived, instrumental guide to decide the question of the
proper scope of governmental intervention in the economy.

Another link in the Smithian-Benthamite edifice was shattered by
Mill and his disciples. The moral assumption, a residue of natural law
moral theory upon which Classical economics had relied in its earlier
days—that the individual is the best judge of his own interests—was dis-

credited. And the harmony-of-interests corollary, that individuals by pursuing their own interests will automatically benefit society, was explicitly repudiated by Mill. Operating in the same direction was Mill's reformulation of the principle of utility which made of it an elitist tool, presuming that some men know better than others what constitutes happiness. The sovereignty of the individual was no longer an article of faith among political economists, and the state was the immediate beneficiary. No longer was all government action intuitively suspect; now, each intervention could be judged on its own merits without any *a priori* principle loading the dice against it.

Pure economics remained in this period pretty much where Ricardo had left it. There were no dramatic changes in what had come to be termed the "science" of political economy, that is, the theories of value, rent, wages, and profit. Thus, the abandonment of the nonintervention principle must be traced primarily to other causes. A revolution in moral theory which had begun earlier with Bentham—from natural rights to utility—was finally driven to its conclusion. Now it became evident that the principle of utility bore no inexorable connection to the laissez-faire doctrine. Since the principle of utility bears no *necessary* connection with either free-market or socialist political theory, the direction in which the principle developed in the hands of Mill and his followers can be attributed in no small part to the growing anti-individualistic agitation of the times. Increasingly virulent opposition of both a socialistic and a reactionary bent contributed substantially to the defensiveness of the political economists and to their ultimate abandonment of laissez-faire. Thus, the most radical changes in the perception by political economists of this period of the proper role of government in the economy came as a result of moral and political upheavals and not from alterations in pure economic theory.

NOTES

1. For a detailed analysis of the anti-Smithian attitude of Mill and Senior to state education, see: E. G. West, "Private Versus Public Education, A Classical Economic Dispute," *The Journal of Political Economy,* Oct. 1964, 72.

2. For a treatment of this topic, consult: Francis Hurst, ed., *Free Trade and Other Fundamental Doctrines of the Manchester School* (New York: Augustus M. Kelley, 1968); William Gampp, *The Manchester School*

of Economics (Oxford: Oxford University Press, 1960); H. Scott Gordon, "The Ideology of Laissez-Faire," in A. W. Coats, ed., *The Classical Economists and Economic Policy* (London: Methuen, 1971); B. Kemp, "Reflections on the Repeal of the Corn Laws," *Victorian Studies,* March 1962, 5.

3. See: Marc Blaug, "The Classical Economists and the Factory Act— A Re-examination," *Quarterly Journal of Economics,* May 1958, 72; and Howard Marvel, "Factory Regulation: A Reinterpretation of Early English Experience," *The Journal of Law and Economics,* Oct. 1977, 20, pp. 379-402. Blaug illuminates Torrens' and McCulloch's support of the Ten Hour Bill and Senior's earlier approval of Althrop's Bill of 1833 limiting child labor. The classical economists did not take a leading position in arguing for such legislation, but they went along with such efforts, usually after the fact. Marvel argues that Althrop's Bill was backed by one group of textile manufacturers in an effort to use the state to penalize their competitors.

4. Of particular note would be the *Quarterly Review* which kept up a constant barrage of opposition to liberal causes; e.g., they favored the dominance of the old landed aristocracy, an unreformed Parliament, religious discrimination, poor laws, factory legislation, public works, large debts, corn laws. See: Frank Fetter, "The Economic Articles in the *Quarterly Review* and Their Authors," *Journal of Political Economy,* Feb. 1958, 66, pp. 47-64, and April 1958, 66, pp. 154-70.

5. See: William Grampp, "Classical Economics and its Moral Critics," *History of Political Economy,* Fall 1973, 5(2), pp. 359-74.

6. Nassau Senior, *Introductory Lecture, 1826,* as quoted in Marian Bowley, *Nassau Senior and Classical Economics* (London: George Allen and Unwin, 1937), p. 43.

7. Nassau Wm. Senior, *An Outline of the Science of Political Economy,* 6th ed. (1st ed. 1836; rpt. New York: Farrar and Rinehart, 1939), p. 2.

8. Ibid.

9. Ibid., p. 3.

10. Ibid.

11. Nassau Wm. Senior, *Industrial Efficiency and Social Economy,* ed. and arranged by S. Leon Levy (New York: Henry Holt and Co., 1928), vol. 1, p. 10.

12. Ibid., p. 27.

13. Ibid., p. 29.

14. John Stuart Mill, "Of the Definition of Political Economy; and on the Method of Investigation Proper to it," in *Essays on Some Unsettled Questions of Political Economy,* 2nd ed. (1st ed. 1836; rpt. London: Longman, Green, Reader and Dyer, 1874), p. 124.

15. Ibid., p. 133.
16. Ibid., p. 137.
17. Ibid., p. 138.
18. Ibid., p. 140.
19. Ibid., p. 143.
20. Henry Sidgwick, *The Principles of Political Economy*, 3rd ed. (1st ed. 1883; rpt. New York: Kraus Reprint Co., 1969), p. 8.
21. Ibid., p. 23.
22. Ibid., quote from Cairnes's *Lectures on the Character and Logical Method of Political Economy*, p. 28.
23. Ibid., p. 8.
24. For the definitive study of Senior, see: Marian Bowley, *Nassau Senior and Classical Economics*.
25. Nassau Senior, *Outline of the Science of Political Economy*, p. 49.
26. Ibid., p. 46.
27. Ibid., p. 102.
28. Ibid., p. 98.
29. Nassau Senior, *Industrial Efficiency*, from an Oxford Lecture of 1847-48, p. 302.
30. Ibid., p. 303.
31. Ibid., p. 287.
32. Ibid.
33. Ibid., p. 286.
34. Ibid., p. 303.
35. Ibid., p. 307.
36. For a comprehensive treatment of the Classical economists' attitudes towards the Irish question, see: R. D. C. Black, *Economic Thought and the Irish Question, 1817-1870* (Cambridge: Cambridge University Press, 1960).
37. Senior, *Industrial Efficiency*, pp. 312-313.
38. Ibid., p. 313.
39. Ibid., p. 316.
40. Ibid., p. 292.
41. Ibid., p. 293.
42. For an account of these influences on Mill, see: R. B. Ekelund, Jr., and E. S. Olsen, "Comte, Mill, and Cairnes: The Positivist-Empiricist Interlude in Late Classical Economics," *Journal of Economic Issues*, Sept. 1973, 7(3), pp. 383-416; Shirley R. Letwin, *The Pursuit of Certainty* (Cambridge: Cambridge University Press, 1965).
43. See: Francis E. Mineka, *The Earlier Letters of John Stuart Mill, 1812-1848, Collected Works*, vol. 12 (Toronto: University of Toronto Press, 1963). In a letter to the St. Simonian, Gustave d'Eichthal, of 8

Oct. 1829, Mill criticizes Comte and the St. Simonians for wanting to put in power the producers, those very individuals who in England he considered to be the most bigotted and narrow (p. 37). He agrees with them that the lower orders must become subject to the higher, but he has difficulty seeing how such a *pouvoir spirituel* could be organized (#28, 7 Nov. 1829). In a subsequent letter (#30, 6 March 1830) he rescinds all but his organizational objections, yet still contending that only a piecemeal approach could be successful in England.

44. John Stuart Mill, *Autobiography* (1873; rpt. New York: The Library of Liberal Arts, The Bobbs-Merrill Co., 1957), p. 107.

45. Ibid., p. 123.

46. J. S. Mill, *Considerations on Representative Government* (1861; rpt. Chicago: Henry Regnery Co., 1962).

47. In his letters to Carlyle particularly, he spoke of the narrowness of his early Utilitarian compatriots and of his own most dramatic departure from them. See: Mineka, *Letters,* vol. 12, #61, 22 Oct. 1832, p. 128.

48. J. S. Mill, "Bentham," *Fortnightly Review,* 1838, in *The Six Humanistic Essays of John Stuart Mill,* ed. Albert Wm. Levi (New York: Washington Square Press, 1963), p. 46.

49. J. S. Mill, "Utilitarianism," in *The Utilitarians* (Garden City, N.Y.: Doubleday and Co., 1961), p. 408.

50. Ibid., pp. 439-440.

51. Ibid., p. 468.

52. Ibid., p. 418.

53. Ibid.

54. Ibid.

55. J. S. Mill, *The Spirit of the Age* (Chicago: University of Chicago Press, 1942). Shirley Letwin goes a bit farther than I care to in interpreting Mill as an elitist (e.g., *Certainty,* p. 306) when she interprets his purpose, even in *On Liberty,* as being contrary to Bentham's. In order to secure ultimate perfection, she contends, he desired liberty to insure the leadership of those who could advance the march of progress, i.e., the intellectuals.

56. J. S. Mill, *Autobiography,* pp. 151-152.

57. See particularly: Mineka, *Earlier Letters,* vol. 13, #432, 6 June 1844, to Comte; #426, 3 April 1844, to Comte; and #442, 8 Nov. 1844, to Chapman. For a detailed analysis of Mill's motives in writing the principles, consult: N. B. de Marchi, "The Success of Mill's Principles," *History of Political Economy,* Summer 1974, 6(2), pp. 119-57. On his methodology, see: J. K. Whitaker, "John Stuart Mill's Methodology,"

Journal of Political Economy, October 1975, 83(5), pp. 1033-49.

58. J. S. Mill, *Principles of Political Economy,* 7th ed. (1st ed. 1848; rpt. from 1909 ed; New York: Augustus M. Kelly, 1969), p. 21.

59. Ibid., Bk. 2, Ch. 16, pp. 428-429.

60. Ibid., p. 430.

61. Ibid., p. 9.

62. J. S. Mill, *Autobiography,* pp. 159-160, also discussed in *Principles,* p. 21, and Bk. 2, Ch. 1, pp. 199-200.

63. J. S. Mill, *Principles,* p. 199.

64. Ibid., p. 200.

65. Ibid., Bk. 1, Ch. 2, p. 32.

66. Mineka, *The Later Letters,* 1849 to 1873, #1569, 26 June 1870, to Charles Eliot Norton, p. 1740.

67. Mill, *Principles,* Bk. 1, Ch. 2, p. 57.

68. Ibid., Bk. 1, Ch. 5, p. 79.

69. For an analysis of this principle and the disparate views taken of it by economists, see: J. H. Thompson, "Mill's Fourth Fundamental Proposition: A Paradox Revisited," *History of Political Economy,* Summer 1975, 7(2), pp. 174-92.

70. Mill, *Principles,* p. 81.

71. Ibid., see p. 86n, and bricklayer-velvet maker example, pp. 81-82.

72. Ibid., p. 89.

73. Ibid., Bk. 1, Ch. 6.

74. Ibid., p. 99.

75. Ibid., p. 115.

76. Ibid., Bk. 1, Ch. 9, p. 143.

77. Ibid., p. 144.

78. Ibid., Bk. 1, Ch. 13, p. 191.

79. Mill was surprised at the reception of the first edition on this issue; he interpreted his remarks on socialism to have been much more favorable than they had been construed by critics. In writing to the socialist Louis Blanc he promised that the second edition would be more explicitly favorable to socialism. Mineka, *Later Letters,* Vol. 14, April 1849, #12, p. 24.

80. J. S. Mill, *Autobiography,* p. 148. The extent to which Mill could be considered a socialist is discussed by Donald Lumis (who discounts the claim): see his "J. S. Mill on Alternative Economic Systems," *American Journal of Economics and Sociology,* Jan. 1971, 30(1), pp. 85-104.

81. In fact, Mill was quite enthusiastic over the 1848 revolution in France, as evidenced by his letters of the period. Mineka, *Earlier Letters,*

vol. 13, #523, 29 Feb., 1848; #524, 7 March 1848; #526, May 1848.
Mill often expressed his desire for a cleansing revolution in England;
e.g., #501, 13 April 1847, p. 713, to John Austin:

> In England . . . I often think that a violent revolution is very
> much needed in order to give the general shake-up to the
> torpid mind of the nation which the French Revolution
> gave to Continental Europe.

And from the same period, in a letter to John Jay on the topic of his
socialist sympathies, he says that while he disagrees with socialists on
completely dispensing with private property, he agrees with them on
many important points. He ends by describing them as the greatest element of improvement (#532, Nov. 1848, p. 741).

82. Mill, *Autobiography*, p. 150.
83. Ibid., pp. 148-149.
84. Mill, *Principles*, Bk. 2, Ch. 1, p. 208.
85. Ibid.
86. Ibid., p. 209.
87. Ibid., p. 210.
88. Ibid., p. 216.
89. Ibid., p. 217.
90. J. S. Mill, "Thornton on Labour and its Claims," from *Fort-nightly Review*, 1869; rpt. in *Essays on Economics and Society, Collected Works*, ed. J. M. Robson, vol. 5 (Toronto: University of Toronto Press, 1967), pp. 680-700.
91. On the doctrine of the wages fund, see: Scott Gordon, "The Wage-Fund Controversy: The Second Round," *History of Political Economy*, Spring 1973, 5(1), pp. 14-35; W. Breit, "Some Neglected Early Critics of the Wages-Fund Doctrine," *Southwestern Social Science Quarterly*, June 1967, 48(1), p. 54-60; R. B. Ekelund, "A Short-Run Classical Model of Capital and Wages: Mill's Recantation of the Wages Fund," *Oxford Economic Papers*, March 1976, 28(1), pp. 66-85; S. Hollander, "The Role of Fixed Technological Coefficients in the Evolution of the Wages-Fund Controversy," *Oxford Economic Papers*, Nov. 1968, 20(3), pp. 320-41; D. G. Phillips, "The Wages Fund in Historical Context," *Journal of Economic Issues*, Dec. 1967, 1(4), pp. 321-34.
92. Despite his recantation Mill did not wholeheartedly endorse all trade union activities. He appealed to unionists to not make demands that would jeopardize the interests of less skilled, unorganized labor and he condemned the restrictive, monopolistic rules of some unions. How-ever, the tone of the piece on Thornton is much more hospitable towards

LIBRARY RATE

TO:

INTERLIBRARY LOAN DEPARTMENT
DUQUESNE UNIVERSITY
LIBRARY
PITTSBURGH, PENNSYLVANIA   15282

RETURN POSTAGE GUARANTEED-ADDRESS CORRECTION REQUESTED

MAY BE OPENED FOR POSTAL INSPECTION IF NECESSARY

_____ PARCEL POST   _____ EXPRESS COLLECT

_____ PREINSURED   _____ EXPRESS PREPAID

$ _____ VALUE

unionism than his much earlier effort of 1845, "The Claims of Labour" (Mill, *Essays on Economics and Society,* pp. 363-90), in which he sought to discredit the philanthropic notion that the poor could be permanently improved by raiding the wealthy classes. Then, he placed greater emphasis upon the eventual recognition of the Malthusian population principle by the poor themselves and the realization that their improvement depended upon themselves. The means of such remediation cited were: voluntary population control, education, removal of government restrictions against joint-stock companies of laborers. Trade unionism was not seen as a vehicle of improvement. For further treatment of this topic, see: Pedro Schwartz, *The New Political Economy of J. S. Mill* (Durham, N.C.: Duke University Press, 1968); and R. Ekelund and R. Tollison, "The New Political Economy of J. S. Mill: The Means to Social Justice," *Canadian Journal of Economics,* May 1976, 9(2), pp. 213-31.

93. J. S. Mill, "Chapters on Socialism," *Fortnightly Review, Jan.-June 1879,* New Series 25, Old Series 31, pp. 217-237, pp. 373-382, pp. 513-530.

94. Ibid., p. 233.

95. Ibid., p. 220.

96. Ibid., p. 222.

97. Ibid., p. 382.

98. J. S. Mill, *Principles,* Bk. 2, Ch. 2, p. 218.

99. Ibid., p. 221.

100. Ibid., p. 233.

101. Ibid.

102. Ibid., pp. 233-234.

103. Ibid., p. 235.

104. Ibid., Bk. 2, Ch. 11.

105. Ibid., p. 362.

106. One of the maddening aspects of Mill is the fact that for almost all his positions on social issues contrary statements can be found in his own writings. For example, on this issue of a right to relief he condemns such a right under the present system (always, of course, looking towards an eventual socialistic state where both production and distribution would be taken over by the state). See: A letter from the same period in *Later Letters,* vol. 14, #24, 22 Jan. 1850, to Edward Herford, p. 44.

107. Mill, *Principles,* Bk. 2, Ch. 13.

108. Ibid., Bk. 2, Ch. 15.

109. Ibid., Bk. 3, Ch. 1, p. 436.

110. Ibid., Bk. 3, Ch. 14.

111. Ibid., Bk. 3, Ch. 17, p. 582.

112. Ibid., Bk. 4, Ch. 3, pp. 724-725.
113. Ibid., p. 791.
114. Ibid., Bk. 4, Ch. 6, p. 749.
115. Ibid., Bk. 4, Ch. 8, p. 792.
116. Ibid., Bk. 5, Ch. 11, p. 578.
117. Ibid., Bk. 5, Ch. 1, p. 800.
118. Ibid.
119. Ibid., Bk. 5, Ch. 11, p. 943.
120. Ibid.
121. Ibid.
122. Ibid., p. 950.
123. John E. Cairnes, "Bastiat," in *Fortnightly Review,* Oct. 1870; rpt. in *Essays in Political Economy* (New York: Augustus M. Kelley, 1965), pp. 312-44.
124. Mill, *Later Letters,* vol. 17, #1598, 15 Sept. 1870, to J. E. Cairnes, p. 1764. For an earlier aspersion upon laissez-faire, see: *Earlier Letters,* vol. 12, #72, 11-12 April 1833, to Thomas Carlyle. Here, Mill expresses the conviction that after its negative work is accomplished, it will soon expire (p. 152).
125. Mill, *Principles,* p. 978.
126. Ibid., p. 954.
127. Ibid., p. 977.
128. Mill, *Autobiography,* pp. 188-189.
129. Mill, *Principles,* p. 99.
130. Ibid., Bk. 2, Ch. 2, p. 219.
131. Ibid., p. 365, and Bk. 5, Ch. 11.
132. Ibid., Bk. 2, Ch. 3.
133. J. S. Mill, "On Liberty," in *The Utilitarians.*
134. J. S. Mill, *Principles,* Bk. 5, Ch. 2.
135. Ibid., Bk. 5, Ch. 9.
136. Ibid., Bk. 1, Ch. 9, and Bk. 5, Ch. 11.
137. Ibid., Bk. 5, Ch. 11.
138. Ibid.
139. Ibid.
140. Ibid.
141. Mill, *Later Letters,* vol. 16, #929, 4 April 1866, to John Campbell, p. 1155.
142. J. E. Cairnes, "Political Economy and Laissez-Faire," An Introductory Lecture delivered at University College, Nov. 1870, in *Essays on Political Economy* (London: Macmillan and Co., 1873), pp. 232-264.
143. Ibid., p. 244.

144. Ibid., p. 246.
145. Ibid., p. 251.
146. Ibid., p. 256.
147. Ibid., p. 257.
148. Ibid., p. 264.
149. Henry Sidgwick, "Political Prophecy and Sociology," *National Review,* December 1894, in H. Sidgwick, *Miscellaneous Essays and Addresses* (London: Macmillan and Co., 1904), pp. 216-234; also: "Economic Socialism," *Contemporary Review,* Nov. 1886, pp. 200-215; "The Economic Lessons of Socialism," *The Economic Journal,* Sept. 1895, pp. 235-248; "The Scope and Method of Economic Science," an address delivered to the Economic Science and Statistics Section of the British Association in 1885, pp. 170-200.
150. Henry Sidgwick, *The Principles of Political Economy,* 3rd ed. (1st ed. 1883; rpt. New York: Kraus Reprint Co., 1969), p. 516.
151. Ibid., Bk. 3, Ch. 2, p. 414.
152. Ibid., p. 417.
153. Ibid., p. 499.
154. Henry Sidgwick, "Economic Socialism," p. 205.
155. Henry Sidgwick, "The Scope and Method of Economic Science," p. 173.

Chapter 4

The Marginalist Revolution and Neo-Classicism: Jevons, Wicksteed, and Marshall

Economic science in the last quarter of the nineteenth century underwent a revolution of shattering proportions.[1] The fundamental principles upon which Classical economics had been founded were reexamined, pronounced defective, and discarded.[2] Primary among these was the labor or cost-of-production theory of value which was overturned completely by Jevons with his final-utility theory of value. Other important components of the Classical framework were also shattered, such as the Malthusian population theory, the projection of a future stationary state, the Ricardian "iron law" of wages, and the macroeconomic approach to determining the shares distributed to each class in the production process. What is truly remarkable, however, is that despite these dramatic alterations in economic theory per se, little direct effect can be seen from this quarter on the question of the government's role in the economy. There was no essential break between J. S. Mill and Jevons in their approaches to this question, for both were Utilitarians, and hence, they both advocated an ad hoc evaluation of each particular proposal for governmental intervention.[3]

The movement away from laissez-faire, which was examined in the last chapter, came in this later period to completion. It was no longer necessary to disavow any connection between economics as a science and the doctrine of laissez-faire, because the latter had become something of a dead issue thanks to the combined influences of Mill, Sidgwick, and Cairnes and their attack upon it, the rise of the trade union movement, and the demands of practical men for an increased regulatory role for the state in order to enable it to deal with the pressing social questions of the day. Thus, for Jevons, Wicksteed, and Marshall it was no longer necessary to proffer even the formalistic, and largely empty, obeisance to laissez-faire that Mill uttered before examining the particular cases for governmental intervention. Their approach, then, was entirely empirical, proceeding with no preconceived preference for either state action or unfettered, free competition. The two were placed more nearly upon an equal footing. In this development, there was no decided break with their immediate predecessors; rather, they completed the disassociation with laissez-faire that the last generation had begun.

Similarly, on the question of the proper scope and method of political economy, or economics as it was now called, the economists of this later period completed the normative-positive distinction which had been first formulated by Senior and Mill. While it is true that Wicksteed conceived of economics as inseparably linked to ethics, politics, and sociology and subject to the same principle, that of differential satisfaction, the general movement in this period was definitely in the opposite direction, that is, to sever the connection between economics and other disciplines.

The influence of Utilitarianism, both as an ethical postulate and as an instrumental, pragmatic approach to policy questions, is particularly evident in this period. The Benthamite pleasure-pain calculus is the foundation upon which Jevons constructed his "final utility" theory of value. The Utilitarian political injunction for maximizing general happiness is the standard which was employed by Jevons and Marshall in evaluating all particular proposals for state intervention in the economy. Bentham's observation that increments of money have a progressively decreasing significance for men once they have an abundance, had a powerful influence over the marginal-utility theorists. It served to substantiate their own contention that greater equality would increase the general happiness by distributing increments of money to those individuals, the poor, to whom it would represent a greater marginal utility.

This final quarter of the nineteenth century and the first decade of the twentieth century represented, then, in one sense a rather revolutionary break with the past, for the marginal-utility theory of value shook the Classical system to its very foundation, and yet on the moral and political level these revolutionaries in economic theory merely continued the work of their immediate predecessors. They put the finishing touches on the Utilitarian victory over the natural rights-inspired doctrine of laissez-faire.

In the political realm, too, this era marked the downfall of laissez-

faire beginning with the massive infusion of social welfare legislation
promulgated by Disraeli in the late 1870s. Under his leadership the
Employer and Workmen Act of 1875 placed masters and workers on an
equal basis with respect to breach of contract, legalized strikes, and
legally protected trade unions; the Public Health Act of 1875 increased
state supervision in every locality; the Artisans' Dwellings Act of 1875
provided for slum clearance; and the Factory Act of 1878 consolidated
and extended the purview of earlier factory legislation. Other pieces of
legislation which followed greatly extended governmental paternalism
and interferences in the contractual freedom of individuals. By the
Worker's Compensation Acts (1897, 1900), workers were forbidden to
contract voluntarily out of the earlier Truck Acts, forbidding payment
in goods; by the Landlord and Tenant Acts with respect to Ireland
(1870, 1881), the rights of the two parties were now to be governed by
custom and law, not the market, and both parties gradually lost the right
to set the terms of their contracts; by the various Arbitration Acts (1867-
1896) government boards of inquiry were established to arbitrate industrial
disputes upon the appeal of both parties; and by the Employer's Liability
Act (1880) and the Workmen's Compensation Act (1897) employers were
compelled by law to insure their workers against industrial accidents.

The collectivist, interventionist temper of the age is particularly
evidenced by the mushrooming legislative interference which altered the
relationship between parent and child. No longer could parents determine
the terms of employment of their children and by successive acts, first
attempting to obligate parents to provide elementary education for their
offspring at their own expense (1870), then dictating compulsory, universal education (1880), and finally providing free elementary education
(1891), they lost the right to determine the extent of education for their
progeny. Whether one empathizes with these developments or condemns
them as rights violations is, of course, entirely irrelevant. What is important,
despite one's sentiments, is that the line of march was indisputably in the
direction of collectivism and away from the conviction that the individual
is the best judge of his own interests.

In foreign policy, also, the old liberal abhorrence of colonialism and
foreign adventures succumbed to an internationalist, imperialist recru-
descence. With the breakup of the Liberal party after the defeat of Gladstone's Home Rule Bill for Ireland in 1886, both Joseph Chamberlain's
Liberal-Unionists and successive conservative governments in the late

1880s and 1890s championed the cause of empire and even that of protectionism.

Contributing in no small measure to this interventionist tidal wave was
the growth of an organized working-class political movement. Both on
the intellectual front, with the founding of the Fabian Society in 1884,
and on the pragmatic level with the birth of the Independent Labour
party in 1893, the socialist movement was on the march. The passage
of the Third Reform Bill, which granted manhood suffrage and tripled
the registers, would revolutionize the party structure of England and
augment the growth of the Labour party to the extent that by 1910 a
Liberal government was dependent upon Labourites for its majority. In
fact, the Liberal party of the early years of the century under David
Lloyd George was liberal, in the old sense, in name only. Free trade
stood alone as a residue from the earlier era of antistatist liberalism. When
it came to social issues, the party was a convert to interventionism.

THE SCOPE AND METHOD OF ECONOMIC SCIENCE

While it is true that during this era there was substantial agreement
concerning the scope of economic science, delimiting it from other sciences and practical arts, there was, nevertheless, considerable and heated
debate over the method proper to the science. Jevons propounded an
extreme, mathematical approach when he sought, in his highly original
work, *The Theory of Political Economy,* first published in 1871, to express all economic relationships in the "fluctional calculus." Others
would not go quite this far, preferring to assimilate the new mathematical
tools to a more traditional method of deductive reasoning combined with
historical examples and analyses. This latter method was employed by
Alfred Marshall. Philip Wicksteed, a disciple of Jevons in respect to the
final utility theory of value, preferred to take a different methodological
approach. He expressed Jevons' complex formulas in ordinary language,
thus rendering them more accessible to those less schooled in advanced
mathematics.

Jevons' approach to economics differed quite radically from that of
the English economists who preceded him, and he took his methodological
inspiration from other sources, particularly certain French, German, and
Italian mathematical economists. On the question of the scope of "econ-

omics" (as he denominated the science in his preface to the second edition of his *Theory*, in 1879, discarding the older term "political economy"),
however, he was in essential agreement with his contemporaries, arguing
that subdivision was needed in economics. Abstract theory must be distinguished from the empirical element and from any detailed treatment
of the practical matters of finance and administration. All practical
branches of economics, what Mill and Senior had called the "art" of
political economy, must be pervaded by general principles developed by
the abstract science. These general principles are simply the unfolding
of the "mechanics of self-interest and utility,"[4] for Jevons was a direct
and avowed disciple of Benthamite Utilitarianism.[5] Thus, economics,
for him, was not one science but many—commercial statics, the mathematical theory of economics, systematic and descriptive economics,
economic sociology, and fiscal sciences—all held together by a common
set of general principles based upon a Benthamite calculus of pleasures
and pains.[6]

Economics, in Jevons' account, must be a mathematical science, and
the issue is simply whether one wants to avow this openly or merely
attempt to phrase necessarily quantitative relationships in rough, approximate, and inaccurate verbal formulations as he charged Smith and his
followers with having done. Economics is necessarily mathematical, he
contended, because even in Smith it treats quantities, equalities, and
proportions. To the extent that this mathematical underpinning was not
made explicit and the practitioners of the science were not aware of its
mathematical nature themselves, Jevons charged them with having been
bad mathematicians, with the result that their "work must fall."[7]

Jevons repeatedly analogizes economics to the science of statical
mechanics, writing in one indicative passage that "the laws of exchange
are found to resemble the laws of equilibrium of a lever as determined
by the principle of virtual velocities."[8] Just as the theory of statics rests
upon the equality of indefinitely small amounts of energy, so the nature
of wealth and value is explained by a consideration of indefinitely small
amounts of pleasure and pain.

This science of economics, which expresses in mathematical terms the
"mechanics of utility and self-interest," is properly a deductive science.
It is subject to verification by the purely empirical science of statistics,
and can also be made an exact science by this same development of statistics.[9] Jevons, then, did not reject the designation by Mill of the deduc-

tive method as the one applicable to economics. He did not accept the approach of Cliffe Leslie, a British critic of Classical economists who adopted the methodology of the German Historical School (which analyzed historical and institutional developments in the economy and largely eschewed theoretical analysis), but rather endorsed the traditional British analytical method. From certain facts of observation, which are in the somewhat peculiar case of economics either known to us immediately by intuition or ready-made from other sciences, the economist proceeds to frame a hypothesis from which he then reasons deductively to the expected results. These results are subsequently examined in light of the facts in question; coincidence confirms the reasoning, while conflict obliges him to seek disturbing causes or abandon his original hypothesis. In this respect, Jevons agreed with the Ricardo-Mill abstract, deductive method, although in other respects, as we shall see, he dissented rather heatedly from their economic theories.

Philip Wicksteed followed Jevons in the utility theory of value, the revolutionary consequences of which are more evident in the disciples' treatment than in the master's, because Wicksteed, being a man of the church, preoccupied with ethical considerations, applied the theory not only to economic relations but to the entire choice mechanism by which men lead their lives. He offered an intriguing explanation of the scope of economics and displayed an acute insight into the economic organization of society, the equal of which had not been seen, perhaps, since Adam Smith. The nature of the economic relationship is precisely this— that if I make some good or perform some activity not because I want it, but because someone else does and that other person will give me what I want or put me in command of the means by which I can get what I want, then I am furthering his purposes as a means of furthering my own. The "mechanism of articulation of the whole complex of such economic relations is the proper scope of economic investigation."[10] The economic organization of society is the spontaneously generated machinery for combining in mutual helpfulness persons whose ends are diverse.[11] "The economic organism," Wicksteed wrote, ". . . of an industrial society represents the instrumentality whereby every man, by doing what he can for some of his fellows, gets what he wants from others."[12]

It was Wicksteed's contention that the theory of differential satisfaction (or marginal utility) was equally applicable to our pursuit of the virtues as it was to our actions in exchanging one good for another or in distributing our resources among the members of our family so that each additional increment goes where it satisfies the most urgent desire. This principle of differential satisfaction harmonizes economics with man's wider ethical, social, and sociological concerns:

> . . . for if we really understand and accept the principle of differential satisfaction we shall realise . . . that Aristotle's system of ethics and our reconstructed system of economics are twin applications of one identical principle or law, and that our conduct in business is but a phase or part of our conduct in life, both being determined by our sense, such as it is, of differential significance and their changing weights as the integrals of which they are the differences expand or contract.[13]

Thus, Wicksteed denied that there were any exclusively economic laws, but he did not conclude that there was no distinct and distinguishable province of economic science. The proper field of economic study was precisely this relationship into which men spontaneously entered when they discovered that they could best serve their own ends by approaching them indirectly by satisfying the needs of their fellows. Mill's efforts to construct psychological laws for a hypothetical "economic man" were misspent, for there are no exclusively economic motives or psychological laws. Economics studies a type of relation, not a type of motive, "and the psychological law that dominates economics dominates life."[14] In a certain sense, Wicksteed reverted to a more Smithian conception of the interrelationship between economics and ethical, social, and political considerations, subsuming all of these under the same principle of differential satisfaction. However, he did separate the purely economic relations from these other fields, constantly emphasizing that the economic mechanism affects no ethical ends other than those pursued by individuals.

Alfred Marshall continued the line of development of the normative-positive distinction first formulated by Senior and the young Mill when he wrote that the laws of economics are statements of tendencies expressed in the indicative mood, not ethical precepts in the imperative. The solution to practical social and political problems depends upon more than purely economic considerations, although such economic factors are important to the resolution of such questions. The economist, however, must not operate in ignorance of ethical forces because altruistic motives, when they operate in a regular fashion, must be taken into account as well as the selfish motives. He agrees with Wicksteed in condemning efforts to construct an abstract science of economics based upon the idealized, singular motivation of an exclusively economic man, but for different reasons. Marshall did not subject all human action to a single principle, as Wicksteed had, but he did think it necessary for economists to take into account altruistic behavior when it operated in the economic realm.[15]

Marshall considered economics to be a science of wealth and also a part of the social sciences dealing with man's efforts to satisfy his wants, to the extent that those efforts and wants are capable of being measured in terms of wealth or its symbol, money.[16] Economics studies the causes by which prices that measure wants are brought into equilibrium with prices that measure efforts. Marshall did not go nearly as far as Senior in limiting the economist to the realm of pure economic theory. Economics, Marshall thought, had a legitimate function to perform for the statesman. It could help the legislator formulate both the ends of policy and the method of attaining such objectives. Rather than distinguishing between economics as an art and a science, he preferred to consider it all as science, but with a pure and an applied aspect.

Marshall was attracted to the study of economics from a desire to mitigate the social condition of the poor, so that he conceived of the science as engaged actively in social issues to an extent that Senior would have rejected. Solving the social problems of the day was the principal objective of the science of economics according to Marshall.[17] In addition to the pure economic questions that the economist confronts—for example, the causes that affect the consumption, production, distribution and exchange of wealth; the organization of industry and trade; foreign trade; the effects of economic freedom; the relationship between wealth and well-being; and so on—the English economist at the turn of the century could be legitimately concerned with social problems that do not lie wholly within the range of his science. Marshall did not eschew the political authority that emanated from being an economist, as Senior had wanted economists to do (although Senior himself was not averse to using his authority as an economist to serve on government commissions, the Poor Law Commission included).

A Marshallian economist, then, could *qua* scientist give advice to the statesman on the following kinds of practical issues: (1) how the state might increase the good and diminish the evil effects of economic freedom; (2) how a more equal distribution of wealth could be realized once such an objective was acknowledged as desirable and the extent to which this purpose should justify changes in the institution of private property, when such changes are likely to diminish aggregate wealth; (3) how far cooperative management is desirable; (4) how far the state should allow individuals and corporations to manage their own affairs and how far monopolies ought to be regulated; and (5) how far the prevailing methods of employing wealth are justifiable.[18] While Marshall did not claim that economics could offer definitive solutions to these social issues, without regard for ethical or political considerations, he did contend that economics *qua* science could offer suggestions towards policy recommendations. In this approach he was much closer to the Mill of the *Principles of Political Economy* than to the Mill of the *Essays* or to Senior. For Smith, the primary allurement of the study of economics was to discover the means by which the wealth of a nation as a whole could be maximized; for Marshall, the purpose has shifted from that of enlarging aggregate wealth to that of (*a*) alleviating poverty, discovering whether it is necessary, as Aristotle thought, to have an underclass in order to provide a high standard of living for the few, and (*b*) effecting a more just, more equal distribution of the national product. Marshall was not indifferent to the Smithian end of maximizing national wealth, but he wanted to achieve the eradication of poverty, provided that such an end would not unduly curtail production.

Marshall acknowledged the benefits of the mathematical approach taken by Jevons but only as a supplement to economic reasoning. He was by no means an enthusiast of the mathematical method to the exclusion of all others.[19] He was a man of eclectic bent, more of a synthesizer of current trends which he considered to be too extreme and one-sided. On the question of value, for example, he managed to combine both Ricardian cost-of-production theory and Jevonian marginal-utility analysis. Similarly, on the question of the method proper to economics, he granted a place to both induction and deduction, to an analytical method and a historical method. In this respect, he is often reminiscent of Smith, reasoning from historical examples and supplementing general principles with examples from the industrial history of various countries. He was influenced by Spencer and his organic approach to society and by the German Hegelians with their emphasis upon society as more than the sum of its individual parts. He combined these elements with the English economic tradition of Ricardo and Mill.

Jevons and Marshall disagreed on another aspect of the nature of economic science, that is, the degree of certainty of which the science is capable. Jevons thought that economics could become as exact as the physical sciences, because even the so-called "exact" sciences depend upon hypotheses that differ from what actually exists. If the method of differential calculus were applied to the motives of wealth and if statistics were fully developed, then there would be nothing to prevent economics from attaining the same degree of precision as the natural sciences. Taking this cue from Bentham's attempt to quantify the moral sciences, he argued that there is no insurmountable hurdle to the quantification of economics. For this purpose it is not necessary to measure directly the feelings of men:

> I hesitate to say that men will ever have the means of measuring directly the feelings of the human heart. A unit of pleasure or of pain is difficult even to conceive; but it is the amount of these feelings which is continually prompting us to buying and selling, borrowing and lending, labouring and resting, producing and consuming; and it is from the quantitative effects of the feelings that we must estimate their comparative amounts.[20]

The physical sciences have the same problems. Gravity can not be measured directly but only through its effects on the motion of a pendulum. "The will is our pendulum," Jevons argued, "and its oscillations are minutely registered in the price lists of the markets."[21]

Now Marshall dissented from this view, contending instead Malthus' point that while economics is the most exact of the social sciences—because the chief business motives can be measured—indirectly, but they can be measured—it can not compare with the precision of the physical sciences.[22] There is a limitation to the measurement of motives by money from the facts that individuals vary in the amount of pleasure they receive from the same sum of money, that individuals with equal incomes would not suffer the same pain from an equal loss, and that the same sum of money represents a greater satisfaction to a poor than a rich man. This source of error is inherent, Marshall thought, in economics, and its effects can be blunted only by dealing with large numbers of individuals and averages. In this way, individual peculiarities can be offset. But economics can never attain the accuracy of the physical sciences.

What has become evident from this discussion of scope and method is that there was in this period considerable disagreement over the extent

to which economics ought to be or can be a mathematical science, with
Jevons arguing that it can only be a mathematical science and Marshall
suggesting that the quantities which are measured in economics are not
a totally accurate indication of men's affections or motives, and, therefore, the mathematical approach is not *the* exclusively proper one in
economics. On the question of the scope of economics there was considerable agreement among the three in isolating pure economics from
moral and political considerations, but there was less reluctance to use
the authority of economics to make policy objectives than was evident
in Senior and Sidgwick. In the latter respect, then, they were more the
heirs of Smith than of Senior.

JEVONS AND THE THEORY OF FINAL UTILITY

The conclusion to which I am ever more clearly coming is that
the only hope of attaining a true system of economics is to fling
aside, once and for ever, the mazy and preposterous assumptions
of the Ricardian school. . . .
    When at length a true system of economics comes to be estab-
lished, it will be seen that that able but wrong-headed man, David
Ricardo, shunted the car of economic science on a wrong line—
and a line, however, on which it was further urged towards confusion by his equally able and wrong-headed admirer, John Stuart
Mill.[23]

With that ringing declaration, Jevons pronounced his independence
from the "false Ricardian doctrines"—the cost of production-labor theory
of value, the wages-fund doctrine, the subsistence theory of wages, and
the class analysis of distribution—and so began his development of the
final- (or marginal-) utility theory of value. This theory was destined to
place economics on a new foundation. Now consumption and men's
desires were to play the key role in determining the ratios of exchange,
rather than the supply factors comprising the Ricardian cost of production. This movement was begun in England by Jevons, although as we
shall subsequently discover, he did not wholly divest his theory from the
contamination of the older theory as his initial, revolutionary declaration
might lead one to expect.
    The general thrust of his doctrine, however, was in the direction of

overturning the misplaced prominence given to production in the work
of J. S. Mill, which seemed at times to have men existing for the sake of
commodities and not the other way around, and replacing the problematic
"objective" standard of value of the Classics with a "subjective" theory
which placed the principal emphasis upon men's judgments of utility.
Jevons credited Malthus and Senior, among English economists, with
having had a clearer view of a true theory of value than the Ricardians
and also the French economists for realizing the importance of utility
in the determination of value.

Jevons was by no means deprecatory toward all English influences,
although he did express much admiration for French and German mathematical economists, for he took as the starting point of his work the psychology and moral system developed by Ricardo's intellectual mentor,
Jeremy Bentham.[24] The Utilitarian theory of morals, the doctrine that
the effect upon human happiness is the sole criterion of what is right
and wrong, is explicitly subscribed to by Jevons. He based his value theory
upon a calculus of pleasures and pains, declaring the object of economics
to be the maximization of happiness by purchasing pleasure at the least
cost of pain.[25] From Bentham, he adopted the notion that the magnitudes
of various pleasures and pains can be estimated by two qualities, their
intensity and duration. And he grants to critics of Utilitarianism the argument that we can not form a conception of a unit of pleasure or pain
because the numerical expression of quantities of feelings seems to be
impossible. For the purposes of economics, however, such a direct calibration of the feelings is unnecessary because each human mind acts as the
final judge of its own feelings, and we can know the results of that process
by the actions taken in the marketplace by that individual, that is, the
resulting action determines which possible choice represents the greatest
pleasure for that individual. "But we only employ units of measurement
in other things to facilitate the comparison of quantities; and if we can
compare the quantities directly, we do not need the units,"[26] Jevons
concluded.

Furthermore, his theory does not attempt to measure total pleasure
or utility but rather, small additions of pleasure brought about by additions of small units of a commodity at the point where an individual is
near indifference between the possession of that final unit or the continued possession of its money price. The complaints of the critics of the
Utilitarian calculus are nullified in addition, Jevons claimed, by the fact

that he never attempts to compare amounts of feeling in one mind with that in another. There are no means by which such a comparison could be accomplished, and the economist need not do this. The weighing of motives is an internal process. Each individual appears to the rest as but a portion of the external world. Thus, Jevons denied the possibility of making interpersonal comparisons of utility, a denial which taken at face value would seem to prohibit any governmental interference with the marketplace to effect the greatest happiness of the greatest number. The reason would be that no one could know what constituted a given magnitude of happiness for any other human being. But Jevons did not consistently develop this position, for he did make assumptions about social utility, and he did advocate certain acts of state intervention in the economy which would seem to be prohibited on his own theoretical assumptions.

Jevons' method was individualistic in the sense that his theory of value and his entire economic system were based upon an investigation of the conditions of single minds and their choice processes. Practically, however, it was in aggregates of individuals that the laws of supply and demand could be detected, because disturbing causes would cancel themselves out in the average. Aggregates of individuals, operating in perfect markets, were the subject matter of his economics.

Jevons' contention was that value depends entirely on utility[27] and not on the quantity of labor. "We have only to trace out carefully," he wrote, "the natural laws of the variation of utility, as depending upon the quantity of commodity in our possession, in order to arrive at a satisfactory theory of exchange, of which the ordinary laws of supply and demand are a necessary consequence."[28] Economics, then, is fundamentally an investigation of utility—that abstract quality by which an object, action, or service satisfies our purposes and becomes entitled to be ranked as a commodity—and must take as its starting point an examination of human wants and desires. One must begin with a theory of consumption. It will be recalled from the last chapter that Mill was criticized at length for placing production ahead of distribution and exchange, implying what we considered to be an inverted causal relationship. Jevons concurred with our objection. "We labour to produce with the sole object of consuming," he contended, with logic on his side of the controversy, "and the kinds and amounts of goods produced must be determined with regard to what we want to consume."[29]

Utility is not an inherent quality of a thing, and although it is a quality of a thing, it would be better described as a circumstance of a thing arising from its relation to man's requirements and desires.[30] All portions of the same commodity which an individual possesses do not have the same utility for him, for after a certain quantity of a given commodity—say, water—was secured by a man, additional increments of water are a matter of comparative indifference. Utility is not proportional to quantity possessed, as Bentham observed in discussing the inequality of wealth, for the same commodity varies in utility depending on how much we already have. Jevons distinguished between total utility, which is the "utility" considered and rejected by Smith as the origin and measure of value, and the utility attaching to any portion of our stock. Each increment of commodity for an individual possesses less utility than the ones which went before because this final portion satisfies a less urgent want. Thus, the water-diamond paradox of the Classical School is dissolved. While water has great total utility, it is so abundant that the final increments of it— which is all that one is concerned about in the normal market situation— are worth little or nothing to people already in possession of all they need. Should a drought occur, people would be willing to pay for water, because the final units they would be getting would fulfill a more urgent need. Diamonds have a high value because they are scarce and men desire them.

The final degree of utility—the utility of the next increment about to be consumed—is, Jevons contended, the function upon which the theory of economics turns. He proposed as a general law the principle that the final degree of utility varies with the quantity of commodity one possesses and ultimately decreases as the quantity increases.[31] Thus, if a commodity is capable of two different uses, for example, if a portion of corn could be used for immediate consumption or to feed cows for future consumption, or if a sum of money in an exchange system could be used to buy some of commodity A or commodity B, then one would be advised to apportion the distribution so that the final degrees of utility of the two uses are equal. A perfectly wise being would consume commodities according to this rule, and he would, in consequence, consume them with a maximum production of utility.[32]

Now, this final-utility theory of value leads directly to the theory of exchange in the marketplace. A market is defined as that state of affairs which results when there is free competition, the ratio of exchange is known to all, each individual exchanges out of regard for his own private interests, and no conspiracies exist.

> A market then, is theoretically perfect only when all traders
> have perfect knowledge of the conditions of supply and
> demand, and the consequent ratio of exchange; and in such
> a market . . . there can be only one ratio of exchange of one
> uniform commodity at any given time.[33]

Jevons considered this perfect market to be real and not simply a model
or construct. Brokers and stock exchanges approximate this theoretical
conception of the perfect market. It is interesting to note in passing one
of the few references to practical politics in this treatise, the remark that
it would be legitimate for the government to compel the publication of
market statistics, because a knowledge of the actual state of supply and
demand is essential to the smooth functioning of the market and the real
good of the community.[34]

> The welfare of millions, both of consumers and producers,
> depends upon an accurate knowledge of the stocks of cotton
> and corn; and it would, therefore, be no unwarrantable inter-
> ference with the liberty of the subject to require any informa-
> tion as to the stocks in hand.[35]

In fact, this was simply an extension of Bentham's contention that the
state had a positive function to perform in disseminating industrial methods
and useful technical knowledge.

Returning to the theory of exchange, Jevons deduces the Law of Indifference, that is, that in the same market, at any one time, there can not
be two prices for any one commodity. When two commodities are identical,
they will be bought with perfect indifference by purchasers. This is the
familiar Classical position which was partially questioned by J. S. Mill.
Jevons argued that in an open market, where increments of different commodities are to be exchanged (e.g., in a stock market) the following principle will govern the exchange—the degree of utility of the commodities exchanged will be in inverse proportion to the magnitude of the increments
exchanged. Thus, if I exchange two apples for one pear, the pear has
twice the final degree of utility for me as an apple.

The general result of exchange is that all commodities—for each individual—
sink to the same level of utility in respect to the last portions consumed. An
equality of utility is produced by the mechanism of exchange so that for
each individual the consumption of different commodities is brought into

equilibrium. Between individuals no such equality will tend to be produced. However, in the next passage Jevons does in fact argue that something like this equality of utility does take place between individuals or at least that what the free market does affect is the maximization of utility. It will be helpful to cite the passage, as Jevons' argument points to a problem that troubled Marshall and Wicksteed also, and it drove them to different conclusions from the free-market one which Jevons seems to endorse:

> But so far as is consistent with the inequality of wealth in every community, all commodities are distributed by exchange so as to produce the maximum of benefit. Every person whose wish for a certain thing exceeds his wish for other things, acquires what he wants provided he can make a sufficient sacrifice in other respects. No one is ever required to give what he more desires for what he less desires, so that perfect freedom of exchange must be to the advantage of all.[36]

Now, it appears that Jevons was not unduly troubled by his opening condition concerning the inequality of wealth. It is not clear from the passage exactly what effect inequality would have on the maximization of utility, but apparently he did not consider this disturbing factor to be a sufficient reason to question the power of the free market to allocate goods in such a way that utility would be the greatest. What he says is that since no one will buy a thing unless he expects some advantage from the purchase, perfect freedom of exchange will, consequently, tend to the maximization of utility.[37] Now, what troubled Marshall and Wicksteed about this assumption was that the rich man, to whom each increment of money has less utility than it does to the poor man, could afford to outbid in money terms the poor man for goods that would have a greater significance to the poor man. Wicksteed thought such ethical concerns fell outside of economics, but Marshall did not, and he used this argument to question the validity of the assumption that the free market produced the maximum satisfaction. Perhaps Jevons did not pursue either of these routes because he considered the price of a commodity to be the only test we can have of the final degree of utility to the purchaser, and he did not deem it necessary or even possible to look beyond this to the means at the disposal of individual consumers. His laws dealt with aggregates of individuals in which differences, such as the inequality of wealth, would be canceled out.

At this point, Jevons, once again, went to considerable length to reiterate the incompatibility of his theory of value with the labor and cost-of-production theories of value.[38] Labor once spent has no influence on the future value of any article. In commerce, commodities are judged anew at every moment, with the value of a thing depending upon someone's estimation of its future utility to them. "Industry is essentially prospective," Jevons lectured his predecessors, "not retrospective; and seldom does the result of any undertaking exactly coincide with the first intentions of its promoters."[39] But from here on, Jevons seems to have smuggled the old cost-of-production element back into the theory of value. What he says is that while labor is never the cause of value, as Smith and Ricardo had contended, in a large proportion of cases it is the determining circumstance. His point seems to be that the final degree of utility of any commodity depends upon the quantity of its supply in the market, and that quantity can be increased by expending more labor on its production. He advances the following causal chain: labor affects supply; supply affects the degree of utility; and the degree of utility governs value or the ratio of exchange. In Jevons' own formulation:

> Cost of production determines supply;
> Supply determines final degree of utility;
> Final degree of utility determines value.[40]

While this does not amount to a complete reversion to a Ricardian cost of production theory, its simplistic formulation is misleading, because in the next breath Jevons declares that labor's (or cost of production's) value is determined by the value of the produce and not the produce by that of labor. The difficulty lies in the fact that Jevons did not entirely dispense with the search for an "objective" standard of value. It appears as though he made supply into the causal factor in determining final degree of utility. But is this not to neglect his own previous arguments about final utility depending upon individual estimations of pleasure and pain? It is to assert, instead, that supply is the key factor in determining value, not demand or the estimations of pleasure made by individuals. What he apparently fails to realize, at this stage of the argument, is that goods only have utility because men desire them. And that the final utility of hoola hoops and hence, the price people are willing to pay, is determined by the intensity with which people desire them, not exclusively by their supply.[41]

The confusion is evident when Jevons offers the conclusion that his theory of value leads to the well-known (Ricardian) law that value in the long run is proportional to cost of production. He offers the following diagram:

QUANTITIES OF COMMODITIES EXCHANGED VARY

DIRECTLY	INVERSELY AS THEIR
as the quantities	(1) value
produced by the	(2) prices
same labor	(3) costs of production
	(4) final degree of utility.[42]

But then he goes on to state that it is not cost of production which rules value but supply and demand and that cost of production is only one circumstance which governs supply and indirectly influences value. What we have here is a rather uneasy attempt to take into account supply factors in the determination of value, an attempt which appears to be at odds with Jevons' earlier ringing pronouncement that utility alone determines value. Such a confusion of two distinct theories is not surprising, considering that Jevons developed his final-utility theory without being aware of any other theories of precisely this kind. He made great strides, but was, quite often, not himself completely aware of the implications of his own theory.

One area in which he was well aware of the revolutionary impact of his theory of value was in the treatment of distribution. He overturned completely the Classical approach, which attempted to define the shares going to the three factors of production, land, labor, and capital, based upon different laws in each case. Wages, according to Jevons, are the shares of produce which the principle of value and the laws of supply and demand enable the laborer to secure; and wages are determined by the same laws of supply and demand as are rents and profits.[43] Each laborer, landowner, and capitalist is regarded as bringing into the common art of production one part of the component elements, with each man bargaining for the best share of the produce which the conditions of the market will allow him to obtain. All are subject to the law of indifference, that is, that in the same free market only one price will exist for the same kind of article. The laborer has a monopoly of labor of each specific kind, just as the landowner or capitalist has a monopoly of land or capital, if property is considered as another name for monopoly. When different individuals own property of the same kind, monopoly is limited by competition. Consequently, no owner of a factor of production can get more for it than others are willing to accept. The result of all this is that wages, profits, and rents are governed by the same laws; rent is determined by the excess of produce in the most profitable employment, and the same is true for wages and interest. The Ricardians claimed that rent was not the cause but the result of high value, and Jevons added that the same must be true of wages, that is, that they are the effect, not the cause of the value of the produce.[44]

Jevons accepted certain of the Ricardian teachings—such as the rent doctrine (but in somewhat modified form) and the notion of fixed and circulating capital—while rejecting others, such as the wages-fund doctrine and the equation which dictated that profits and wages varied inversely. The wages-fund theory he considered to be a mere truism, providing no means of determining how much capital would at any time be forthcoming for the maintenance of labor. Rather he argued that the amount of capital appropriated for the payment of wages in any trade will depend on the amount of the anticipated profits, and that the competition to obtain properly skilled workmen will tend to secure to them their legitimate share of the produce.[45] Ricardo's contention that wages tend to a subsistence level and his theoretical assumption of a uniformity of labor were rejected entirely by Jevons.

One important consequence of Jevons' consumption orientation was to dispense with the distinction made by J. S. Mill and other Classical writers between productive and unproductive labor. "The sole end of all industry is to satisfy our wants,"[46] Jevons instructed, and therefore, all labor is productive which satisfies wants by producing utilities. And all goods in the hands of consumers are capital.

Certain essential consequences of the Classical economics were accepted by Jevons, particularly the Say-Mill contention that a general glut or overproduction throughout the economy was not possible. It is perfectly conceivable that overproduction might occur in particular trades. If

people are satiated with silk products, for example, they will not buy
them at a ratio of exchange sufficient to compensate the labor expended
on their production, but such a state of affairs is not possible throughout
an entire nation, on the Classical grounds that supply creates its own demand. The Neo-Classical economists generally accepted this view, while
Hobson dissented, arguing in a fashion similar to Malthus that undercon-
sumption could become a general condition throughout industry. Another
Classical position which Jevons endorsed was the Smithian projection that
as society progresses and capital accumulates, the rate of profit (or interest)
tends to fall. He argued that unless there were constant progress in the
state of the arts of industry, the rate of profit would eventually sink
towards zero. His reasons for such a scenario are different from Smith's
(the competition of accumulated capital) or Ricardo's (the fall of profits
due to a rise of wages to pay for increases in agricultural products). His
argument appears to be that in a highly developed country capital will
be abundant while the demand for it will not be urgent, and hence, profits
will be low. He disagrees with the Ricardians, however, when he contends
that the returns of capital and labor are independent of each other.

One interesting result of Jevons' final-utility theory is that, just as the
consumer pays only the value of the final unit of a commodity, getting
the rest of the units at the same lower value, the borrower of capital pays
a rate of interest based upon the advantage secured by the last increment
of capital, and he gets all previous units at the same rate even though
their advantage would be much greater. Thus, the capitalists can never
exact from the laborers or borrowers the whole advantage which their
capital confers.

> The general result of the tendency to uniformity of interest
> is that employers of capital always get it at the lowest pre-
> vailing rate; they always borrow the capital which is least
> necessary to others, and either the labourers themselves, or
> the public generally as consumers, gather all the excess of
> advantage.[47]

This chain of reasoning tends, one would anticipate, to put profits or
interest on capital (and Jevons, like the Classicals, tends to use the terms
interchangeably) on a securer foundation than did the Classical position,
for Jevons emphasized the benefit to the workers and the consumers

resulting from the accumulation of capital, which the Classical economists had recognized and also the fact that the borrowers pay only a fraction of the capital's true value to the capitalist for the benefit of its use, which the Classical writers had not realized.

The problem for economics, as Jevons conceived it, was to discover the best mode of employing the labor of a country so as to maximize the utility of the produce.

> Given a certain population, with various needs and powers
> of production, in possession of certain lands and other
> sources of material; required, the mode of employing their
> labour which will maximize the utility of the produce.[48]

Adam Smith's purpose for economics was to increase the total product for the nation; Jevons' objective was to maximize the *utility* of the produce. This latter end could be achieved by individuals apportioning their consumption in such a way that the final utilities of the last increment of each good consumed would be equal; by workers going to those trades in which their product would be greatest and their wages will, therefore, be the highest; and capital seeking the employment in which it can contribute the greatest net addition of output.

Jevons' approach to economics overthrew the Classical attempt to define the shares distributed to each factor of production which had led to a class analysis of industry and society. He also divested Ricardo's rent doctrine of some of its potentially anti-free-market import, by claiming, instead, that rent was determined on the same basis as the shares of the other factors of production. Perhaps the most significant consequence of the final-utility theory of value was that it placed the pricing system for all factors of production on the same footing, not subject to different laws, as in the Classical system.

Jevons' political theory and his attitude toward governmental intervention were quite scrupulously kept distinct from his abstract economic theory as expounded in the *Theory of Political Economy.* In a later volume published in 1882, entitled *The State in Relation to Labour,* he gave a detailed treatment of his practical, political views and their relationship to his economic doctrines. Each science, he thought, was a composite of natural laws which resolve themselves into probabilities, with the legislator called upon to consult all the sciences whose probabilities bear on the end to be sought. In matters of trade, the legislator ought not decide on solely economic probabilities but must also look to other considerations, moral, sanitary, political, and so on.[49] Economics is related to legislation as science to practice, and thus, Jevons endorsed the Senior-Mill-Sidgwick distinction.

Being opposed rather vehemently to any "metaphysical" principles, a familiar Benthamite position, Jevons argued that legislation must be Baconian, that is, that legislation must proceed upon grounds of experience, invoking the experimental methods of the natural sciences.[50] He endorsed Mill's fondness for attempting social experiments on a small scale, and he advised the legislator to reason from proximate and analogous experience. The effects of legislative changes ought to be judged by "that which is not seen, as well as that which is seen," to turn Bastiat's phrase against him, for Bastiat laid down that injunction in the process of denouncing governmental meddling, while Jevons employed it for the opposite purpose.

The by now empty and formalistic obeisance is paid to the general rule of laissez-faire at the opening of *The State in Relation to Labour,* but its effect is quickly rendered nugatory. The future course of the argument undercut explicitly any such sweeping generalization. No hard-and-fast rules can be laid down *a priori;* every case must be treated on its merits with experience as the guide. In large categories of cases governmental interference, local or central, ought to be invoked.[51]

All "metaphysical" ideas and expressions were anathema to Jevons. The right to dispose freely of one's own labor should mean nothing more to the legislator than that in the majority of instances the individual will, in fact, be a better judge of his own interests than would the legislator. Yet, in those cases in which this presumption is shown by experience not to hold true, the legislator is perfectly justified in intervening.[52] Thus, in dealing with legislation pertaining to labor, for example, the statesman must distinguish between those cases where the individual is the best judge and where he ought, therefore, to be left free, from those cases in which some superior authority should intervene because the individual is not the best judge.

Liberty, for Jevons, is not an indefeasible right but rather an instrumental means toward the attainment of a given end. In social matters there are no abstract rights, absolute principles, inalterable rules, or anything of an eternal and indefeasible nature.[53] "The liberty of the subject," he declared, "is only the means towards an end; it is not itself the end; hence, when it fails to produce the desired end, it may be set aside and other means employed."[54] But what is this end, to which liberty is but a means only? It is precisely the Benthamite, Utilitarian objective of the greatest happiness of the greatest number.

> It may be fearlessly said that no social transformation would be too great to be commended and attempted if only it could be clearly shown to lead to the *greatest happiness of the community*. No schemes of Bellers, or Babeuf, or Robert Owen could be resisted if only their advocates could adduce scientific evidence of their *practicality* and *good tendency*. No laws, no customs, no rights of property, are so sacred that they may not be made away with, if it can be clearly shown that they stand in the way of the greatest happiness. *Salus populi, supreme lex.*[55]

The radical import of this declaration—more extreme in language, if not content, than anything Mill wrote, even in his most socialistic phases—was negated, as it was in Senior, by the economist's concern for sufficient evidence that a proposed change would actually secure the greatest sum of happiness before any overhaul or overthrow of the present system could be endorsed. The present social system has at least this minimal presumption in its favor—that it does exist and that it is tolerated. Hence, there is a heavy burden of proof placed upon those who advocate a restructuring of society. Despite this practical warning, Jevons' theoretical stance is the boldest we have confronted since Senior. A good accomplished, he stated, is justification enough for any governmental act, with the proviso that no countervailing evil would be equal to or outweigh its effect.[56] This is Utilitarianism in its most elemental form, unadulterated by any holdover from a natural rights presumption in favor of liberty or property, the taint of which was still apparent in the work of J. S. Mill. " . . . I conceive that the State is justified in passing any law, or even doing any single act which, without ulterior consequences, adds to the sum total of human happiness."[57] This is Utilitarianism stripped to its barest essentials and carried to its logical limit.

Jevons distinguished between the provinces of morals and legislation in a way that acknowledged a much greater cleavage between the two than any of the theorists whose works we have previously examined. Legislation deals only with outward acts, and consequently, the law has nothing to do with conscience, religion, or moral right and wrong as determined by individuals, and it knows nothing of absolute principles from which we can not diverge.[58] It is simply an aggregate of arbitrary rules, changed from century to century, different from one country to another, and founded upon experience and trial. In a way, then, Jevons has left more room for the legislator to operate upon the body politic to maximize happiness than did Mill, but he left less sanction for the legislator to sit as a judge upon the value or quality of the happiness pursued by individuals than Mill had with his mechanism of the wise man from the *Utilitarianism* essay. Jevons was also less individualistic than Mill, for he did not make a special case for absolute liberty in those provinces of one's behavior which only affected oneself. He is willing to have the legislator declare certain factory practices illegal on the grounds of their dangerousness or unhealthful tendencies, even if people have been perfectly willing to work under those conditions, and even if they are injuring only themselves. The ignorant can not protect themselves simply because they are ignorant; therefore, the government is justified in intervening on their behalf.

It is interesting to note in passing that Jevons argued, in direct opposition to Herbert Spencer, that as society progresses and the instruments and institutions of civilization multiply, the result will not be the withering away of the state's control over the economy but rather a growing complication of relations and the consequent growth of governmental regulation.[59]

Now, as Jevons gets down to specific cases, it will become apparent that he did not go radically beyond his immediate predecessors in advocating specific acts of governmental regulation, but he did continue their drift toward interventionism. Adults should, as a general rule, take care of themselves, for the practical reason that if they are but sheep under the whip of an overseer, they will become heedless of unforeseen dangers, and they will be sapped of their strength and no new leaders will emerge. There are, of course, exceptions to the rule. If a large number of people get maimed in factory accidents, then the government is justified in intervening. Individuals have not used their liberty to good purpose—the purpose that Jevons wishes them to pursue—therefore, they must lose a portion of it. In fact, Jevons argues, the factory owners in England did not pay the trifling expense for safety until it was mandated by the government. Similarly, in the case of the Factory Acts relating to child labor and the

Elementary Education Act, he contended that the very fact there had been practically no education going on before the act proved that the parents were not the best judges of their children's true interests. The state, as a result, was justified in interfering on the children's behalf.

Jevons, in addition, designated a role for the state in testing, stamping, and guaranteeing the purity of certain commodities. Individuals are not the best judges of the worth of some goods, and in those cases the government may legitimately act as their protector. The majority of transactions may safely be left free, as they are merely cases of individual preference, but in those instances in which an expert is the best judge it is an advancement of the principle of division of labor for the government to provide that expert's opinion as a public service. Such an expenditure would create utility. Government inspection does not really infringe or limit the liberty of the purchaser, argued Jevons, because nobody wishes to purchase defective merchandise. Bentham was nearer to the mark when he called a spade a spade and took the consequences. All legislative acts are an infringement of liberty, Bentham said, and it is merely a case of whether they produce a preponderance of good or not. Jevons' government inspectors do limit the freedom of the consumer (and the producer), and the real question, on Utilitarian grounds, ought to be not whether it is an infringement, but whether it is a desirable infringement.

In regard to the Factory Acts, Jevons described them as "one of the brightest achievements of legislation," for these economic regulations were not, as others were in the past, motivated by class selfishness. Future limitations on adult male labor ought to be judged by the standard of expediency. Although he did not think that the time was ripe for limitations of the hours of work of adult males, he claimed that the case for regulation of female labor was much stronger because of the dependence of future generations upon maternal care, thus providing in this latter case a legitimate province for state regulation. In his essay, "Married Women in Factories,"[60] he argued that the abuses caused by the employment of childbearing women in factories warranted the intervention of the legislator. He even went so far as to advocate the "ultimate complete exclusion of mothers of children under the age of three years from factories and workshops."[61] He explicitly dismissed the natural-liberty, freedom-of-contract arguments in this instance. All these rights or principles are merely presumptions of good. "But surely probability is rebutted or destroyed by contrary certainty."[62]

On other issues pertaining to governmental policy, a progression can be clearly deciphered in Jevons' thought over the period of the late 1860s until his death in 1882. While his theoretical stance remained unchanged—that is, his rejection of *a priori*, metaphysical principles and endorsement of social experimentation—as time went on, he saw more and more opportunities for constructive state economic activity.[63] But there is certainly a greater sympathy for governmental inactivity in such earlier works as *The Coal Question* and the "Inaugural Address as President of the Manchester Statistical Society"[64] than in any of his later efforts. In the former work he argued that Britain's prosperity depended on coal, and as that natural resource was strictly limited and would eventually be exhausted, that fact combined with increased competition from abroad would cause an end to prosperity by the close of the century. With admirable foresight, he predicted that a Conservative party would then arise to call for protectionist legislation. Jevons would have none of it. Legislative intervention could produce nothing salutary in averting the inevitable decline. The only remedies Jevons suggests were that the national debt be paid off during the present prosperity, that a general system of education be provided to upgrade the working classes, and that further restrictions on child labor be enacted. Protectionism abroad and internal interferences would exacerbate the situation and breach the "principles of industrial freedom of Adam Smith."[65]

Such encomiums to natural liberty and Adam Smith are conspicuously absent from his later reflections on policy questions. From such comparatively mild incursions upon the laissez-faire principle as his advocacy of state provision of public parks, music, gardens,[66] public libraries, museums, art galleries, and clocks,[67] his principle of utility gradually stretched to sanction governmental takeover of the telegraph industry[68] and the parcel post,[69] governmental licensing and regulation of the liquor trade,[70] governmental oversight but not ownership of the railroads,[71] and government condemnation of old housing and superintendence of the building of new houses.[72] Experience, only, can determine which industries the state ought to monopolize:

> My own strong opinion is that no abstract principle, and no absolute rule, can guide us in determining what kinds of industrial enterprises the state should undertake, and what it should not.[73]

In place of a general, *a priori* principle he offers four empirical conditions in which state management is likely to be efficient: (1) where numerous operations can only be coordinated efficiently by a single, extensive government system; (2) where the operations possess an invariable, routinized character; (3) where they are performed immediately under the public eye; (4) where there is little capital expenditure.[74] The railroads fail to meet these criteria, but the telegraph qualifies. Jevons' only regret with the state's takeover of the telegraphs in 1870 was that it was executed so poorly that it would provide ammunition for those opposed to future takeovers by the government.[75] Thus on grounds of the maximization of utility, Jevons went quite far, indeed, in undermining the principle of "be quiet."

Jevons' attitude toward trade unions was a direct result of his final-utility theory of value and its resultant theory of wages. Since no simple principle can determine the shares which go to any individual worker, each must bargain for his share, and what he gets will depend on his ability and the state of supply and demand in his particular trade. The price which an owner of labor, land, or capital can get is limited by the price at which others are willing to work, rent out their land, or loan their capital. This theory is in contrast to the wages-fund doctrine, to the Millian notion that demand for commodities forms no part of demand for labor, to the trade union doctrine that wages come out of the employers' pockets (they are actually a share of the product, not of the capitalist's property), and to the Ricardian tenet that when wages rise, profits automatically fall. Depending on the conditions of the market, the supply of the product and the demand for it, the employer may be able to pass on wage increases. High wages often accompany high profits. Thus, the putative conflict between labor and capital, a conflict bred into the Ricardian system and adopted by the trade unionists of Jevons' day, is a delusion. The real conflict, he maintained, is between the producer and the consumer, in the settling of price in the marketplace.[76]

He concluded from all this that trade unions can not bring about permanent increases of wages, that such would depend on alterations in the state of supply and demand in the market, and that to the extent they are successful in securing monopolies for themselves, they lead to great loss and injury to the community.[77] From a different theoretical underpinning, Jevons arrived at the same position in regard to trade unions as did the Classical wages-fund-doctrine advocates. The effects of strikes are difficult to judge by experience given the multiplicity of causes which affect wages. The only true system, then, is for each individual himself to "strike" for higher wages by seeking the employment at which he will get the greatest remuneration. While generally antagonistic to trade unions, Jevons did not wish to instigate any legislative prohibitions against them, for such had been tried and found fruitless in the past. As to the future, Jevons urged trade unionists to become their own capitalists and engage in cooperative ventures, a typically Millian position.[78] In his address to the trade unionists' political association delivered in 1887, he applauded trade unions for their activities to promote the welfare of their members and to shorten the hours and make more healthful the conditions of labor, but he deplored their monopolistic, restrictive attempts to raise wages artificially. Throughout his works, he expressed his sympathy for the movement to uplift the working class.

While the state ought to do nothing to prohibit labor unions, it could intervene in industrial matters in other ways. Among these were the promulgation of laws of industrial conspiracy; laws to order men to stay at their jobs when a strike was called which threatened vital industries such as coal; and laws to promote conciliation and arbitration. All legislation to regulate industry and all other industrial problems ought to be solved, Jevons concluded, by an estimation of the "total utilitarian results." Neither wholesale state interference nor blanket laissez-faire ought to be the aim of the legislator; rather he should entertain various points of view, various estimations of general happiness. Individuals may legitimately differ over their Utilitarian estimations; that is they agree to differ about means but not ends. Everyone ought to uphold the greatest happiness of the greatest number as the end.

Jevons revolutionized abstract or pure economic theory with his final-utility theory of value, but this dramatic and fundamental reorientation on the theoretical level did not carry over into a radically different theory of governmental intervention in the economy. While it is true that his theoretical challenge to the class analysis of society of the Ricardian school negated any arguments which were based upon that doctrine and which reasoned from it to a contention that rent, as an unearned income, should be confiscated, and that capitalists were the natural enemies of workers, such conclusions had never been reached by the orthodox Classical economists (with the exception of J. S. Mill) but by socialists claiming them as their authorities.

Jevons' theory of the marketplace as maximizing utility would have logically been expected to lead him to a more laissez-faire position than the Classical economists maintained, but it did not. The final utility theory is potentially a much sounder foundation for laissez-faire, because it ceases to lead to the conclusion that profit is a capitalist's extortion, it no longer views wages as kept to a subsistence level, and it dissolves the Ricardian class antagonisms. Yet in the final analysis, it was Jevons' Utilitarian moral principle which had far greater influence upon his attitude towards state intervention in the economy. This principle of greatest happiness led him to overrule individual choices in the marketplace and to advocate restrictive labor legislation even if such were not desired by the recipients of the concern. And it led him to champion certain state industries. On the art-science distinction, he maintained that other concerns than the purely economic ought to be taken into account in making policy decisions. For Jevons, this resulted in placing the probabilities drawn from the science of economics in a subservient role to the principle of maximizing general happiness. It is not clear how such a position can be reconciled with his economic doctrine that it is impossible to make interpersonal comparisons of utility, for is it not true that in order to maximize social utility, to increase general happiness, one has to assume that such interpersonal comparisons can, in fact, be made?

Jevons was more extreme than Mill in his enthronement of utility and expediency as respectively the objective and the test of legislation, and in the all but complete disavowal of laissez-faire as the regnant principle governing state intervention in the economy. When it came down to actual proposals, Jevons was, however, not quite as adventurous as Mill, and he did not display Mill's enthusiasm for socialistic ventures, although he had no preconceived hostility towards them. He was perfectly willing to adopt such measures if they proved their suitability for maximizing general happiness. While Adam Smith on several occasions, as we saw earlier, dismissed various state activities by saying that they constituted violations of the right to property, Jevons says *any* violation of property is valid so long as it can be scientifically shown to increase the general good. The contrast between the moral theories of natural rights and utility as they affected the question of the proper role of the government in the economy could not be more sharply focused than by this comparison of Jevon with Smith.

WICKSTEED AND THE CLAIM THAT THE MARKET
DOES NOT REALIZE HIGHER MORAL VALUES

Philip Wicksteed was Jevons' disciple in the final-utility theory of value, or as Wicksteed preferred to call it, the theory of marginal satisfaction. Although he was not an originator in economic doctrine as Jevons had been, he contributed interpretations of his own which helped clarify and popularize the innovations of his great mentor. To the considerable extent, then, in which Wicksteed's pure economic theories parallel those of Jevons, it would be superfluous to our purposes to engage in a detailed analysis of his treatise, *The Common Sense of Political Economy*.[79] It will be sufficient to mention briefly the few significant differences between the expositions of marginal utility given by the two men. The principal disparity lies in the fact that Wicksteed gave what has come to be termed an "ordinal" approach to individual preferences, speaking of individual preference orders, rather than the "cardinal" approach advanced by Jevons in which it was assumed that a definite quantity of pleasure could be assigned to each commodity desired by an individual. Wicksteed's approach involved looking at the preference orders of each individual consumer, in which various goods would be ranked—first, second, third, and so on—and from these individual rankings a composite, communal preference order would be arrived at in a market. Value, or price, would depend in a given market, for a certain commodity, on the extent of the supply and the marginal significance of the good to the consumers.

Wicksteed clarified some of the confusion that we observed in Jevons' conclusion that the final-utility theory of value amounts to the same thing as the cost-of-production theory in the long run. Wicksteed contended that utility is the only thing that determines value, but that in the long run those products will not continue to be produced whose marginal utility falls short of their cost of production, with cost being conceived of as opportunity cost. Instead of Jevons' rigid and inaccurate aphorism that "cost of production determines supply," Wicksteed said a product's cost will be a factor in determining whether it will be produced, because if its projected costs exceed the anticipated price of the good, it will not be produced. While none of this was really a departure from Jevons' intent, it did clarify what had become muddled in Jevons. Cost of production was unambiguously ruled out as a determining factor of price.

Wicksteed followed Jevons in the development of a differential theory
of distribution, and he was especially precise in denying any special status
to land as a factor whose share would have to be determined by a different
law from other commodities. To a man desiring to purchase land the commodity presents itself in exactly the same way as any other. If he is willing to pay the going price, then he will be able to purchase as much of
land as he would of any other good. There is not a special problem, as
the Classical economists thought, arising from the fact that land is limited
and unexpansible in quantity. He also helped develop the equilibrium
theory of exchange which was of such moment to all the Neo-Classical
economists, and he adopted Mill's version of depressions, arguing that they
were a result of speculative overconfidence, followed by failure of confidence throughout the economy, and that they were not the result of a
Malthusian general glut.

Wicksteed is important to us for two reasons. First, he offered a definition of political economy which held the seeds of a collectivist orientation within it, and second, he qualified his appreciation of the market as
a mechanism for satisfying our wants indirectly by satisfying the needs
of others with the repeated observation that the market does not guarantee
that the ends pursued by individuals will be noble or socially advantageous
or that those who receive the goods produced by industry will get them
in proportion to their efforts or the social worth of their work.

As indicated above, when Wicksteed was described as offering an
ordinal version of marginal utility, this approach takes the study of man's
psychological choice process as primary and does not, as Jevons did, look
beyond this and claim that precise quantitative measurements can be made
of pleasure. Thus, for Wicksteed the choice process is fundamental, while
for Jevons a Utilitarian attempt to quantify pleasures was taken to be the
starting point of economic theory. The logical movement of Wicksteed's
economics was, then, from a study of choice as it would be made by the
individual in administering his own resources or by a mother in allocating
the household's resources, and then proceeding to special applications of
the theory to commercial and industrial life.[80]

The proper field of economic investigation includes everything which
enters the circle of exchange, that is, the things men do for each other
in an impersonal way. These economic relations can not be permanently
separated from noneconomic relations. The term "economy" means to

Wicksteed what it meant for Aristotle: "the administration of the affairs
and resources of a household in such a manner as to avoid waste and
secure efficiency." And the term "political economy"—which Wicksteed,
unlike most of his contemporaries, still found acceptable because he saw
economics as more intimately connected with moral and political considerations than they did—he defined as "the administration in the like manner,
of the affairs and resources of a State, regarded as an extended household
or community and regulated by a central authority." The study of political
economy would, consequently, entail "a study of the principles on which
the resources of a community should be so regulated and administered
as to secure the communal ends without waste."[81] Now since worth is the
regulating principle of every act of administration and our estimations of
worth depend on our values and our ends, political economy must: (1)
either assume or inculcate certain ends as proper for the state to advance,
and (2) evaluate the ways in which the central authority can administer
state resources to the accomplishment of its ends. Wicksteed criticizes
previous works on political economy for failing to do this; they have in
large part neglected to treat the deliberate directing of communal means
to communal ends. Political economy must be predicated upon a knowledge of how men spontaneously administer their resources and enter
into relations of exchange with each other.

Wicksteed's conception of the scope and purpose of political economy,
as distinguished from economy, is Smithian in the sense that it sets a purpose for the state to fulfill and it includes a recognition of the scope of
economics as being inextricably bound up with considerations of a moral
and political nature. But it is *not* Smithian in another sense in that it
proposes to introduce ends other than Smith's singular one of maximization of production, an end that could be achieved by individual spontaneity
alone, Smith thought. Wicksteed's definition assumes that a central authority ought to operate the way a mother of a household does, apportioning goods to her children so that the marginal or final unit will go to fulfill the most urgent need, and the whole supply will be allocated in such
a way that the marginal utility to each child will be equal. Clearly, this
holds out the prospect for a much more active state than would be possible
in Smith's account of the nature of political economy. Wicksteed never
actually went as far in this direction of social apportionment of goods
as his definition would allow, but he does go part of the way. What he
does contend is that when the market, the mechanism whereby individuals
spontaneously arrange to exchange satisfactions, fails to satisfy social pur-

poses, social ends, the government is justified in intervening. Clearly, then, Wicksteed built into the very definition of political economy what might be described as a bias in favor of collective ends and communal interests, but the reverse might be said of Smith, that his conception of political economy held an inherent prejudice in favor of individual ends and individual interests. Smith was concerned only with maximizing production, and all the economists we have examined agreed that by and large the individual could best accomplish that purpose. But Wicksteed was interested in how the total product of the community was administered so that utility could be maximized. This later objective raises the whole question of redistribution and apportioning goods on other than a purely market criterion.

Now, to return to our second point, Wicksteed's reservations about the market system revolved around the realization that the market was an "ethically indifferent instrument," and consequently it would not necessarily produce ethically desirable results. This was not meant as a wholesale condemnation of the market system, for Wicksteed was an admirer of its efficiency and its limited social tendencies in that it forced men to satisfy their needs by trying to anticipate the needs of their fellows. But he was by no means an unqualified admirer of the market. By seeking my ends in serving the ends of others, there is absolutely no guarantee that those ends served will be admirable, decent, or socially desirable. The worthiness of the ends is suspect, and so is the moral worth of the means. Wicksteed, the religious enthusiast, also questioned the desirability of satisfying our ends indirectly, arguing that there was a psychic loss involved in being a monetary contributor rather than an artisan producing an entire product or a missionary. But this familiar socialistic complaint against industrial society was not his primary objection. What troubled him most was that "The economic forces, then, have no tendency whatever to direct my efforts to the most vitally important ends or the supply of the most urgent individual needs."[82] His point was that, for example, the offer of a halfpenny to a merchant by a millionaire or a pauper provides the same inducement to the merchant in both cases, despite the fact that their respective need for the good may vastly differ. The market ignores the social or human point of view—it permits the millionaire to spend fifty pounds on an extra ruby when that fifty pounds could provide a great service by purchasing 24,000 red herrings for the poor—and so it is found wanting on moral grounds.

The Smithian assumption that the market will satisfy the most urgent wants is condemned as a gross confusion. The wants that the merchant can get the greatest remuneration by supplying can not be taken to be the most urgent wants without committing a grave error. It is false to assume that because A will give more for a marginal increment of one good than B would for another, A is more urgently in need of the one than B is of the other, for such an assumption would ignore the possible disparities of incomes of the two and the social importance of the functions of the goods. When dealing with a single individual, it is perfectly legitimate to conclude that the good for the marginal unit of which A will pay more is what he wants the most, but it is illegitimate to assume that if A will pay more for a marginal increment of a good than B will for another, that A is in more urgent want of that good than B is of the other.

The importance of this point is that it represents a frontal assault upon the Smithian principle that by pursuing one's own interests one is led inevitably to pursue that course which is most beneficial to society.

> A whole school of cheerful optimism has been based upon the creed that if every man pursues his own interests in an enlightened manner we shall get the best of possible results, because it will be to his interest to apply his energies where they are *"most useful to others."*[83]

But the problem is that those others who are served are precisely those who already have most of everything. "This automatic action of the economic forces is at the service of every man exactly in inverse proportion to the urgency of his wants."[84]

What Wicksteed is objecting to, here, is the moral outcome of market activities. They do not favor the poor, because they do not give to the poor more than their services are worth, that is, more than their services have produced. He concedes that the market gives to every man what his product is worth or what his contribution to a product is worth; the problem lies in the fact that, in the case of the poor, they are not worth enough. Clearly, this is a moral judgment on Wicksteed's part, a fact which he cheerfully acknowledges, for he says continually that economics can not be separated from such moral considerations. The moral question, then, comes down to this—should those who have produced reap the equivalent of their efforts, or rather should those whose needs are greater (the "unprivileged," to use Wicksteed's quaint term) have some claim on a share of the products of others? The market does not make this latter kind of distribution, and for this reason he found it wanting. Wicksteed has a valid

point against those he terms the "economic optimists," for they over-
stepped their case when they asserted that under free competition effort
is directed to those activities which are most beneficial to society or most
necessary. All they could justifiably claim was that in an open market
goods will go to those who are willing to pay the most for them, the
assumption being that those with larger incomes have derived them from
production or the fruits of past abstinence, that is, from satisfying to a
large extent the needs of other individuals.

It was this "absolute moral and social indifference" of the market
which Wicksteed could not abide. And he concluded that the state is
justified, where practicable and not unduly harmful to production, in
channeling private ends into coherence with social ends. The enlightened
student of political economy should see that

> . . . it is our business in every instance to endeavour to yoke
> those forces, when we can, to social work, and to restrain
> them, when we can, from social devastation; . . . and no more
> to take it as axiomatic that they will work for social good, if left
> alone, than we would take it for granted that lightening will in-
> variably strike things that are better felled.[85]

But is the market really morally indifferent as Wicksteed claims? Rather,
is it not true that the market embodies another moral code, a theory of
justice which he rejects? The market objectifies the proposition that those
who produce *should* (a moral imperative) enjoy the fruits of their own
labor, and that those who do not produce, or do not produce enough to
satisfy their hypothetical "needs," should not enjoy the fruits of the
labor of others.

Wicksteed also objects to the fact that individual specializations of
capacity are acts of administration of the collective capacity, but they
are made not on any communal evaluation of worthiness but simply on
individual judgments. "Political" or communal resources are not collectively directed to communal purposes, to the *general good;* there is not
now any "comprehensive and deliberate scheme" for effecting social ends.
While individual and domestic resources are directed towards an end by
each individual, no such communal evaluation is undertaken in the realm
of political economy. The prospect of economic advantage will establish
a drift toward the supply of wants that stand higher on the collective preference scale, but this cannot be equated with a spontaneous movement
toward the general good. The rank on the collective scale of a particular

want does not correspond with the urgency of that want, precisely because an insignificant want on the part of the wealthy man will rank above
the most critical want on the part of the pauper.

> Only if we acquiesce entirely in the law "to him that hath
> shall be given," and only if we are further content to accept
> each man's purposes as worthy to be accomplished in propor-
> tion to his eagerness to accomplish them can we hold optimistic
> views of the social significance of this spontaneous tendency.[86]

Wicksteed's conclusion was that we must comprehend the economic forces
so that, where necessary, we can control them for social purposes. He preferred, however, to harness socially desirable works when possible to the
direct governance of economic forces, because individuals are effective in
superintending their own affairs, whereas government supervision of the
business of individuals requires constant vigilance. The trick, then, was
to discover how individuals can be made to use their energies for social
purposes. Economic forces must be harnessed to the "social car."

Wicksteed's suggestions for governmental intervention could be classified as mildly socialistic. Public education was desirable because it would
fit more individuals for higher-level positions, jobs on the open market
which were understocked due to the expense of higher education. As a
result of this, the socialistic, utopian dream of higher pay for manual
work might be approached even on the free market. Also, underpayment
of workers, in the sense not that they receive less than they are worth on
the open market, because such is not the case, but that they are worth
so little, can be rectified by government programs for making people
worth more.[87] A Poor Law, or a graduated income tax—a departure from
the Classical rejection of such a progressive tax, which was assented to
even by Mill—to make the rich and successful help the unfortunate poor,
Wicksteed found totally acceptable.[88] However, he was not unaware of
the possibly deleterious effects on productivity of such schemes as minimum wage legislation with the government as employer of last resort;
but he displayed considerable enthusiasm for proposals to get for workers
more than they are worth by the appropriation of communal funds or by
government programs to shift workers from work that is worth comparatively little to industries in which they would be more productive. A redistribution of wealth in either of these ways would be socially justifiable,

he claimed, because it would help those in the most deplorable conditions while actually increasing the total revenue of the community.

One perversity, or paradox, of the market from the individualistic point of view is that each person wishes that scarcity should reign in the commodity he provides and is immediately threatened by abundance in that product, while he hopes for plenty in all the goods which he consumes. When we pass to the social point of view, we see how ludicrous such a predicament appears. On this ground, Wicksteed was as willing to criticize monopolistic trade unions that tried to limit the supply of labor of their particular kind as he was to fault merchants for their narrow, individualistic, and antisocial perspective.[89] To the extent, however, that local distress to particular industries or workers is caused by conditions that are generally beneficial to society as a whole, the government, he concluded, is justified in diverting some of this social benefit to the relief of those who have been made to suffer.

> To mitigate the penalties of failure, without weakening the incitements to success, and to effect an insurance against the disaster incident to advance, without weakening the forces of advance themselves, is the problem which civilization has not yet solved.[90]

It was doubts like these—partially the traditional concern of the Classical economists that efforts at social amelioration would curtail production by limiting incentive—that kept Wicksteed from wholeheartedly embracing the socialist movement, on the fringes of which he remained throughout his life. He could not abandon the economists' caution. The market serves certain functions quite well, and Wicksteed was unwilling to dispense with its mechanism entirely. So far as the market was social, it was beneficial. It made men serve other men's wants. But this was not the final answer to the social problem.

> But the more we analyze the life of society the less can we rest upon the "economic harmonies;" and the better we understand the true function of the "market," in its widest sense, the more fully shall we realize that it never has been left to itself, and the more deeply shall we feel that it never must be. Economics must be the handmaid of sociology.[91]

Equality was one objective which the market did not spontaneously approximate or drift toward, and therefore, Wicksteed was willing to employ government taxing powers to move society in what he considered to be a morally desirable direction. With the ascendancy of democratic sentiment and governments, he felt that a more even distribution of wealth would gradually come to be viewed as a desirable end, and taxation, which diverts funds from those channels in which the individual would naturally employ them, could then be utilized as a means of redistributing wealth.[92] This was, of course, a pronounced departure from the position of the Classical economists and of Jevons. Similarly, he rejected the enthusiasm of Senior for the workhouse system of Poor Law administration, arguing that men no longer considered a subsistence level of existence provided by the state as a hindrance to energy and thrift. He endorsed public works for the benefit of the poor and old age pensions because they would not lower the wages of productive labor. Generally, then, Wicksteed favored what we have come to call "redistributive" social programs, but only those he thought could work; consequently, he disparaged minimum wage laws because the government can not decree by legislative fiat that a man will be worth more than he is; the only result would be unemployment for those not worth the minimum rate. The problem of poverty was to make workers worth more, not to rail at the employers, for they were not exploiting the workers, as Marx had thought, but were paying them exactly what they were worth on the open market.

Wicksteed's concern for alleviating the plight of the poor was as pronounced as the socialists', even if his solutions were less apocalyptic. The poor had a claim on the fortunate and the successful, and therefore, he favored a tax on the "unearned increment," the unearned income of the rich, as well as a tax on high earned incomes. He claimed that such a tax would make the rich more industrious, not less—a dubious asseveration to be sure. Land nationalization was an enthusiasm of his, but in his typically skeptical attitude toward socialistic proposals, for which he himself had a natural proclivity, he wondered, in the *Common Sense,* whether land can really be separated theoretically from other commodities.

Wicksteed was a fervent democrat. Privilege must be abolished; the democratic spirit must prevail; men must learn to rejoice in the common wealth, and to respect and take pride in communal property, for only then can men "prepare for the kingdom."[93] Social purposes—the relief of poverty, the elevation of the laborer, the redistribution of wealth, and

the subsumption of individual interests to social purposes—can only be
realized in a democratic spirit if it is to be accomplished without bitter-
ness. Revolutionary socialism was, then, implicitly disparaged. He did not,
however, wish to accomplish this quasi-socialistic "kingdom" by wholesale nationalization of all industries. It was perfectly permissible, he
thought, for the government to acquire some of the means of production,
but it should never prohibit individuals from engaging in private enterprise, for such a blanket condemnation would be to misperceive the function of industry. Every man who has made a tool has benefited society
much more than the advantage that accrues to himself. Thus, he criticized
the socialists for condemning capital as an evil when in private hands.[94]
And he chastized the socialists for failing to realize that if the government
were the only employer, a profound difficulty would arise—the problem
being how to fix wages. (This argument anticipated a much later one by
Ludwig von Mises, of the Austrian School, who argued that socialism
could not provide a pricing mechanism for any kind of commodity.) His
solution was to permit both private and public industries so that opportunities would be extended, individual initiative would not be stifled, and
the government industries would have some idea of whether they were
proceeding along economically feasible lines.

It is interesting to observe the connection between Wicksteed and the
Fabians whom he influenced through George Bernard Shaw. In the year
1884, Wicksteed published an article entitled "The Marxian Theory of
Value,"[95] which appeared in the socialist journal, *To-Day*. He subjected
the Marxian labor theory of value to the withering attack of the marginal-
utility theory. Shaw, who at the time endorsed the Marxian labor theory,
vehemently objected, and the two carried on a rather heated exchange
in the pages of *To-Day*. Shaw eventually succumbed, and his contribution to the *Fabian Essays* on the economic question is a Jevonian exposition of marginal utility. Wicksteed's complaint against the market as
failing to realize social purposes was adopted by the Fabians to support
their contentions that unearned incomes ought to be confiscated by the
government, and large-scale industries nationalized.

What we have seen, then, with Jevons and Wicksteed is fundamentally
the same marginal-utility theory of value being employed to restructure
economic theory. But when it came to the question of governmental intervention in the economy, we have witnessed a parting of the ways. Jevons,
the Utilitarian, remained more circumspect about the role of the govern-

ment in the economy. Wicksteed, impelled by his doubts about the social desirability of the ends pursued in the market and his Aristotelian moral framework, ended by endorsing redistribution, equality, government ownership of industries, and progressive taxation—all on the grounds that the government can know better than individuals how to spend their incomes for social purposes.

ALFRED MARSHALL: THE NEO-CLASSICAL APPROACH

Jevons, the originator of the marginal-utility theory in England, went to considerable pains to underscore his break with the economics of Ricardo and Mill, and like many innovators he perhaps overstated his case. Such was the opinion, at any rate, of Alfred Marshall, who can truly be termed a Neo-Classical economist because he attempted to synthesize the newer marginal-utility theory of value with the Ricardo-Mill cost-of-production theory and to reassert the centrality of supply factors in the determination of value. While Wicksteed denied the separate existence of a supply curve, arguing that what had been designated a supply curve was really part of the demand curve because it really only represented the reserved demand of the producers, Marshall ended by placing the long-range determinant of value entirely on the supply factor, cost of production. He rejected the Marginalists' conception of costs as opportunity costs, or foregone alternatives, reverting instead to a "real-cost" conception similar to the Classical position. Ricardo and the Ricardians were not the misguided villains of economic history, malevolently casting aside the utility inklings of Malthus and Senior, as they had been for Jevons. They were, in Marshall's estimation, the proponents of a valid approach to value theory who went a bit too far in one direction, just as the Jevonians had gone much too far in the opposite direction. Marshall, not Jevons, was destined to become the leading force in British economics for the next generation.[96]

Marshall was initially attracted to the study of economics by a passionate concern for the plight of the poor, and as he came to investigate both abstract theory and the operations of industry and the effects of technology in England and elsewhere, he gradually became more skeptical of the attraction of his youthful years to socialism.[97] As he related in his monumental work of his final years, *Industry and Trade*, his fascination with socialism was solidified by a reading of Mill's posthumous "Chapters on Socialism" in the *Fortnightly Review*.[98] For a decade after this (that would be, roughly, the 1880s), he related, he considered the question of socialism to be of paramount importance, but gradually his enthusiasm for radical change ebbed. He familiarized himself with the workings of the market, and this investigation led him to the realization that inherent market forces were moving in the direction of greater social justice through a natural filtering down of wealth to the masses, a spontaneous movement of capital to those individuals whose energy and foresight would drive them to employ it most profitably despite their initial lack of pecuniary means. A consequent upward mobility of the working class would result. That the distribution of wealth was changing for the better he could not deny, and therefore, he rejected radical cures. However, he never endorsed the halcyon expectations of Adam Smith for the unregulated, free market. When the market failed to realize the ends of social justice, he was perfectly willing to have the government intervene—to regulate monopolies, to tax for the benefit of the poor, to educate, to subsidize industries subject to increasing returns, and so forth.

Central to Marshall's economic system was the theory of equilibrium of supply and demand. It was, he said, the fundamental idea running through the problems of distribution and exchange.[99] He offers a marginal-utility analysis of how individual estimations of the utility of increments of a commodity result in a composite demand curve for a particular good in a market, but he does not contend, as Jevons and Wicksteed had, that marginal utility (demand) is the ultimate determinant of value. In the immediate short run, demand governs value and price, which means that utility or demand preponderated in the determination of market values (prices), because the stock of commodities in the market is given, and the equilibrium price will depend on the strength of consumer demand. Over a slightly longer period, in which the supply can be increased within the given plant capacity, and in the longer run, in which productive facilities can be increased, cost of production preponderates. What Marshall ends up with, then, is a two-tier value system, similar to the Classical distinction between natural and market values, in which marginal utility (demand) is the causal factor in the setting of market value, while cost of production is the causal factor in establishing normal, long-range value.

This must not be confused with the contention of Jevons and Wicksteed that there will be a coincidence between marginal utility and cost of production in the long run, for they explicitly denied any causal properties to cost of production in the determination of value. Wicksteed, who gave the clearer explanation of the two, states that cost of production entered the picture only when the producer considered whether it was profitable to continue production given the market value (as determined by a ranking of the commodity on the communal preference order, based on individual estimates of its marginal utility) of his commodity, and the foregone alternatives, the costs, it would entail for him to keep on producing. If the price were above this cost, he would continue to produce; if below, he would not. Marshall's difference with Jevons and Wicksteed lay precisely in the fact that he did assign causal properties to cost of production, conceived not as opportunity costs, but in the Classical fashion as real costs. "We might," he challenged Jevons, "as reasonably dispute whether it is the upper or the under blade of a pair of scissors that cuts a piece of paper, as whether value is governed by utility or cost of production."[100] A theory of value is suspect precisely because it is lucid[101] and offers a one-sided explanation of the determinants of value. All that can be maintained is that as a general rule the shorter the period considered, the greater must be the attention given to demand on value, while the longer the period, the more important will be cost of production on value.[102]

Equilibrium occurs, then, when the amount produced is such that supply price equals demand price, for at that point sellers are just sufficiently compensated for their efforts, and production will continue at that level. However, Marshall was interested in more than this stable or static equilibrium. Over time, the demand and supply schedules do not remain unchanged because tastes are constantly in flux. Thus, in practice the equilibrium amount and the equilibrium price are constantly changing. The real world of dynamic change presents, consequently, only a loose connection between supply price and the real cost of production.[103] He was concerned with what he called organic growth and not merely statical equilibrium.

Marshall offers a fuller explanation of producers' costs than did Ricardo, but it was essentially the same kind of explanation. Supply price (or the price sufficient to command the services of the factors of production) equals the sum of the prices of raw materials, depreciation of machines and buildings, interest and insurance of capital, wages, and gross earnings of management.[104] It is interesting to note that in this account the ordinary rate of profits, which so concerned the Classical economists, becomes subsumed under interest, insurance, and gross earnings of manage-

ment. Profits in excess of this customary rate would depend on temporary
market factors that would occur when the market value exceeded the cost
of production or supply price. In a certain sense, this is an improvement
over the Smith-Ricardo account, in which profits seemed to be something
automatically added on to costs, since it made profits per se depend on
the pricing mechanism in the market.

In several important ways Marshall presented definite improvements
over the Classical position: he developed the notion of elasticity of demand,
when he observed that the consumption of certain goods seems to respond
greatly to upward or downward changes in prices while other goods are
relatively inelastic in their consumption patterns; he gave greater emphasis
to the demand side of the relationship than the Ricardians had; he contended that purchasers enjoy a consumers' surplus every time they buy
a good because they pay a price equivalent not to its total utility to them,
but to its marginal utility, thus enjoying all earlier units of the same good
at the lower price of the final one; and he dispensed with J. S. Mill's error
when he stated that demand for commodities is indirectly demand for
labor and the other factors of production.

He adapted from his Classical predecessors the division of the factors
of production into land, labor, and capital, with an additional element
of his own added, which he termed "organization." This latter factor depended on the state of progress in industry (external economies of scale),
on the efficiency of management of particular industries (internal economies
of scale), on the education of the people, on climate, and so on. Marshall's
investigation of this factor is undertaken as a historical, or what one would
now call sociological, study. He analogizes the industrial organism to the
natural organism of an advanced animal, wherein development involves a
subdivision of functions and a growing interdependence.[105] An essential
unity exists, then, between the laws of nature in the physical and moral
world. Here, Marshall exhibits the evolutionist, organismic approach to
society which was so popular in the last decades of the nineteenth century under the influence of Darwinian biology and Spencerian sociology.
Marshall's vision of the effects of evolution differed quite markedly from
Spencer's, for Spencer conceived of progress as demanding a nonaltruistic
morality whereby no provisions should be made by the fit for the unfit,
while Marshall envisioned a growing interdependency in which those
civilizations would survive whose members were the most ready to sacrifice private to public interests. The one argued that progress would cause

the withering away of governmental regulation of the economy, while the other saw a growing role, and a more propitious environment, for state intervention. As Marshall wrote, in a totally un-Spencerian fashion:

> Thus the struggle for existence causes in the long run those races of men to survive in which an individual is most willing to sacrifice himself for the benefit of those around him; and which are consequently the best adapted collectively to make use of their environment.[106]

What is interesting for our purposes is that Marshall undertook this investigation of industrial organization with the intention of discovering means by which it could be improved—that is, other than natural or market means, for he explicitly stated that the doctrine of natural organization (that if a certain organization of industry was more beneficial, the market would have arrived at it spontaneously), taken from Smith's discussion of the division of labor, had been carried entirely too far by his followers. It is perfectly legitimate, then, to inquire how industrial organization might be altered in a manner that would enable the lower grades of industry to develop their latent mental faculties; men to fit themselves for better organization; industry to increase production in the future; and society to distribute wealth more equally. Thus, Marshall's conception of society, as an organism composed of interdependent men who are compelled by nature to be altruistic to a certain degree in order to survive, allowed for a potentially much more activist role for the state in the economy than had Smith's individualistic, natural rights ethic, or Bentham's early Utilitarianism suffused with individualistic content carried over from the natural rights position.

In the process of analyzing industrial organization, Marshall became one of the earliest developers of the theory of the firm. Setting up a model of an average firm with a rational manager, he dissected the way in which this manager would select among a mix of factors of production in order to maximize output, minimize costs, and consequently maximize profits. He isolated those cases in which industry would enjoy increasing returns to scale, and those trades, particularly agriculture, in which there would be a diminishing return to scale. This approach was in harmony with the Classical perspective, but on a much more sophisticated level.

The account given by Marshall of the distribution of "national income" smacks of the Classical economists much more than the Marginalists. Al-

though he did acknowledge that in regard to labor and interest, the shares
of the recipients are determined by their marginal productivity and their
contributions to production and that there is a reflex influence operating
here of demand on supply, he had a separate theory to determine the
share that would go to land. In fact, he modified the Ricardian rent
theory for this purpose, and his reason for entertaining a separate theory
in regard to land was the same as it had been for his mentors, that is,
land could not be expanded in quantity in response to consumer demand.
This position, it will be recalled, was completely rejected by Wicksteed
and Jevons. Another Classical element in Marshall, one which was shared
by the Marginalists, was the explanation of depressions offered by Mill
and founded upon Say's Law. Malthus' population doctrine was, in large
part, dispensed with by Marshall.[107] Even though he acknowledged the
tendency of population to outstrip the food supply in the past, he argued
that as a result of the importation of food from abroad and England's
continual technological advancement, the checks of misery and starvation would not present an immediate problem, if ever. Thus, his economics was much more optimistic than that of the early Classical
economists or Mill, for that matter. Increased numbers, rather than threat-
ening humanity with starvation and a shortage of jobs, would present
increased opportunities for a greater efficiency of labor and capital and
increased efficiencies of scale.

Also, Marshall dispensed with the imminent projection of a stationary
state which played such a prominent part in the pessimistic strain of the
Classical School. The stationary state had not occurred despite a substantial rise in population throughout the century. The real wages of labor
had, in fact, risen over that period, and the subsistence theory of wages
of Malthus and Ricardo had been proved illusory in practice and suspect
in theory. Actually, there was a natural redistribution occurring in a manner
that would benefit the working class. Rent had not eaten up the substance of society; profits had not fallen; and real wages had not gone down.
Marshall recognized these errors in the Ricardian system as a result of the
fact that predictions, which directly resulted from Ricardian theory, had
not come about. But he did not, for this reason, reject what he considered
to be valuable from the Ricardian School—the explanation of cost of production as determining supply and value. What he was left with, then, was a
much more optimistic projection for the future than his predecessors
could have conceived, with their population doctrine and their iron law
of wages. And even the threat of growing monopolies, the natural result

of efficiencies of scale, could not really dampen the generally hopeful tone of his economics, for here government regulations could curtail most harmful effects.

On the debate over whether the market maximizes satisfaction, Marshall sided with Wicksteed rather than Jevons. As a direct result of his analysis of goods that obey either the law of diminishing or increasing returns, Marshall questioned the assertion of Jevons and Walras that the market tends to produce the maximum of satisfaction. One exception to the doctrine that maximum satisfaction is achieved when each individual spends his income as he sees fit was apparent in the case where an individual spends his income in such a manner as to increase the demand for services of the poor with the result that their incomes would rise. If, instead, he had spent his money on something that would end up in the pockets of the rich, he would have added less to the total happiness of the community than in the first case because the happiness provided by an additional shilling is much greater for the poor than the rich.[108] This argument is, of course, reminiscent of Mill. But a further exception to the doctrine of maximum satisfaction is evidenced by a hypothetical case in which it is assumed that a shilling represents equal importance to all people. For, even then

> . . . we would have to admit that the manner in which a person spends his income is a matter of direct economic concern to the community. For in so far as he spends it on things which obey the law of diminishing returns, he makes those things more difficult to be obtained by his neighbors, and thus lowers the real purchasing power of their incomes; while in so far as he spends it on things which obey the law of increasing returns, he makes those things more easy of attainment by others, and thus increases the real purchasing power of their incomes.[109]

Marshall did not take this reflection to its absurd, logical limit of the state dictating the consumer choices of all individuals, but he did contend that the state would be justified in taxing the population on the goods they purchased which obeyed the law of diminishing returns in order to give bounties or subsidies to industries obeying the law of increasing returns.[110] If this were done, he argued, the aggregate, communal satisfaction would be increased.[111] This is a reversal of the whole tenor of Classi-

cal economics, for those economists, including Mill, were of one voice
in condemning special bounties to industry.

Marshall was a cautious man, and he concluded these somewhat radical
reflections with the hedge that further statistical work must be done to
discover the effects of such a program before these conclusions could
provide a valid ground for governmental interference. Statistics, he thought,
would enable us to discover "what are the limits of the work that society
can with advantage do towards turning the economic actions of individuals
into those channels in which they will add the most to the sum total of
happiness."[112] Here, Marshall displayed his thoroughly Utilitarian, experimental approach to the solution of so-called social problems and his equally
Utilitarian attitude toward the end which the market ought to be made to
serve when it did not do so spontaneously, that is, the greatest good of
society, the sum total of happiness. Out of this argument, born of Bentham's
reflection that succeeding increments of wealth add declining increments
of utility or happiness, he also concluded that redistribution of wealth
was a valid social instrument to achieve the maximization of aggregate
satisfaction. He contended that ". . . the aggregate satisfaction can *prima
facie* be increased by the distribution, whether voluntary or compulsory,
of some of the property of the rich among the poor."[113]

When it came to the question of the proper role of government in the
economy,[114] Marshall displayed the traditional, Utilitarian propensity
to abjure general edicts, and evaluate each case on its merits. Rights of
property ought to be based not on abstract principles, this heir of Bentham
declared, but on the observation that in the past the recognition of such
rights has been inseparable from solid progress. The presumption is on
the side of maintaining them, and movements to modify or abrogate them
must proceed cautiously. Where the market can not be counted upon to
achieve socially desirable results, Marshall urged that the government was
perfectly justified in intervening.

Marshall's preoccupation with the improvement of the working class
endured for a lifetime, and in his pronouncements on this subject his
flirtation and eventual disillusionment with extreme socialism can be seen
most clearly. In one of his earliest works, "The Future of the Working
Class,"[115] published in 1873, he advocated a gradual, and it is important to
note, not a revolutionary, transition to a new society in which the distinction between workingman and gentleman will be eradicated. While his
halcyon projection for the future is socialistic in flavor—hours of work

will be few, manual and intellectual labor will be engaged in by everyone—the means of attaining this utopia are anything but radical. Rather, an evolutionary process, already much in evidence, is envisioned in which improved education for all, the encouragement of refinement in the working class, and the increased employment of machinery will bring about a society in which "by occupation at least, every man is a gentleman."[116] The state can further this process by making it compulsory that all children receive an education and by punishing delinquency by parents as "treason to the state."[117] Cooperative industries will prevail, but private capitalists will coexist with them. In all his later pronouncements, the same elements of compulsory education, gradualism, enthusiasm for the cooperative movement,[118] and a moral condemnation of competition[119] would prevail, but what appeared to fade somewhat was the utopianism of his earlier vision.

In his lectures on "Progress and Poverty,"[120] published in 1883, Marshall sought to combat Henry George's land nationalization as a panacea for poverty, although he does sanction radical land reform in the future. Trade unionism,[121] too, was dismissed, for the usual reasons of the economists, as a source of permanent or widespread amelioration. Rather, he advances several steps for making the labor of the poor worth more: (1) that the working class should marry later, bring up their children better, or emigrate to decrease their numbers; (2) that they should dispense with the wages of their children, and the state should provide for their education at nominal cost; (3) that charity should only be given to the deserving poor; (4) that the government should increase factory and sanitary inspection; (5) that cooperative societies, trade unions, and boards of conciliation should help educate the working class to the fact that curtailing production in one trade injures all others; and (6) that everyone ought to develop a higher sense of duty, family ties should be strengthened, and drinking and criminality should be curtailed. With the exceptions of his advocacy of state provision for education *and* factory and sanitary legislation, this is an essentially free-market scenario for improvement. Of course, it is supplemented by a plea for an elevated social consciousness.

This theme of universal brotherhood is enshrined in his work, "Social Possibilities of Economic Chivalry,"[122] which appeared in 1907. What he proposes, finally, is what he terms "National Socialism" in which the wealthy classes, through a refinement of character—"economic chivalry"—will provide public benefits to the poor. He contrasts this to bureaucratic collectivism which will stifle this progress. By collectivism he means the total nationalization of all land and industries, and to this, but not to a modified socialism, he is opposed.

> We are told sometimes that everyone who strenuously endeavours to promote the social amelioration of the people is a Socialist— at all events, if he believes that much of this work can be better performed by the State than by individual effort. In this sense nearly every economist of the present generation is a Socialist.[123]

The press of social forces in his day—parliamentary reform, the spread of education, cooperation, the zeal of the churches, the influence of statesmen and social critics—had combined to increase the scope for beneficial state intervention even beyond what J. S. Mill had envisioned. Laissez-faire is given a new meaning which turns it on its head:

> Let everyone work with all his might, and most of all let the government arouse itself to do that which is vital, and which none but government can do efficiently.[124]

Thus, Marshall endorsed government nationalization of natural monopolies and regulation but not ownership of other large industries, government control over city planning[125] and building codes, and government powers to protect the consumer from tawdry goods and to inspect and arbitrate. In other essays, Marshall endorsed a graduated income tax to effect a redistribution in income between rich and poor,[126] the Social Welfare Budget of the Liberal Party in 1909 which heavily taxed the rich for social purposes,[127] the Old Age Pension Act,[128] severe death duties,[129] and public works to relieve unemployment.[130]

It is quite evident that he did share a common moral end with the socialists, despite his general aversion to their extremist means, for he did wish to move society towards a condition of greater equality of conditions and a more regulated use of the products of human industry for communally approved purposes.[131] "The drift of economic science during many generations," he wrote, "has been with increasing force towards the belief that there is no real necessity, and therefore no moral justification for extreme poverty side by side with great wealth."[132] Here, Marshall quite explicitly displays his Utilitarian, instrumentalist approach to moral questions; in other words, if X is no longer deemed necessary for economic reasons (that is, for securing the maximum productivity), then it is now morally right to do away with it. The same kind of reasoning prompted the movement from the Ricardo-Malthus opposition to the Poor Law to Senior's endorsement of it, for Senior thought that given the then current state of progress in industry, certain measures could be safely taken to alleviate poverty which could not have been undertaken earlier because they would have dangerously curtailed production. Now, Marshall says that civilization and industry have progressed to the point where the prevailing level of inequality has become intolerable, and the means for its remediation lie in hand without unduly disturbing production. Consequently, inequality of wealth must be viewed as a "serious flaw in our economic organization."[133] For the "residium" of unemployables, Marshall proposed a social program along the German line, calling for great expenditures of public funds, and a "more strict subordination of personal freedom to public necessity."[134]

Can any consistent position be attributed to Marshall on the question of governmental intervention? If he changed in his enthusiasm for socialism, it was an alteration in style rather than substance.[135] He was never, even in his earliest days, enamored of complete collectivism, and in the end that is what he opposed. However, he remained what we would call today a welfare statist throughout his life, forecasting the platform that both the Liberal and Labour parties in Britain would eventually embrace, i.e., government regulation, some nationalization, and social provision.

The drift toward ever greater governmental intervention is quite apparent in Marshall. His general moral precept, the principle of utility, combined with his growing doubts about the market's ability to realize his social goals—maximizing satisfaction, alleviating poverty, generating equality of conditions—led him to view state intervention in the marketplace as a beneficent force in a large number of cases.

CONCLUSION

What we have seen in this period is the birth of a radically innovative value theory, the marginal-utility theory of value, which set economics on an entirely different foundation from the labor and cost-of-production theories of value and exchange. Under the inspiration of this theory, such established fixtures of Classical economics as the subsistence theory of wages, Malthus' population theory, the projection of a stationary state for the future, the separate theories of distribution for land, labor, and capital, and the antipathy between wages and profits, laborers, and capitalists which was built into the Ricardian system, were all discredited. Although Marshall tried to assimilate certain features of the Classical position to the Marginalist economics, he did not dissent from this general casting aside of the central tenets of Classicism.

The truly remarkable aspect of this revolution in pure theory was that it had so little effect upon the treatment by these economists of the question of governmental intervention in the economic realm.[136] These men were all drawn to economics by a desire to mitigate social evils—to resolve the problems of poverty and inequality of wealth. Still under the sway of both the Utilitarian moral principle and the experimental, ad hoc, case-by-case approach to questions of governmental interference, Jevons and Marshall followed the lead of J. S. Mill in remaining open to future socialistic ventures, while in the present world willingly accepting the government's regulatory intervention and even nationalization when the market putatively failed to achieve their own moral goal—the maximization of general happiness for the community. Wicksteed, though not an avowed Utilitarian and more of an Aristotelian in morals, still favored socialistic schemes for the nebulously defined objective of securing the "general good." Consequently, there was substantial agreement among the three men that the government had a positive function to perform in modifying the results of the free play of individual interests. In fact, the only tenet of the old laissez-faire economic policy which they did not partially or completely abandon was free trade, and Marshall was rather shaky on that also.[137] Revolutionaries in pure theory, in policy these men were the direct heirs of John Stuart Mill.

NOTES

1. In the recent literature there has been an extensive treatment of the status of the so-called Marginalist revolution, with critics attempting to discover whether there was either a Kuhnian or Lakatosian-type scientific revolution or alteration in research program in this period. See particularly: A. W. Coats, "Is There A Structure of Scientific Revolutions in Economics," *Kyklos,* 1969, 22; M. Bronfenbrenner, "The Structure of Revolutions in Economic Thought," *History of Political Economy,*

270   MORAL REVOLUTION AND ECONOMIC SCIENCE

Spring 1971, 3(1), pp. 136-51; Kunin and Weaver, "On the Structure of
Scientific Revolutions in Economics," *History of Political Economy,*
Fall 1971, 3; M. Blaug, "Kuhn Versus Lakatos, or Paradigms Versus Re-
search Programmes in the History of Economics," *History of Political
Economy,* 1975, 7(4); M. Blaug, "Was There a Marginal Revolution,"
History of Political Economy, Fall 1972, 4(2), pp. 269-80; M. DeVroey,
"The Transition from Classical to Neo-Classical Economics: A Scientific
Revolution," *Journal of Economic Issues,* September 1975, 9(3), pp.
415-39; L. Reynolds, "The Nature of Revolutions in Economics," *Inter-
mountain Economic Review,* Spring 1976, 7(11), pp. 25-33; R. D. C.
Black, "W. S. Jevons and the Foundation of Modern Economics,"
History of Political Economy, Fall 1972, 4(2), pp. 364-78.

   2. The following articles are particularly good on this transition:
A. W. Coats, "The Economic and Social Context of the Marginal Revolution of the 1870's," *History of Political Economy,* Fall 1972, 4(2), pp.
303-24; N. B. DeMarchi, "Mill and Cairnes and the Emergence of Marginalism in England," *History of Political Economy,* Fall 1972, 4(2),
pp. 344-63; T. W. Hutchison, "The Marginal Revolution and the Decline
and Fall of English Classical Political Economy," *History of Political
Economy,* Fall 1972, 4(2), pp. 442-68; R. N. Soffer, "The Revolution
in English Social Thought, 1880-1914," *American Historical Review,*
December 1970, 75(7), pp. 1938-64.

   3. For a concurring interpretation, see Blaug, "Was There a Marginal
Revolution":

   In matters of economic policy, there was in fact continuity
   with classical thinking, and when Jevons and Walras wrote.
   on policy questions, as they did, there was little or no connection between practical recommendations and their views
   on value theory. (p. 269)

   4. W. Stanley Jevons, *The Theory of Political Economy,* 2nd ed.
(Middlesex, England: Penguin Books, 1970), p. 50.
   5. See W. S. Jevons, "John Stuart Mill's Philosophy Tested—Utilitarianism," *Contemporary Review,* 1879, 36, pp. 521-38, in which he argues
the Benthamite position that feelings are quantifiable in terms of money;
also, R. D. C. Black, "Jevons, Bentham and DeMorgan," *Economica,* May
1972, 39(154), pp. 119-34.
   6. Jevons, *Theory of Political Economy,* p. 44.
   7. Ibid., p. 54.
   8. Ibid., p. 44.
   9. Ibid., p. 90.

10. Philip H. Wicksteed, "The Scope and Method of Political Economy in the Light of the 'Marginal' Theory of Value and Distribution," *The Economics Journal*, March 1914, 24(93), reprinted in Philip H. Wicksteed, *The Common Sense of Political Economy*, ed. Lionel Robbins (New York: Augustus M. Kelley, 1967), Vol. 2, pp. 772-773.

11. Ibid., p. 781.

12. Ibid., p. 773.

13. Ibid., pp. 779-780.

14. Ibid., p. 780.

15. Alfred Marshall, *Principles of Economics*, 8th ed. (1930; rpt. London: Macmillan and Co., 1961), p. vi.

16. Ibid., Bk. 2, Ch. 1, p. 49.

17. Ibid., Bk. 1, Ch. 4, p. 42.

18. Ibid., Bk. 1, Ch. 4, pp. 41-42.

19. Marshall's attitude towards mathematical methods in economics is discussed in: R. H. Coase, "Marshall on Method," *Journal of Law and Economics*, April 1975, 18(1), pp. 25-31; and a critical view of Marshall's condemnation of mathematics is taken by H. Brems, "Marshall on Mathematics," *Journal of Law and Economics*, October 1975, 18(2), pp. 583-5.

20. Stanley Jevons, *The Theory of Political Economy*, p. 83.

21. Ibid.

22. Alfred Marshall, *Principles of Economics*, Bk. 1, Ch. 2, pp. 14-19.

23. Stanley Jevons, *The Theory of Political Economy*, pp. 67 and 72. For an evaluation of the accuracy of Jevons' charges against the Mill faction in monopolizing the teaching of economics in the universities, see: N. B. DeMarchi, "The Noxious Influence of Authority: A Correction of Jevons' Charge," *Journal of Law and Economics*, April 1973, 16(1), pp. 179-90. He argues that there was no conspiratorial intention.

24. Jevon, *Political Economy*, p. 55.

25. Ibid., pp. 91 and 101.

26. Ibid., p. 84.

27. Ibid., p. 77.

28. Ibid.

29. Ibid., p. 102.

30. Ibid., p. 105.

31. Ibid., p. 111.

32. Ibid., pp. 115-116.

33. Ibid., p. 134.

34. Ibid.

35. Ibid.

36. Ibid., p. 171.
37. Ibid., p. 174.
38. Ibid., pp. 185-196.
39. Ibid., p. 186.
40. Ibid., p. 187.
41. Marshall also pointed out the Ricardian element in Jevons' theory: see his "Mr. Jevons' Theory of Political Economy" (1872), reprinted in A. C. Pigou, ed., *Memorials of Alfred Marshall* (New York: Kelley & Millman, 1956), pp. 93-4.
42. Jevons, *Political Economy,* p. 205.
43. Ibid., pp. 68-69.
44. Ibid., pp. 70-71.
45. Ibid., pp. 257-258.
46. Ibid., p. 251.
47. Ibid., p. 248.
48. Ibid., p. 254.
49. W. Stanley Jevons, *The State in Relation to Labour,* 4th ed. (1882; rpt. New York: Augustus M. Kelley, 1968), p. 29.
50. This position is clearly enunciated in an earlier piece, "Experimental Legislation and the Drink Traffic," *Contemporary Review,* February 1880, reprinted in W. S. Jevons, *Methods of Social Reform* (1883), (New York: Augustus M. Kelley, 1965), in which Jevons argues for direct social experiments "upon the living social organism." (p. 255-6)
51. Jevons, *State in Relation to Labour,* p. vi.
52. Ibid., p. 17.
53. Ibid., p. 6.
54. Ibid., p. 13.
55. Ibid., p. 12.
56. A similar statement was delivered by Jevons as early as 1870 to the British Association for the Advancement of Science, reprinted in *Methods of Social Reform:*

The laws of property are purely human institutions, and are just so far defensible as they conduce to the good of society. (p. 198)

57. Jevons, *State in Relation to Labour,* p. 13.
58. Ibid., p. 7.
59. Ibid., p. 15.
60. W. S. Jevons, "Married Women in Factories," *Contemporary Review,* June 1882, reprinted in *Methods of Social Reform.*
61. Ibid., p. 172.

62. Ibid., pp. 176-77.

63. T. W. Hutchison interprets Jevons' development in the same way in his excellent article, "Economists and Economic Policy in Britain After 1870," *History of Political Economy,* 1969, 1, pp. 233-4.

64. W. S. Jevons, *The Coal Question: An Inquiry Concerning the Progress of the Nation and the Probable Exhaustion of Our Coal Mines,* 1st ed., 1865, 3rd ed., 1906 (New York: Augustus M. Kelley, 1965); and "Inaugural Address as President of the Manchester Statistical Society on the Work of the Society in Connection with the Questions of the Day," November 10, 1869, reprinted in *Methods of Social Reform.* In the latter piece, Jevons criticizes medical charities and the poor-law medical service for relaxing the habits of providence and self-help in the working class.

65. Ibid., p. 447.

66. W. S. Jevons, "Amusement of the People," in *Contemporary Review,* October 1878, 33, reprinted in *Methods of Social Reform.*

67. W. S. Jevons, "Rationale of Free Public Libraries," in *Contemporary Review,* March 1881, 39. Here, he involves the principle of the multiplication of utility: the "enormous increase in public utility which is thereby acquired for the community at a trifling cost." (p. 29)

68. W. S. Jevons, "On the Analogy Between the Post Office, Telegraphs, and Other Systems of Conveyance of the United Kingdom, As Regards Government Control," Manchester Statistical Society, April 10, 1867, reprinted in *Methods of Social Reform.*

69. W. S. Jevons, "A State Parcel Post," *Contemporary Review,* January 1879, 34, reprinted in *Methods of Social Reform.*

70. W. S. Jevons, "On the United Kingdom Alliance and its Prospects of Success," Manchester Statistical Society, March 8, 1876, and "Experimental Legislation and the Drink Traffic," both reprinted in *Methods of Social Reform.*

71. W. S. Jevons, "The Railways and the State," Manchester, 1874, in *Methods of Social Reform.*

72. W. S. Jevons, "Introductory Lecture at University College," reprinted in *The Principles of Economics and Other Papers* (1905), ed. H. Higgs (New York: Augustus M. Kelley, 1965).

73. W. S. Jevons, "On the Analogy Between the Post Office," p. 278.

74. Ibid., pp. 279-280.

75. W. S. Jevons, "The Post Office, Telegraphs and Their Financial Results," *Fortnightly Review,* December 1875, 18, reprinted in *Methods of Social Reform.*

The financial failure of the Telegraph Department must be deeply regretted, because it puts an almost insuperable ob-

stacle in the way of any further extension of government
industry in the present generation. (p. 304)

76. Jevons, *State in Relation to Labour,* p. 101.
77. Ibid., p. 109.
78. W. S. Jevons, "Trade Societies, Their Objects and Policies," delivered to the Trade Unionists' Political Association, Manchester, March
31, 1868, reprinted in *Methods of Social Reform.*
79. Philip H. Wicksteed, *The Common Sense of Political Economy
and Selected Papers and Reviews on Political Economy* (New York:
Augustus M. Kelley, 1967).
80. Ibid., Vol. 1, Introduction.
81. Ibid., Vol. 1, p. 14.
82. Ibid., Vol. 1, p. 189.
83. Ibid., Vol. 1, p. 191.
84. Ibid.
85. Ibid., Vol. 1, pp. 191-192.
86. Ibid., Vol. 1, p. 334.
87. Ibid., Vol. 1, p. 340.
88. Ibid., Vol. 1, pp. 341-342.
89. Ibid., Vol. 1, pp. 351-352.
90. Ibid., Vol. 1, p. 357.
91. Philip Wicksteed, "The Scope and Method of Political Economy,"
p. 784.
92. P. Wicksteed, *Common Sense of Political Economy,* Vol. 2, Ch. 2.
93. Ibid., Vol. 2, p. 710.
94. Ibid., Vol. 2, p. 680.
95. Philip Wicksteed, "The Marxian Theory of Value," *To-Day,* October 1884, reprinted in *Common Sense of Political Economy.*
96. A. W. Coats presents a thorough analysis of the dominance of the
Marshallian, Cambridge School economists. See his: "Sociological Aspects
of British Economic Thought (1880-1930)," *Journal of Political Economy,*
October 1967, 75(5), pp. 706-29. Despite the foundation of the London
School of Economics, he views the ascendancy of the Marshallians as due
primarily to lack of opposition. Also consult his article: "Alfred Marshall
and the Early Development of the London School of Economics: Some
Unpublished Letters," *Economica,* November 1967, N.S., 34(136), pp.
408-17. Of interest, also, is: N. Jha, *The Age of Marshall: Aspects of
British Economic Thought, 1890-1915* (London: Franklass, 1963).
97. Hutchison concurs in this general drift in Marshall's thought
toward less enthusiasm for socialistic solutions, but he points to certain
anomalies in his position and to the difficulty in tracing a definite pattern

due to his delays in publishing many of his works. (Hutchison, "Economists and Economic Policy in England.") The same progression is documented and attributed to an emotional, not intellectual alteration by R. McWilliams-Tulberg in "Marshall's Tendency to Socialism," *History of Political Economy,* September 1975, 7(1), pp. 75-111.

98. Alfred Marshall, *Industry and Trade,* 3rd ed. (London: Macmillan and Co., 1920), p. viii.

99. Alfred Marshall, *Principles of Economics,* p. viii.

100. Ibid., p. 348.

101. Ibid., p. 368.

102. Ibid., p. 349.

103. Ibid., p. 347.

104. Ibid., p. 343.

105. Ibid., p. 241.

106. Ibid., p. 243.

107. Although, in an earlier period, Marshall was still arguing from a Malthusian position. See his: "The Pressure of Population on the Means of Subsistence," delivered at Toynbee Hall, September 10, 1885, summary in *The Malthusian,* Oct. 1885.

108. Marshall, *Principles,* p. 474.

109. Ibid., pp. 474-475.

110. Ibid., p. 475.

111. Ibid., pp. 472-473.

112. Ibid., p. 475.

113. Ibid., pp. 471-472.

114. For a discussion of Marshall's attitude towards state intervention which treats him as much less of a welfare statist than I do, see: G. K. Fry, "The Marshallian School and the Role of the State," *Bulletin of Economic Research,* May 1978, 28(1), pp. 23-35. On this topic, also: J. K. Whitaker, "Some Neglected Aspects of Alfred Marshall's Economic and Social Thought," *History of Political Economy,* Summer 1977, 9(2), pp. 161-97.

115. Marshall, "The Future of the Working Class" (1873), in A. C. Pigou, *Memorials of Alfred Marshall* (New York: Kelley and Millman, 1956).

116. Ibid., p. 102.

117. Ibid., p. 114.

118. Marshall, "Co-Operation," address to the Twenty-first Annual Co-Operative Congress, 1889, in Pigou, *Memorials.* He states that cooperation is the greatest scheme for social reform because its business basis is the strongest (p. 255).

119. A. Marshall, "Farewell Address to Bristol," September 29, 1881, in Pigou, *Memorials:*

> The work I have set before myself is this—How to get rid of the
> evils of competition while retaining its advantages. (p. 16)

Marshall described competition as "crude, ugly, harsh," but his customary
ambivalence is apparent in his criticism of the Christian Socialists Kingsley
and Maurice for failing to see the intimate connection between freedom
and competition. See his: Letter to Bishop Wescott, January 20, 1901,
in Pigou, *Memorials,* pp. 394-5.

    120. A. Marshall, "Three Lectures on Progress and Poverty," *Journal
of Law and Economics,* April 1969, 12(1), pp. 184-226.

    121. Marshall's attitude toward trade unionism was similar to Jevons';
i.e., a general sympathy but opposition to their attempts to "make work"
and artificially raise wages. He was particularly concerned with England's
retrogression in the face of competition from America and Central
Europe, blaming both the unions and the enervation of her capitalists.
He was incensed by the engineers' strike and went so far as to declare
that:

> I have often said that T. U.'s are a greater glory to England than
> her wealth. But I thought then of T. U.'s in which the minority,
> who wanted to compel others to put as little work as possible into
> the hour, was over-ruled. Latterly, they have, I fear, completely
> dominated the Engineers' Union. I want these people to be beaten
> at all costs: the complete destruction of Unionism would be as
> heavy a price as it is possible to conceive, but I think not too
> high a price.

From a letter to Edward Caird, October 22, 1897, in Pigou, *Memorials,*
p. 400. A. Petridis traces Marshall's change in attitude, although not in
doctrine, from a generally favorable one, to increasing ambiguity, and
eventual antipathy. See his: "Alfred Marshall's Attitudes to the Economic
Analysis of Trade Unions: A Case of Anomalies in a Competitive System,"
History of Political Economy, Spring 1973, 5(1), pp. 165-98.

    122. A. Marshall, "Social Possibilities of Economic Chivalry" (1907),
in Pigou, *Memorials.*

    123. Ibid., p. 334.

    124. Ibid., p. 336.

    125. In another work ("Where to House the London Poor," February
1884, in Pigou, *Memorials*) he went so far as to propose such strict enforcement of the sanitary codes that the excess population of London
would be forced to relocate in the countryside. Government subsidies
could be provided to aid their transfer to industrial colonies established
by private charities.

126. E.g., Letter to Bishop Wescott, January 24, 1900, in Pigou, *Memorials,* p. 386; "Co-Operation," p. 229.

127. A. Marshall, "Rates and Taxes on Land Value," letter to *The Times,* November 16, 1909.

128. A. Marshall, "The Aged Poor," prepared for the Royal Commission, 1893.

129. A. Marshall, "The Equitable Distribution of Taxation" (1917), in Pigou, *Memorials.*

130. A. Marshall, "Political Economy and Outdoor Relief," a letter to *The Times,* February 15, 1886; letter to Percy Austin, January 28, 1903, in Pigou, *Memorials,* p. 447; and letter to Louis Fry, November 7, 1919, in *Memorials,* p. 486.

131. A. Marshall, *Industry and Trade,* p. vi.

132. Alfred Marshall, *Principles of Economics,* p. 714.

133. Ibid.

134. Ibid., p. 714*n.*

135. For a perfect example of Marshall's ambivalence towards socialism see his letter to Lord Reay, November 12, 1809, in which he calls socialism the "greatest present danger to human well-being" (*Memorials,* p. 462), while endorsing redistribution.

136. Hutchison agrees: see his "Economists and Economic Policy," p. 232-3.

> Regarding the relation between economists' theorizing and such policy proposals as they undertake, I would simply venture the impressionist judgment or guess that although I am sure there are some important exceptions to this generalization, perhaps increasingly from this period onwards, economists' policy proposals, much more often than they usually admit, have only a fairly tenuous base if any firm base at all, in any kind of systematic or empirically tested theory.

137. In his "An Export Duty on Coal" (1901), in Pigou, *Memorials,* he argues that defense of free trade is not based on any absolute *a priori* reasoning, but rather on a study of the details of the case. And while he condemned the government's move to tax the export of coal, he stated, "but I admire the courage of the Chancellor." (p. 322)

Conclusion

The preceding investigation of the influence of changes in economic and moral theory upon the question of the proper role of the government in the economy has placed in doubt the distinction drawn by Lord Robbins, for one, between the various individualistic movements of the nineteenth century. He distinguished the French School, which advocated a system of economic freedom spontaneously generated under conditions of minimal state intervention and grounded on principles of natural law and natural right, from the English Classical School, which sprang from the Utilitarian moral principle and eschewed all universally applicable general rules in regard to state intervention in the economy.[1] There is, of course, a large element of truth embodied in this view, but one must respectfully demur from the classification of the Classical School as being entirely in the Utilitarian mold. It did not begin that way, for Adam Smith was not a Utilitarian in his morals; he did not advocate an entirely empirical approach to state interference, and he did invoke natural rights at critical points in his rejection of specific acts of intervention in the market. Smith's conception of the universe as exhibiting a natural harmony in which each element performs its function in a benevolently organized scheme was something he brought from his moral system to the study of political economy, and it led quite logically to the principle which was central to his economic system, that is, that each individual by pursuing his own interests will be naturally led to that course which is most beneficial to society.

With the ascension of Bentham and the admixture of the Utilitarian moral system to Smithian economics, there remained, for a time, a large element of noninterventionism, individualism, and natural-harmony theory which accrued to Utilitarianism from the natural-rights-inspired suspicion of government, to which Smith gave lasting expression. Bentham's conviction that the individual is the best judge of his own interests led him to acknowledge laissez-faire as the general principle, but it was grounded now on *a posteriori* evidence, not *a priori* assumptions of natural rights, as in Smith. It was only a matter of time before the principle of utility, the greatest happiness for the greatest number, undercut this general rule of government noninterference, because it simply instructed the legislator to intervene in any instances, whether of an economic nature or not, in which the greatest happiness was not being furthered by individualistic means. Such large-scale intervention waited only upon economic arguments to the effect that in a certain category of actions the choices of individuals in the free market would not maximize communal happiness. While Bentham presented a substantial list of his own in this regard, it was left for Mill and Sidgwick to do the real damage to the Smithian conception of the individual pursuit of self-interest leading naturally to the harmony of interests in society. In the words of the great historian A. V. Dicey:

> In 1830 the despotic or authoritarian element latent in Utilitarianism was not noted by the statesmen of any party. The reformers of the day placed, for the most part, implicit faith in the dogma of *laissez-faire* and failed to perceive that there is no necessary connection between it and that "greatest happiness principle," which may, with equal sincerity, be adopted either by believers in individual freedom or by the advocates of paternal government. . . . And, oddly enough, the tendency of Benthamite teaching to extend the sphere of State intervention was increased by another characteristic . . . —that is, by the unlimited scorn entertained by every Benthamite for the social contract and natural rights.[2]

As Utilitarianism gradually removed from itself the *a priori*, individualistic elements of the older, natural-rights position, the economist as political theorist came to doubt whether the market and the free choices of individuals would maximize pleasure. Thus, J. S. Mill flirted with socialism; its ideals of equality and social justice were not incompatible with the utility principle of morality. The empirical, experimental approach to social and political questions which was an essential feature of Utilitarianism left it open to economic arguments of Mill's kind—that monopolies prevented the market from operating for the general interest, that individuals often do not know their own interests, that custom and sectional interests prevent the market from operating as it did in the idealized models of the economists—that undercut the economic conclusions of the earlier Utilitarians, which had led them to view the market as largely benevolent. Once these instrumental arguments for a free market were cast into doubt, there was no philosophical resistance, as there would have been on a natural rights defense of the free market, left to the expansion of government regulation of the market.

Our difference with Lord Robbins, then, lies only in this: that Classical economics held within it the seeds of both the movements which he sought to distinguish—both the French natural rights, minimal-state position, and the Utilitarian, experiential approach—and that they existed together for a time in the Classical School, with Utilitarianism eventually winning out as laissez-faire was finally expunged as the general principle in regard to state intervention in the economy. Thus, the laissez-faire principle was not an integral consequence of the utility principle of morality as it was for the natural rights moral system. The power of the natural rights position to withstand the interventionist *zeitgeist* of the late nineteenth century can be seen most vividly in the figure of Herbert Spencer. He denounced the utility principle and championed natural rights with the result that in economic policy he was the strictest of laissez-fairists. In contrast, Utilitarianism placed noninterventionism on an ad hoc, contingent foundation which eroded quite rapidly as the progression from Bentham to Mill to Jevons and Marshall demonstrates.

The tremendous influence of the greatest-happiness principle and the pragmatic approach to questions of governmental policy which it engendered were seen in their most graphic form when the views on state interference of the Marginalist Jevons and the Neo-Classicist Marshall were examined. The marginal-utility theory of value wreaked havoc on both the foundations of Classical economics and almost its entire superstructure. Gone were the Malthusian population theory, the stationary state, the separate theories of distribution, the Millian emphasis upon production over consumption, and so on. But on the question of economic policy Jevons and Marshall both, despite their differences, acknowledged general happiness as the social end and willingly entertained government regulation, even nationalization, when they thought that in specific cases the market would not accomplish this end if left to itself. Individual choice was only an instrument for the realization of general happiness; it was not an end in itself. Marshall was quite emphatic on that point, when he argued that the "residium" of the poor might have to sacrifice some personal freedom to have the government fit them for society—certainly a very un-Smithian position.

We also observed how the marginal-utility theory was used by Jevons, Wicksteed, and Marshall to reach different conclusions about the extent to which the free market produces a maximization of satisfaction. This is illustrative of a larger point. The marginal-utility theory of value could be employed by either enthusiastic interventionists, like these men, or by believers in a generally free market, like the Austrians Böhm Bawerk and later von Mises to support their positions. In the same fashion, the labor theory of value had been employed by the Classical economists to buttress their moral case for the free-market system and by the socialists Thompson and Marx to attack that system as morally bankrupt. In the words of Lord Robbins, with which we concur: "A theory of economic policy, in the sense of a body of precepts for action, must take its ultimate criterion from outside economics."[3] Hence, changes in pure economic theory were not the crucial determining factor in the demise of laissez-faire.

As political economy developed into economics, under the influence primarily of the Senior-Mill distinction between art and science, it became clear that moral, political, physical, and other considerations had to be entertained by the legislator in addition to those of a purely economic nature. Political economy in the early days, particularly with Adam Smith, assumed an intimate connection between pure theory and questions of governmental intervention in the economy, and moral suppositions were inextricably bound up with the deduction of economic principles. Economics as a discipline was far more aware of its bounds, and much more reluctant to lay down general precepts either in outright condemnation or endorsement of state interference in the economy. Under the influence of this development in the discussion of the scope and method of political economy and economics, laissez-faire was dealt another blow, a blow that in concert with others delivered by Utilitarianism, both as a moral precept and as a method of proceeding in the social sciences, proved fatal.

Thus, we have discovered that the theoretical movement towards ever greater governmental intervention in the economy in nineteenth-century Britain was caused principally by a change in moral perspective and not

by alterations in pure economic theory. As the Utilitarian moral imperative of general happiness supplanted the natural rights position, an expanded
role for the government in the economic realm was the logical result.
While changes in the conception of the scope and method of political
economy and in pure economic theory largely paralleled the effect of the
utility principle in undermining laissez-faire, they were contributing factors
only, not the catalyst. Finally, it has been argued that the laissez-faire
principle was not a logically necessary deduction from the Utilitarian
moral principle as it had been from the natural-rights position.

NOTES

1. Lionel Robbins, *The Theory of Economic Policy in English Classical
Political Economy* (London: Macmillan and Co., 1952).
2. A. V. Dicey, *Lectures on the Relation Between Law and Public
Opinion in England During the Nineteenth Century* (London: Macmillan
and Co., 1905), pp. 307 and 308.
3. Robbins, *Theory of Economic Policy*, p. 177.

Bibliography

ARTICLES

Anspach, R. "The Implications of the Theory of Moral Sentiments for Adam Smith's Economic Thought," *History of Political Economy,* Spring 1972, 9(1), p. 176-206.

Anspach, R. "Smith's Growth Paradigm," *History of Political Economy,* Winter 1976, 8(4), p. 494-514.

Atkinson, R. F. "J. S. Mill's Proof of the Principle of Utility," *Philosophy,* 1957, 32, p. 158-67.

Barkai, H. "The Empirical Assumption of Ricardo's 93 Per Cent Labour Theory of Value," *Economica,* November 1967, N.S., 34(136), p. 418-23.

Black, R. D. C. "Jevons, Bentham and DeMorgan," *Economica,* May 1972, 39(154), p. 119-34.

Black, R. C. "Jevons, Marginalism and Manchester," Manchester School Economic and Social Studies, March 1972, 40(1), p. 2-8.

Black, R. D. C. "W. S. Jevons and the Foundation of Modern Economics," *History of Political Economy,* Fall 1972, 4(2), p. 364-78.

Blaugh, M. "Kuhn Versus Lakatos, or Paradigms Versus Research Programs in the History of Economics," *History of Political Economics,* Winter 1975, 7(4), p. 399-433.

Blaugh, M. "Was There A Marginal Revolution?" *History of Political Economy,* Fall 1972, 4(2), p. 269-80.

Bowley, M. "The Predecessors of Jevons—The Revolution That Wasn't," *Manchester School Economic and Social Studies,* March 1972, 40(1), p. 9-29.

Breit, W. "Some Neglected Early Critics of the Wages Fund Doctrine," *Southwestern Social Studies Quarterly,* June 1967, 48(1), p. 54-60.

Brems, H. "Marshall on Mathematics," *Journal of Law and Economics,* October 1975, 18(2), p. 583-85.

Bronfenbrenner, M. "The 'Structure of Revolutions' in Economic Thought," *History of Political Economy,* Spring 1971, 3(1), pp. 136-51.

Buchanan, J. M. "Adam Smith on Public Choice," *Public Choice,* Spring 1976, 25, pp. 81-82.

Cairncross, A. "The Market and the State," in T. Wilson and A. Skinner, *The Market and the State,* pp. 111-134.

Chaloner, W. H. "Jevons in Manchester: 1863-1876," *Manchester School Economic and Social Studies,* March 1972, 40(1), pp. 73-84.

Coase, R. H. "Adam Smith's Views of Man," *Journal of Law and Economics,* October 1976, 19(3), pp. 529-46.

Coase, R. H. "Marshall on Method," *Journal of Law and Economics,* April 1975, 18(1), pp. 25-31.

Coats, A. W. "Adams Smith's Conception of Self-Interest in Economic and Political Affairs," *History of Political Economy,* Spring 1975, 7(1), pp. 132-6.

Coats, A. W. "Alfred Marshall and the Early Development of the London School of Economics: Some Unpublished Letters," *Economica,* November 1967, N.S., 34(136), pp. 408-17.

Coats, A. W. "The Economic and Social Context of the Marginal Revolution of the 1870's," *History of Political Economics,* Fall 1972, 4(2), pp. 303-24.

Coats, A. W. "Is There a Structure of Scientific Revolution in Economics," *Kyklos,* 1969, 22.

Coats, A. W. "Sociological Aspects of British Economic Thought (c. 1880-1930)," *Journal of Political Economy,* October 1967, 75(5), pp. 706-29.

deMarchi, N. B., and Sturges, R. R. "Malthus and Ricardo's Inductivist Critics: Four Letters to William Whewell," *Economica,* November 1973, N.S., 40(160), pp. 379-93.

de Marchi, N.B. "Mill and Cairnes and the Emergence of Marginalism in England," *History of Political Economy,* Fall 1972, 4(2), pp. 344-63.

deMarchi, N. B. "The Noxious Influence of Authority: A Correction of Jevons' Charge," *Journal of Law and Economics,* April 1973, 16(1), pp. 179-90.

deMarchi, N. B. "The Success of Mill's Principles," *History of Political Economy,* Summer 1974, 6(2), pp. 119-57.

deVroey, M. "The Transition From Classical to Neo-Classical Economics: A Scientific Revolution," *Journal of Economic Issues,* September 1975, 9(3), pp. 415-39.

Dow, L. A. "Malthus on Sticky Wages, the Upper Turning Point, and General Glut," *History of Political Economy,* Fall 1977, 9(3), pp. 303-21.

Eatwell, J. L. "The Interpretation of Ricardo's Essay on Profits," *Economica,* May 1975, 42(166), pp. 182-87.

Ekelund, R. B., Jr. "A Short-Run Classical Model of Capital and Wages: Mill's Recantation of the Wages Fund," *Oxford Economic Papers,* March 1976, 28(1), pp. 66-85.

Ekelund, R. B., Jr., and Olsen, E. S. "Comte, Mill, and Cairnes: The Positive-Empiricist Interlude in Late Classical Economics," *Journal of Economic Issues,* September 1973, 7(3), pp. 383-416.

Ekelund, R. B., Jr., and Tollison, R. D. "The New Political Economy of J.S. Mill: The Means to Social Justice," *Canadian Journal of Economics,* May 1976, 9(2), pp. 213-31.

Fetter, F. W. "The Authorship of Economic Articles in the Edinburgh Review, 1802-47," *Journal of Political Economy,* 1953, 61, pp. 232-59.

Fetter, F. "The Economic Articles in *Blackwood's Edinburgh Magazine,* and Their Authors, 1817-1853," *Scottish Journal of Political Economics,* June 1960, 7, pp. 85-107, and November 1960, 7, pp. 213-31.

Fetter, F. "The Economic Articles in the *Quarterly Review* and Their Authors, 1809-1852," *Journal of Political Economy,* February 1958, 66, pp. 47-64, and April 1960, 66, pp. 154-170.

Fetter, F. "Economic Articles in the *Westminister Review* and Their Authors," *Journal of Political Economy,* 1962, 70, pp. 570-96.

Fetter, F. W. "The Rise and Decline of Ricardian Economics," *History of Political Economy,* Spring 1969, 1(1), pp. 67-84.

Fry, G. K. "The Marshallian School and the Role of the State," *Bulletin of Economic Research,* May 1976, 28(1), pp. 23-35.

Gee, J. M. A. "Adam Smith's Social Welfare Function," *Scottish Journal of Political Economy,* November 1968, 15(8), pp. 283-99.

Gordon, H. S. "The Wage-Fund Controversy: The Second Round," *History of Political Economy,* Spring 1973, 5(1), pp. 14-35.

Gordon, H. S. "The London *Economist* and the High Tide of Laissez-Faire," *Journal of Political Economy,* December 1955, 63, pp. 461-88.

Grampp, W. D. "Classical Economics and its Moral Critics," *History of Political Economy,* Fall 1973, 5(2), pp. 359-74.

Grampp, W. D. "Malthus and His Contemporaries," *History of Political Economy,* Fall 1974, 6(3), pp. 278-304.

Hollander, S. "The Development of Ricardo's Position on Machinery,"

History of Political Economy, Spring 1971, 3(1), pp. 105-35.

Hollander, S. "The Reception of Ricardian Economics," *Oxford Economic Papers,* July 1977, 29(2), pp. 221-57.

Hollander, S. "Ricardo and the Corn Laws: A Revision," *History of Political Economy,* Spring 1977, 9(1), pp. 1-47.

Hollander, S. "The Role of Fixed Technical Coefficients in the Evolution of the Wages-Fund Controversy," *Oxford Economic Papers,* November 1968, 20(3), pp. 320-41.

Hollander, S. "The Role of the State in Vocational Training: The Classical Economists' View," *Southern Economic Journal,* April 1968, pp. 513-25.

Hume, J. "Myrdal on Jeremy Bentham: Laissez-Faire and Harmony of Interests," *Economica,* August 1969, 36(143), pp. 295-303.

Hutchison, T. W. "Adam Smith and the Wealth of Nations," *Journal of Law and Economics,* October 1976, 19(3), pp. 507-28.

Hutchison, T. W. "Bentham as an Economist," *Economic Journal,* June 1956, pp. 288-306.

Hutchison, T. W. "The Marginal Revolution and the Decline and Fall of English Classical Political Economy," *History of Political Economy,* Fall 1972, 4(2), pp. 442-68.

Jadlow, J. M. "Adam Smith on Usury Laws," *Journal of Finance,* September 1977, 32(4), pp. 1195-1200.

Kaushil, S. "The Case of Adam Smith's Value Analysis," *Oxford Economic Papers,* March 1973, 25(1), pp. 60-71.

Kemp, B. "Reflections on the Repeal of the Corn Laws," *Victorian Studies,* March 1962, 5.

Kerton, R. B. "Hours at Work: Jevons' Labor Theory After 100 Years," *Industrial Relations,* May 1971, 10(2), pp. 227-30.

Kolb, P. R. "The Stationary State of Ricardo and Malthus: Neither Pessimistic nor Prophetic," *Intermountain Economic Review,* Spring 1972, 3(1), pp. 17-30.

Kuninih and Weaver. "On the Structure of Scientific Revolutions in Economics," *History of Political Economy,* Fall 1971, 3.

Lewis, T. J. "Adam Smith: The Labor Market as the Basis of Natural Rights," *Journal of Economic Issues,* March 1977, 11(1), pp. 21-50.

Losman, D. L. "J. S. Mill on Alternative Economic Systems," *American Journal of Economics and Sociology,* January 1971, 30(1), pp. 85-104.

MacLennan, B. "Jevon's Philosophy of Science," *Manchester School Economic and Social Studies,* March 1972, 40(1), pp. 53-71.

Maital, S., and Haswell, P. "Why Did Ricardo (Not) Change His Mind? On Money and Machinery," *Economica,* November 1977, 44(176), pp. 359-368.

Marshall, A. "The Old Generation of Economists and The New," *Quarterly Journal of Economics*, 1897.

Marshall, A. "Three Lectures on Progress and Poverty," *Journal of Law and Economics*, April 1969, 12(1), pp. 184-226.

Marshall, A. "Where to House the London Poor," *The Contemporary Review*. February 1884.

McWilliams-Tulberg, R. "Marshall's Tendency to Socialism," *History of Political Economy*, Spring 1975, 7(1), pp. 75-111.

Meek, R. L. "New Light on Adam Smith's Glasgow Lectures on Jurisprudence," *History of Political Economy*, Winter 1976, 8(4), pp. 439-477.

Moss, L. C. "The Economics of Adam Smith: Professor Hollander's Reappraisal," *History of Political Economy*, Winter 1976, 8(4), pp. 564-574.

Myers, M. L. "Philosophical Anticipations of Laissez-Faire," *History of Political Economy*, Spring 1972, 4(1), pp. 163-75.

Myint, H. "Adam Smith's Theory of International Trade in the Perspective of Economic Development," *Economica*, August 1977, 44(175), pp. 231-48.

Ohno, T. "Marshall's Principles in the Setting of the Classical Tradition," *Economic Studies Quarterly*, November 1968, 19(3), pp. 40-57.

Petralla, F. "Benthamism and the Demise of Classical Economics," *History of Political Economy*, Summer 1977, 9(2), pp. 215-36.

Petridis, A. "Alfred Marshall's Attitudes to the Economic Analysis of Trade Unions: A Case of Anomalies in a Competitive System," *History of Political Economy*, Spring 1973, 5(1), pp. 165-98.

Phillips, D. G. "The Wages Fund in Historical Context," *Journal of Economic Issues*, December 1967, 1(4), pp. 321-334.

Prasad, K. N. "The Classical Approach to the Nature of Economic Science: An Appraisal—II," *Economic Affairs*, March 1976, 21(3), pp. 108-14.

Ralph, L. J. "Adam Smith's Theory of Inquiry," *Journal of Political Economy*, November/December 1969, 77(6).

Rashid, S. "Malthus' Model of General Gluts," *History of Political Economy*, Fall 1977, 9(3), pp. 366-83.

Reynolds, L. "The Nature of Revolutions in Economics," *Intermountain Economic Review*, Spring 1976, 7(1), pp. 25-33.

Rosenberg, N. "Adam Smith on Profits—Paradox Lost and Regained," *Journal of Political Economy*, November/December 1974, 82(6), pp. 1177-90.

Rosenberg, N. "Adam Smith, Consumer Tastes, and Economic Growth," *Journal of Political Economy*, May/June 1968, 76 (3), pp. 361-74.

Roychowdhury, K. C. "Ricardo's Theory of Economic Growth," *Indian Economic Journal*, April/June 1975, 22(4), pp. 273-94.

Samuels, W. J. "Adam Smith and the Economy as a System of Power," *Review of Social Economy*, October 1973, 31(2), pp. 123-37.

Skinner, A. S. "Adam Smith: The Development of a System," *Scottish Journal of Political Economy*, June 1976, 23(2), pp. 111-32.

Skinner, A. S. "Of Malthus, Lauderdale and Say's Law," *Scottish Journal of Political Economy*, June 1969, 16(2), pp. 177-95.

Soffer, R. N. "The Revolution in English Social Thought, 1880-1914," *American Historical Review*, December 1970, 75(7), pp. 1938-64.

Spiegel, Henry W. "Adam Smith's Heavenly City," *History of Political Economy*, Winter 1976, 8(4), pp. 478-493.

Stigler, G. J. "Alfred Marshall's Lectures on Progress and Poverty," *Journal of Law and Economics*, April 1969, 12(1), pp. 181-83.

Stigler, G. J. "The Ricardian Theory of Value and Distribution," *Journal of Political Economy*, 1952, 60, pp. 187-207.

Stigler, G. J. "Ricardo and the 93 Per Cent Labour Theory of Value," *American Economic Review*, 1958, 48, pp. 357-67.

Stigler, G. J. "Smith's Travels on the Ship of State," *History of Political Economy*, Fall 1971, 3(2), pp. 265-77.

Thompson, J. H. "Mill's Fourth Fundamental Proposition: A Paradox Revisited," *History of Political Economy*, Summer 1975, 7(2), pp. 174-92.

Viner, J. "Adam Smith and Laissez-Faire," *Journal of Political Economy*, April 1972, 35(2), pp. 192-232.

West, E. G. "Adam Smith's Economics of Politics," *History of Political Economy*, Winter 1976, 8(4), pp. 515-529.

West, E. G. "Adam Smith's Public Economics: A Re-Evaluation," *Canadian Journal of Economics*, February 1977, 10(1), pp. 1-18.

West, E. G. "Private Versus Public Education, A Classical Economic Dispute," *The Journal of Political Economy*, October 1964, 72, in A. W. Coats, *The Classical Economists and Economic Policy* (London: Methuen, 1971), pp. 123-143.

Whitaker, J. K. "John Stuart Mill's Methodology," *Journal of Political Economy*, October 1975, 83(5), pp. 1033-49.

Whitaker, J. K. "The Marshallian System in 1881: Distribution and Growth," *Economic Journal*, March 1974, 84(333), pp. 1-17.

Whitaker, J. K. "Some Neglected Aspects of Alfred Marshall's Economic and Social Thought," *History of Political Economy*, Summer 1977, 9(2), pp. 161-97.

Woolheim, R. "John Stuart Mill and the Limits of State Action," *Social Research*, Spring 1973, 40(1), pp. 1-30.

BOOKS

Albee, Ernest. *A History of English Utilitarianism.* New York: Collier Books, 1962.

Alexander, Edward. *Matthew Arnold and John Stuart Mill.* New York: Columbia University Press, 1965.

Anschutz, R. P. *The Philosophy of J. S. Mill.* Oxford: Clarendon Press, 1953.

Atkinson, Charles M. *Jeremy Bentham, His Life and Work.* New York: Augustus M. Kelley [1905], 1969.

Bain, Alexander. *John Stuart Mill: A Criticism With Personal Recollections.* New York: Augustus M. Kelley [1882], 1969.

Barber, William J. *A History of Economic Thought.* Middlesex, England: Penguin Books, 1967.

Barber, William J. *A History of Economic Thought.* New York: Praeger [1967], 1968.

Barker, Ernest. *Political Thought in England: 1848-1914.* London: Oxford University Press, 1963.

Bastiat, Frederic. *Economic Harmonies.* Irvington-on-Hudson, N.Y.: The Foundation for Economic Education, 1964.

Bastiat, Frederic. *Selected Essays on Political Economy.* Irvington-on-Hudson, N.Y.: The Foundation for Economic Education, 1964.

Baumgardt, D. *Bentham and the Ethics of Today.* Princeton, N.J.: Princeton University Press, 1952.

Beer, Max. *A History of British Socialism.* London: George Allen and Unwin, 1940.

Beer, Samuel H. *British Politics in the Collectivist Age.* New York: Random House, 1965.

Bentham, Jeremy. *Bentham's Handbook of Political Fallacies.* Ed. Harold A. Larrabee. New York: Thomas Y. Crowell Co., 1952.

Bentham, Jeremy. *The Correspondence of Jeremy Bentham.* Ed. Timothy Sprigge. London: Athlone Press, 1968.

Bentham, Jeremy. *A Fragment on Government.* Ed. F. C. Montague. Oxford: Clarendon Press, 1951.

Bentham, Jeremy. *Jeremy Bentham's Economic Writings.* 3 volumes, Ed. W. Stark. London: George Allen and Unwin, 1952.

Bentham, Jeremy. *The Principles of Political Economy.* New York: Hafner Publishing Co., 1948.

Bentham, Jeremy. *Theory of Legislation.* London: Kegan Paul, 1904.

Bentham, Jeremy. *The Works of Jeremy Bentham.* Ed. John Bowrind. Edinburgh: William Tait, 1839.

Birne, Arthur. *An Economic History of Europe: 1760-1939.* London: University Paperbacks, Methuen, 1962.

Blaugh, Marc. *Economic Theory in Retrospect.* Homewood, Ill.: Richard D. Irwin [1962], 1968.

Blaugh, Marc. *Ricardian Economics.* New Haven, Conn.: Yale University Press, 1958.

Bonar, James. *Letters of David Ricardo to Thomas Robert Malthus: 1810-1823.* Oxford: Clarendon Press, 1887.

Bonar, James. *Malthus and His Work.* London: Macmillan and Co., 1885.

Bonar, James. *Malthus and His Work.* London: G. Allen, 1924.

Bonar, James. *Philosophy and Political Economy: In Some of Their Historical Relations,* 3rd ed. London: George Allen and Unwin, 1967.

Bonar, James (ed.) *A Catalogue of the Library of Adam Smith.* New York: Augustus M. Kelley, 1966.

Bonar, James (ed.) *Letters of David Ricardo to Hutches Tower and Others.* Oxford: Clarendon Press, 1899.

Bowley, Marian. *Nassau Senior and Classical Economics.* London: George Allen and Unwin, 1937.

Briggs, Asa (ed.) *Fabian Essays.* London: George Allen and Unwin, 1962.

Brinton, Crane. *English Political Thought in the Nineteenth Century.* Cambridge, Mass.: Harvard University Press, 1949.

Cairnes, John E. *Essays in Political Economy.* New York: Augustus M. Kelley, [1873], 1965.

Cairnes, John. *Political Essays.* New York: Augustus M. Kelley, 1967.

Campbell, T. D. *Adam Smith's Science of Morals.* London: George Allen and Unwin, 1971.

Coats, A. W. (ed.) *The Classical Economists and Economic Policy.* London: Methuen, 1971.

Clark, John M., et al. *Adam Smith, 1776-1926.* Letters to Commemorate the Sesquecentennial of the Publication of *The Wealth of Nations.* Chicago: University of Chicago Press, 1928.

Cole, G. D. H. *A History of Socialist Thought,* 3 volumes. London: Macmillan and Co., 1956.

Cole, Margaret. *The Story of Fabian Socialism.* Stanford, Calif.: Stanford University Press, 1961.

Cowling, Maurice. *Mill and Liberalism.* Cambridge: Cambridge University Press, 1963.

Cropsey, Joseph. *Polity and Economy.* The Hague: Martinus Nijhoff, 1957.

Dankert, Clyde. *Adam Smith: Man of Letters and Economist.* Hicksville, N.Y.: Exposition Press, 1974.

Dicey, Albert Venn. *Lectures on the Relation Between Law and Public Opinion in England During the Nineteenth Century.* London: Macmillan and Co., 1905.

Eagly, Robert V. *Structure of Classical Economic Theory.* New York: Oxford University Press, 1974.

Ensur, Robert. *England: 1870-1914.* Oxford: Clarendon Press, 1936.

Everett, Charles W. *Jeremy Bentham.* London: Weidenford and Nicolson, 1966.

Franklin, Burt, and G. Legman. *David Ricardo and Ricardian Theory, A Bibliographical Checklist.* New York: Burt Franklin, bibliographical series, No. 1, 1949.

Fraser, David. *The Evolution of the British Welfare State.* London: Macmillan and Co., 1973.

Gootzeit, Michael. *David Ricardo.* New York: Columbia University Press, 1975.

Grampp, William. *Economic Liberalism.* New York: Random House, 1965.

Grampp, William. *The Manchester School of Economics.* Oxford: Oxford University Press, 1960.

Gregg, Pauline. *Modern Britain: A Social and Economic History Since 1760.* New York: Pegasus, 1965.

Halevy, Elie. *The Growth of Philosophical Radicalism.* London: Faber and Faber, 1952.

Halevy, Elie. *A History of the English People.* New York: Harcourt, Brace and Co., 1924.

Halliday, Richard. *John Stuart Mill.* London: George Allen and Unwin, 1976.

Hamburger, Joseph. *Intellectuals in Politics: John Stuart Mill and the Philosophic Radicals.* New Haven, Conn.: Yale University Press, 1965.

Haney, Lewis H. *History of Economic Thought,* 4th ed. London: Macmillan and Co., 1949.

Havard, William. *Henry Sidgwick and Later Utilitarian Political Philosophy.* Gainesville, Fla.: University of Florida Press, 1959.

Himmelfarb, Gertrude. *On Liberty and Liberalism.* New York: Alfred A. Knopf, 1974.

Hollander, Jacob H. *David Ricardo: A Centenary Estimate.* New York: Augustus M. Kelley [1910], 1965.

Hollander, S. *The Economics of Adam Smith.* London: Heinemann, 1973.

Hoselitz, Bert (ed.) *Theories of Economic Growth.* New York: The Free Press, 1960.

Hurst, Francis W. (ed.) *Free Trade and Other Fundamental Doctrines of the Manchester Shop.* New York: Augustus M. Kelley, 1968.

Hutchison, T. W. *'Positive' Economics and Policy Objectives.* London: George Allen and Unwin, 1964.

Hutchison, T. W. *A Review of Economic Doctrines: 1870-1929.* Oxford: Clarendon Press, 1966.

Jevons, W. S. *The Coal Question: An Inquiry Concerning the Progress of the Nation, and the Probable Exhaustion of Our Coal Mines.* Ed. A. W. Flux, 1st ed., 1865; 3rd ed., 1906. New York: Augustus M. Kelley, 1965.

Jevons, William S. *Methods of Social Reform.* New York: Augustus M. Kelley, [1883], 1965.

Jevons, William S. *Money and the Mechanism of Exchange.* New York: A. Appleton, 1876.

Jevons, William S. *Papers and Correspondence of W. Stanley Jevons.* London: Macmillan and Co., 1972.

Jevons, William S. *The Principles of Economics and Other Papers.* Ed. H. Higgs, 1905.

Jevons, William Stanley. *The State in Relation to Labour,* 4th ed. New York: Augustus M. Kelley, 1968.

Jevons, William Stanley. *The Theory of Political Economy.* Ed. R. D. Collison Black. Middlesex, England: Penguin Books, 1970.

Jha, Narmadeghwar. *The Age of Marshall. Aspects of British Economic Thought, 1890-1915.* London: Franklass, 1963.

Johannsson, Harldur. *Mercantilist and Classical Theories of Foreign Trade. An Introduction.* Kuala Lumpur: Raybooks, 1968.

Keynes, John Neville. *The Scope and Method of Political Economy,* 4th ed. Clifton, N.J.: Reprints of Economic Classics, Augustus M. Kelley [1890, 1912], 1973.

Landreth, Harvey. *History of Economic Thought.* Boston: Houghton Mifflin, 1976.

Letwin, Shirley Robin. *The Pursuit of Certainty: David Hume, Jeremy Bentham, John Stuart Mill, Beatrice Webb.* Cambridge: Cambridge University Press, 1965.

Levy, S. Leon. *Nassau W. Senior 1790-1864: Critical Essayist, Classical Economist, and Advisor of Governments.* New York: Augustus M. Kelley [1943], 1970.

Lindgren, J. Ralph. *The Social Philosophy of Adam Smith.* The Hague: Martinus Nijhoff, 1973.

Locke, John. *The Second Treatise of Government.* Indianapolis: The Bobbs-Merrill Co., 1952.

Long, Douglas. *Bentham on Liberty.* Toronto: University of Toronto Press, 1977.

Lowenthal, Esther. *The Ricardian Socialists.* New York: Columbia University Press, 1911.

Lurdin, Hilda. *The Influence of Jeremy Bentham on English Democratic Development.* Iowa City: The University, 1920.

Lyons, David. *In the Interest of the Governed.* Oxford: Clarendon Press, 1973.

Macafie, A. *The Individual in Society.* London, 1967.

McBriar, A. M. *Fabian Socialism and English Politics, 1884-1918.* Cambridge: Cambridge University Press, 1962.

Mack, Mary P. *Jeremy Bentham: An Odyssey of Ideas, 1748-1792.* New York: Columbia University Press, 1963.

MacKay, Thomas. *History of English Poor Law.* London: P. S. King and Sons, 1898-1899.

Malthus, Thomas R. *An Essay on the Principle of Population.* London: J. Johnson, 1798.

Malthus, Thomas R. *An Essay on the Principle of Population.* Rpt. from last edition. London: Ward, Lock and Co., 1890.

Malthus, Thomas R. *Occasional Papers of T. R. Malthus.* Ed. Bernard Semmell. New York: B. Franklin, 1963.

Malthus, Thomas R. *The Pamphlets of Thomas Robert Malthus.* New York: Augustus M. Kelley [1800], 1970.

Malthus, Thomas R. *Principles of Political Economy Considered With a View to Their Practical Application.* London: William Pickering, 1836.

Malthus, Thomas R. *Three Essays on Population: Thomas Malthus, Julian Huxley, Frederick Osborn.* New York: The New American Library, 1960.

Mandeville, Bernard. *The Fable of the Bees.* Ed. Philip Harth. Middlesex, England: Penguin Books, 1970.

Marshall, Alfred. *Industry and Trade.* London: Macmillan and Co., 1920.

Marshall, Alfred. *Principles of Political Economy.* London: Macmillan and Co., 1920.

Meek, Ronald L. (ed.) *Precursors of Adam Smith.* London: Rowman & Littlefield, 1973.

Mill, James. *Essay on Government.* Indianapolis: The Bobbs-Merrill Co., 1955.

Mill, John Stuart. *Autobiography.* Indianapolis: The Bobbs-Merrill Co., 1957.

Mill, John Stuart. *Collected Works.* Ed. Francis Mineka and D. Lindley. Toronto: University of Toronto Press.

Mill, John Stuart. *Considerations on Representative Government.* Chicago: Henry Regnery Co., 1962.

Mill, John Stuart. *Dissertations and Discussions.* Boston: W. V. Spencer, 1865-68.

Mill, John Stuart. *Essays on Economics and Society.* Ed. J. M. Robson. Toronto: University of Toronto Press, 1967.

Mill, John Stuart. *Essays on Politics and Culture.* Ed. Gertrude Himmelfarb. Garden City, N.Y.: Doubleday and Co., 1962.

Mill, John Stuart. *Essays on Sex Equality.* Ed. Alice S. Rossi. Chicago: University of Chicago Press, 1970.

Mill, John Stuart. *Essays on Some Unsettled Questions of Political Economy.* London: Longman, Green, Reader, and Dyer, 1874.

Mill, John Stuart. *The Letters of John Stuart Mill.* Ed. Hugh Elliott. London: Longmans, Green and Co., 1910.

Mill, John Stuart. *Principles of Political Economy: With Some of Their Applications to Social Philosophy.* Ed. Sir William Ashley. New Edition 1909. New York: Augustus M. Kelley, 1969.

Mill, John Stuart. *The Six Great Humanistic Essays of John Stuart Mill.* New York: Washington Square Press, 1963.

Mill, John Stuart. *A System of Logic: Ratiocinative and Industive.* London: Longman, 1970.

Mill, John Stuart, and Jeremy Bentham. *The Utilitarians.* Garden City, N.Y.: Doubleday and Co., 1961.

Mini, Piero V. *Philosophy and Economics: The Origins and Development of Economic Theory.* Gainesville, Fla.: University of Florida Press, 1974.

Mises, Ludwig von. *Socialism: An Economic and Sociological Analysis.* London: Jonathan Cape, 1969.

Mitchell, Wesley C. *Types of Economic Theory: From Mercantilism to Institutionalism.* Ed. Joseph Dorfman. New York: Augustus M. Kelley, 1969.

Morrow, Glenn R. *The Ethical and Economic Theories of Adam Smith.* New York: Augustus M. Kelley [1923], 1969.

Myrdal, Gunnar. *The Political Element in the Development of Economic Thought.* Cambridge, Mass.: Harvard University Press, 1954.

Nesbitt, George. *Benthamite Reviewing: The First Twelve Years of the Westminister Review.* New York: Columbia University Press, 1934.

Newman, Philip C. (ed.) *Source Readings in Economic Thought.* New York: W. W. Norton and Co., 1954.

O'Brien, D. P. *The Classical Economists.* London: Clarendon Press, 1975.

O'Brien, D. P. *J. R. McCulloch: A Study in Classical Economics.* New York: Barnes & Noble, 1970.

Oser, Jacob. *The Evolution of Economic Thought.* New York: Harcourt, Brace & World [1963], 1970.

Owen, Robert. *A New View of Society*. London: Everyman's Library, J. M. Dent, 1966.

Paglin, Morton. *Malthus and Lauderdale: The Anti-Ricardian Tradition*. Clifton, N.J.: Augustus M. Kelley [1961], 1973.

Parekh, Bhikhn. *Jeremy Bentham: Ten Critical Essays*. London: Cass, 1971.

Pease, Edward R. *The History of the Fabian Society*. New York: Barnes & Noble, 1963.

Pigou, A. C. (ed.) *Memorials of Alfred Marshall*. New York: Kelley and Millman, 1956.

Plamenatz, John. *The English Utilitarians*. Oxford: Basil Blackwell, 1966.

Plump, J. H. *England in the Eighteenth Century*. The Pelican History of England, number 7. Middlesex, England: Penguin Books, 1950.

Rees, John. *Mill and His Early Critics*. Leicester, England: University College, 1956.

Reisman, David. *Adam Smith's Sociological Economics*. London: Harper & Row, 1976.

Ricardo, David. *Letters of David Ricardo to John Ramsay McCulloch*. New York: The Macmillan Co., 1895.

Ricardo, David. *Principles of Political Economy and Taxation*. Ed. R. M. Martwell. Middlesex, England: Penguin Books, 1971.

Ricardo, David. *The Works and Correspondence of David Ricardo*. Ed. Piero Sraffa. Cambridge: Cambridge University Press, 1952.

Robbins, L. *The Evolution of Modern Economic Theory and Other Papers on the History of Economic Thought*. London: Macmillan and Co., 1970.

Robbins, Lionel. *Political Economy: Past and Present: A Review of Leading Theories of Economic Policy*. New York: Columbia University Press, 1976.

Robbins, Lionel. *The Theory of Economic Development in the History of Economic Thought*. London: St. Martin's Press, 1968.

Robbins, Lionel. *The Theory of Economic Policy*. London: Macmillan and Co., 1953.

Robson, John, and Michael Laine (eds.) *James and John Stuart Mill: Thought of John Stuart Mill*. London: Routledge and Kegan Paul, 1968.

Robson, John, and Michael Lanine (eds.) *James and John Stuart Mill: Papers of the Centenary Conference*. Toronto: University of Toronto Press, 1976.

Ryan, Alan. *John Stuart Mill*. London: Routledge and Kegan Paul, 1974.

St. Clair, Osward. *A Key to Ricardo*. New York: Augustus M. Kelley,1965.

Samuels, Warren. *The Classical Theory of Political Economy.* Cleveland: World Publishing Co., 1966.

Say, Jean-Baptiste. *A Treatise on Political Economy: on the Production, Distribution and Consumption of Wealth.* Philadelphia: J. B. Lippincott and Co., 1855.

Schneewind, Jerome. *Mill: A Collection of Critical Essays.* Garden City, N.Y.: Anchor Books, Doubleday, 1968.

Schumpeter, Joseph A. *Economic Doctrine and Method: An Historical Sketch.* New York: Oxford University Press [1912, 1954], 1967.

Schumpeter, Joseph A. *History of Economic Analysis.* New York: Oxford University Press, 1954, 1976.

Schwartz, Pedro. *The New Political Economy of J. S. Mill.* Durham, N.C.: Duke University Press, 1972.

Senior, Nassau W. *Industrial Efficiency and Social Economy.* Ed. S. Leon Levy. New York: Henry Holt and Co., 1928.

Senior, Nassau W. *An Outline of the Science of Political Economy.* New York: Farrar and Rinehart, 1939.

Senior, Nassau W. *Selected Writings on Economics.* New York: Augustus M. Kelley, 1966.

Senior, Nassau W. *Three Lectures on the Cost of Obtaining Money.* London: John Murray, 1830.

Shaw, Bernard. *The Road to Equality: Ten Unpublished Lectures and Essays, 1884-1918.* Boston: Beacon Press, 1971.

Shoup, Carl S. *Ricardo on Taxation.* New York: Columbia University Press, 1960.

Sidgwick, Henry. *The Elements of Politics.* London: Macmillan and Co., 1897.

Sidgwick, Henry. *Lectures on the Ethics of T. H. Green, Mr. Herbert Spencer, and J. Martineau.* London: Macmillan and Co., 1902.

Sidgwick, Henry. *Miscellaneous Essays and Addresses.* London: Macmillan and Co., 1904.

Sidgwick, Henry. *The Principles of Political Economy.* 3rd ed. New York: Kraus Reprint Co., 1969.

Skinner, A. S., and T. Wilson. *Essays on Adam Smith.* Oxford: Clarendon Press, 1975.

Smith, Adam. *Adam Smith's Moral and Political Philosophy.* Ed. Herbert W. Schneider. New York: Harper & Row, 1948.

Smith, Adam. *The Correspondence of Adam Smith.* Ed. E. C. Mosner and I. S. Ross. Oxford: Clarendon Press, 1977.

Smith, Adam. *The Wealth of Nations.* London: George Routledge and Sons, 1908.

Sowell, Thomas. *Classical Economics Reconsidered*. Princeton, N.J.:
    Princeton University Press, 1974.
Sowell, Thomas. *Say's Law: An Historical Analysis*. Princeton, N.J.:
    Princeton University Press, 1972.
Spencer, Herbert. *The Man Versus the State*. Caldwell, Idaho: The Caxton
    Printers, Ltd., 1965.
Spencer, Herbert. *The Principles of Sociology*. 3 volumes. New York: D.
    Appleton and Co., 1895.
Spiegel, H. W. (ed.) *The Development of Economic Thought: Great
    Economists in Perspective*. New York: John Wiley and Sons, 1952.
Stephen, 'Leslie. *English Utilitarians*. 3 volumes. London: Duckworth,
    1900.
Stephen, Leslie. *History of English Thought in the Eighteenth Century*.
    3rd ed. New York: Harcourt, Brace and World, 1962.
Strauss, Leo, and Joseph Crapsey. *History of Political Philosophy*.
    Chicago: University of Chicago Press, 1963.
Steintrager, James. *Bentham*. Ithaca, N.Y.: Cornell University Press,
    1977.
Sturges, R. P. (compiler) *Economists' Papers, 1750-1950: A Guide to
    Archives and Other Manuscript Sources for the History of British and
    Irish Economic Thought*. Durham, N.C.: Duke University Press, 1975.
Thomas, David. *England in the Nineteenth Century*. The Pelican History
    of England, number 8. Middlesex, England: Penguin Books, 1950.
Thornton, William. *On Labour, Its Wrongful Claims and Rightful Dues,
    Its Actual Present and Possible Future*. London: Macmillan and Co.,
    1869.
Tocqueville, Alexis de. *Correspondence and Conversations of Alexis de
    Tocqueville With N. W. Senior (1836-1859)*. Ed. M. C. M. Simpson.
    2nd edition. New York: Augustus M. Kelley, 1968.
Trevelyan, G. M. *British History in the Nineteenth Century, 1782-1919*.
    New York: Harper & Row, 1966.
Viner, J. *The Role of Providence in the Social Order*. Philadelphia: Ameri-
    can Philosophical Society, 1972.
Watson, J. Steven. *The Reign of George III: 1760-1815*. Oxford: Clarendon
    Press, 1960.
Webb, Sidney. *English Poor Law History*. London: Longman, Green and Co.,
    1927-29.
West, E. G. *Adam Smith*. New Rochelle, N.Y.: Arlington House, 1969.
Whitaker, J. K. (ed.) *The Early Writings of Alfred Marshall, 1867-1890*.
    2 volumes. New York: The Macmillan Co.; Free Press, 1975.
Wicksteed, Philip. *The Alphabet of Economic Science*. New York:

Augustus M. Kelley [1888], 1970.
Wicksteed, Philip H. *The Common Sense of Political Economy*. 2 volumes. Ed. Lionel Robbins. New York: Augustus M. Kelley, 1967.
Wilson, Thomas, and A. Skinner. *The Market and the State: Essays in Honor of Adam Smith*. Oxford: Clarendon Press, 1976.
Winch, Donald. *Economics and Policy: An Historical Study*. New York: Walker [1969], 1970.
Wood, Anthony. *Nineteenth Century Britain: 1815-1914*. New York: David McKay Co., 1960.
Woodward, Llewellyn. *The Age of Reform: 1815-1870*. 2nd ed. Oxford: Clarendon Press, 1962.

Index

Gladstone, W. E., 120, 221
Godwin, William, 82
Gold standard, 83, 107, 184
Governmental intervention in
  the economy, 3, 28-29, 31-
  34, 51, 66-80, 86, 88, 90-93,
  103-09, 139-46, 204-09, 219,
  239-47, 253-58, 262, 265-68,
  279-83; and natural rights, 5,
  36-38; and utilitarianism, 5,
  60-61, 78-80, 187-99, 209,
  269

Halevy, Elie, 76
Hobson, John A., 238
Human nature: in Bentham, 52;
  in Smith, 15-16, 18-19,
  39n.14
Hume, Joseph, 46
Hutcheson, Francis, 13
Hutchison, T. W., 20

Impartial spectator, 14, 152
Industry and Trade (Marshall),
  258-59
Inquiry into the Nature and
  Causes of the Wealth of
  Nations, An, 9, 17-38, 59,
  82; natural rights in, 20-
  22; and The Theory of
  Moral Sentiments, 10, 16,
  18, 19, 32
Institute of Political Economy
  (Bentham), 62, 64, 67
Interest rate, 34, 67-68, 75
Introductory Lecture (Senior),
  123

Jevons, William Stanley, 3, 6; art-
  science distinction, 240; and
  Bentham, 230, 243; on busi-

ness cycle, 237-38; on class
analysis, 239, 245, 246; on
education, 243; and factory
legislation, 242, 243; final
utility theory of value, 7,
229-39; on free trade, 244;
and governmental intervention,
239-47; and laissez-faire principle, 240; law of indifference
in, 233; and Marshall, 258,
264; on maximization of
utility, 234; and Mill, 242,
247; on monopoly, 244; on
nationalization, 244-45; natural rights, attack on, 240-41;
profit, theory of, 237, 238;
rent, theory of, 237; and
Ricardo, 229; scope and method,
222-24; and socialism, 241; on
trade unionism, 245-46; and
utilitarianism, 230, 241;
wages, theory of, 236-37; and
wages-fund doctrine, 237; and
Wicksteed, 248, 249; The Coal
Question, 244; "Inaugural
Address as President of the
Manchester Statistical Society,"
244; "Married Women in Factories," 243; The State in Relation to Labour, 239-47;
The Theory of Political
Economy, 222
Justice: in Adam Smith, 13-14;
  in Wicksteed, 249, 251-53

Keynes, John Maynard, 81, 88,
  90

Labor theory of value. See Value
Laissez-faire, 283; and Malthus'
  population theory, 6; and

108; on poor laws, 104; on
profit, 97-98; rent theory, 6,
98-100; and Say's Law, 88, 90,
105; scope and method, 94;
and Senior, 136-38; and
Smith, 93-94, 96-97, 102, 108;
socialism, 104, 108; and stationary state, 101-02; on
taxation, 95, 105-06; theory
of value in, 95-98; and
theory of wages, 100-01; on
wages-fund doctrine, 105;
"Plan for a National Bank,"
107; *Principles of Political
Economy and Taxation*, 95
Riviere, Mercier de la, 5
Robbins, Lionel, 20, 76, 279,
281, 282
Rousseau, Jean-Jacques, 153

St. Simonians, 148, 154, 156,
169, 170, 212n.43
Say, Jean-Baptiste, 88, 107, 136
Say's Law, 88-91, 105, 184
Scope and method of political
economy, 4, 17, 40n.31,
57-63, 81-82, 94, 121-22,
123-34, 155-57, 220, 222-29
Self-interest, 10-13, 19, 20, 39n.2,
56-57, 61-62, 193, 194-95,
204-05, 240
Senior, Nassau William, 6, 181;
on factory acts, 143; governmental intervention in, 139-
46; on the Irish question, 144;
on Malthusian population
theory, 134-35; and poor law
reform, 139, 144-45; profit,
theory of, 137-38; and Ricardo,
136-38; on sanitation and
housing legislation, 143;
scope and method, 123-29;

on socialism, 145; value,
theory of, 136-37; wages,
theory of, 135-36; wages-fund
doctrine, 135; *Introductory
Lecture*, 123; *An Outline of
Political Economy*, 124, 134,
139, 156
Shaw, George Bernard, 257
Sidgwick, Henry, 6, 58, 175; on
governmental intervention,
204-07; laissez-faire, critique
of, 203-07; and Mill, 206;
scope and method, 132-34; on
socialism, 203-04; "Economic
Socialism," 207; *Principles of
Political Economy*, 132, 200
Sismondi, Jean Charles Leonard
Simonde de, 88
Six Acts of 1819, 46
Smith, Adam, 3, 5; Aristotelian ele
ments in, 13, 14, 18, 37; and
Bentham, 45, 47, 51, 58-60,
61, 72, 73, 75, 76, 78-80;
and Cairnes, 202; and class
analysis, 10, 26-28; colonial
policies in, 36; division of
labor in, 16, 18-19, 40n.32;
and free trade, 21-22, 35-36;
and governmental intervention in the economy, 28-29,
31-34; and harmony of
nature, 11, 16, 27-29; and
impartial spectator, 14; justice in, 13-14; and labor
theory of value, 9, 23-25,
42n.56; and Malthus, 80, 88,
91, 92-93; and Marshall, 259,
262; and Mill, 128, 152, 155-
56, 160, 196; and moral system, 10-17; and natural
rights, 10, 20-23, 37, 41n.42,
73; political economy, concep-

ABOUT THE AUTHOR

Ellen Frankel Paul is a visiting assistant professor in the Political Science Department of Miami University in Oxford, Ohio. Her articles have appeared in such journals as *The Personalist, The Journal of Libertarian Studies* and the *Journal of the History of Ideas.*